HABEAS VISCUS

HABEAS VISCUS

Racializing Assemblages, Biopolitics,

and Black Feminist Theories of the Human

ALEXANDER G. WEHELIYE

Duke University Press   Durham and London   2014

Library of Congress Cataloging-in-Publication Data
Weheliye, Alexander G., 1968–
Habeas viscus : racializing assemblages, biopolitics, and
black feminist theories of the human / Alexander G. Weheliye.
pages cm
Includes bibliographical references and index.
ISBN 978-0-8223-5691-2 (cloth : alk. paper)
ISBN 978-0-8223-5701-8 (pbk. : alk. paper)
1. African Americans—Study and teaching. 2. Blacks—
Study and teaching. 3. Feminist theory. 4. Spillers,
Hortense J. 5. Wynter, Sylvia. I. Title.
E184.7.W43 2014
305.4201—dc23
2014000761

Cover art: Wangechi Mutu, Untitled, 2002. Collage, ink on
paper, 12 × 9 inches. Courtesy of the artist.

For Aaliya and Marlena Weheliye

CONTENTS

Acknowledgments ix

INTRODUCTION: Now 1

1   **BLACKNESS**: The Human 17

2   **BARE LIFE**: The Flesh 33

3   **ASSEMBLAGES**: Articulation 46

4   **RACISM**: Biopolitics 53

5   **LAW**: Property 74

6   **DEPRAVATION**: Pornotropes 89

7   **DEPRIVATION**: Hunger 113

8   **FREEDOM**: Soon 125

Notes 139

Bibliography 181

Index 205

ACKNOWLEDGMENTS

I thank the following individuals, who either read or discussed parts of the book with me, for their valuable insights: Richard Iton, Ruth Wilson-Gilmore, Fred Moten, Saidiya Hartman, Dylan Rodriguez, Katherine McKittrick, Andrea Smith, Alondra Nelson, Dwight McBride, Hortense Spillers, Jodi Kim, John Keene, Nicola Lauré Al-Samarai, Joseph Chaves, Ulla Haselstein, Ewa Ziarek, Annette Schlichter, Anna Parkinson, Samuel Weber, and the anonymous readers at Duke University Press. Many thanks also to the participants in the UCHRI research group Between Life and Death: Necropolitics in the Era of Late Capitalism, as well as the audiences at Reading Race Today at Brown University, Critical Ethnic Studies Conference at UC Riverside, the Program in American Studies and Ethnicity at USC, the John F. Kennedy Institute for American Studies at the Free University Berlin, the English Department at University of Wisconsin–Madison, the annual meetings of the American Studies and Modern Language Association, the Comparative Literature Department at UC Irvine, and the faculty colloquium in the English Department at Northwestern for allowing me to test out the ideas of the book and for their valuable feedback. Of course, I am extremely thankful for Sylvia Wynter's and Hortense Spillers's brilliance in charting the paths of future inquiry, of what needs to be done, for us.

While producing *Habeas Viscus*, I learned a great deal from the graduate students in my seminars Man and Animal, Terror and Freedom, Post-soul Blackness, and Expressive Arts and Culture, especially Rickey Fayne, Brittnay Proctor, Cecilio Cooper, Chad Benito Infante, Mohwanah Fetus, Jared Richardson, Pablo Lopez-Oro, Sam Tenorio, La TaSha Levy, and Keeanga Taylor. Special thanks to Nora Eltahawy for proofreading an earlier version of the manuscript, to Cecilio Cooper and Christine Goding for preparing the index, and to Ken Wissoker, Jade Brooks, and Christine Choi at Duke University Press for their work in bringing this book to publication.

Many thanks to my colleagues in the Department of African American Studies at Northwestern: John Marquez, Celeste Watkins-Hayes, Sherwin Bryant, Mary Pattillo, E. Patrick Johnson, Nitasha Sharma, Sylvester Johnson, Barnor Hesse, Martha Biondi, Sandra Richards, Darlene Clark Hine, Michelle Wright, and Tracy Vaughn. Much gratitude also goes out to Marjorie McDonald, Suzette Denose, and Kathy Daniels. Parts of the book have been published previously in the following journals: an earlier and shorter incarnation of chapter 6 appeared as "Pornotropes" in *Journal of Visual Culture* 7.1 (April 2008), while other sections of *Habeas Viscus* incorporate materials from my essay "After Man," which appeared in *American Literary History* 20.1–2 (spring 2008).

Finally, I owe immense gratitude to my family: Barbara Christine and Nur Ahmed Weheliye, Samatar, Ayaan, and Asli Weheliye, Daud Ahmed and Qadiiya Isaac, Asli-Juliya Weheliye, Jan Wiklund, Safiya Weheliye, Said Ahmed, Eedo Biod and Eedo Safia, as well as my friends Patrick Hosp, Roya Djaberwandi, Arndt Weisshuhn, Aki Hanne, Andrea Wiedermann, Christian Schwabe, Jamila Al-Habash, Patricia Bembo, Manfred Bertelmann, and Sonja Boerdner.

This book is dedicated to my daughters, Marlena and Aaliya.

INTRODUCTION: NOW

On the one hand, *Habeas Viscus* is concerned with rectifying the short-comings of "bare life and biopolitics discourse," and on the other hand, it suggests—from the vantage point of black studies—alternate ways of conceptualizing the place of race, or racializing assemblages, within the dominion of modern politics. Focusing on the layered interconnectedness of political violence, racialization, and the human, I contend that the concepts of bare life and biopolitics, which have come to dominate contemporary scholarly considerations of these questions, are in dire need of recalibration if we want to understand the workings of and abolish our extremely uneven global power structures defined by the intersections of neoliberal capitalism, racism, settler colonialism, immigration, and imperialism, which interact in the creation and maintenance of systems of domination; and dispossession, criminalization, expropriation, exploitation, and violence that are predicated upon hierarchies of racialized, gendered, sexualized, economized, and nationalized social existence.[1] Although my argument resides in the same conceptual borough as Agamben's bare life, Foucault's biopolitics, Patterson's social death, and, to a certain extent, Mbembe's necropolitics, it differs significantly from them, because, as I show later, these concepts, seen individually and taken as a group, neglect and/or actively dispute the existence of alternative modes of life alongside the violence, subjection, exploitation, and racialization that define the modern human.

Building on Hortense Spillers's distinction between body and flesh and the writ of habeas corpus, I use the phrase *habeas viscus*—"You shall have the flesh"—on the one hand, to signal how violent political domination activates a fleshly surplus that simultaneously sustains and disfigures said brutality, and, on the other hand, to reclaim the atrocity of flesh as a pivotal arena for the politics emanating from different traditions of the oppressed. The flesh, rather than displacing bare life or civil death, excavates the social (after)life of these categories: it represents racializing assemblages of subjection that can never annihilate the lines of flight, freedom dreams, practices of liberation, and possibilities of other worlds. Nonetheless, genres of the human I discuss in *Habeas Viscus* ought not to be understood within the lexicons of resistance and agency, because, as explanatory tools, these concepts have a tendency to blind us, whether through strenuous denials or exalted celebrations of their existence, to the manifold occurrences of freedom in zones of indistinction. As modes of analyzing and imagining the practices of the oppressed in the face of extreme violence—although this is also applicable more broadly—resistance and agency assume full, self-present, and coherent subjects working against something or someone. Which is not to say that agency and resistance are completely irrelevant in this context, just that we might come to a more layered and improvisatory understanding of extreme subjection if we do not decide in advance what forms its disfigurations should take on.

When I initially began thinking about this book I wondered about the very basic possibility of agency and/or resistance in extreme circumstances such as slave plantations or concentration camps. The initial inquiry, then, led me to broader methodological questions facing minority discourse: Why are formations of the oppressed deemed liberatory only if they resist hegemony and/or exhibit the full agency of the oppressed? What deformations of freedom become possible in the absence of resistance and agency? I don't intend for *Habeas Viscus* to provide final answers to these questions as much as to ask them in novel ways and leave the resulting fragments reverberating around the room of collective scholarly inquiry with the hope that we will be able to pose the problem of subjection qua agency and resistance in different, heretofore nonexistent ways. How might we go about thinking and living enfleshment otherwise so as to usher in different genres of the human and how might we accomplish this task through the critical project of black studies?

I locate my argument principally within black studies as a (non)disciplinary formation that brings to the fore blackness, and racializing assemblages more generally, as one of the major political, cultural, social, and economic spaces of exception, although clearly not the only one, within modern western humanity. Nevertheless, my points are also relevant to and draw on other forms of racialized minority discourse (Asian American studies, Latino/a studies, ethnic studies, Native American studies, postcolonial studies, etc.). Overall, I construe race, racialization, and racial identities as ongoing sets of political relations that require, through constant perpetuation via institutions, discourses, practices, desires, infrastructures, languages, technologies, sciences, economies, dreams, and cultural artifacts, the barring of nonwhite subjects from the category of the human as it is performed in the modern west.

While black studies became an institutional and disciplinary formation in the mainstream U.S. university in the 1960s, it has existed since the eighteenth century as a set of intellectual traditions and liberation struggles that have borne witness to the production and maintenance of hierarchical distinctions between groups of humans. Viewed in this light, black studies represents a substantial critique of western modernity and a sizeable archive of social, political, and cultural alternatives. As an intellectual enterprise, black studies investigates processes of racialization with a particular emphasis on the shifting configurations of blackness. If racialization is understood not as a biological or cultural descriptor but as a conglomerate of sociopolitical relations that discipline humanity into full humans, not-quite-humans, and nonhumans, then blackness designates a changing system of unequal power structures that apportion and delimit which humans can lay claim to full human status and which humans cannot. Conversely, "white supremacy may be understood as a logic of social organization that produces regimented, institutionalized, and militarized conceptions of hierarchized 'human' difference."[2] Although much of the critical, poetic, and quantitative work generated under the auspices of black studies has been concerned with the experiences, life worlds, struggles, and cultural productions of black populations around the world, the theoretical and methodological protocols of black studies have always been global in their reach, because they provide detailed explanations of how techniques of domination, dispossession, expropriation, exploitation, and violence are predicated upon the hierarchical ordering of racial, gender, sexual, economic, religious, and national differences. Since blackness has functioned as one of the key signifiers for the sociopolitical articulation of visual distinctions among human groups in modernity, black studies has developed a series of comprehensive analytical frameworks—both critical and utopian—in the service of better understanding and dismantling the political, economic, cultural, and social exploitation of visible human difference. In sum, black studies illuminates the essential role that racializing assemblages play in the construction of modern selfhood, works toward the abolition of Man, and advocates the radical reconstruction and decolonization of what it means to be human. In doing so, black studies pursues a politics of global liberation beyond the genocidal shackles of Man.[3]

As will become evident, habeas viscus is but one modality of imagining the relational ontological totality of the human. Yet in order to consider habeas viscus as an object of knowledge in the service of producing new formations of humanity, we must venture past the perimeters of bare life and biopolitics discourse and the juridical history of habeas corpus, because neither sufficiently addresses how deeply anchored racialization is in the somatic field of the human. Where bare life and biopolitics discourse aspires to transcend racialization via recourse to absolute biological matter that no longer allows for portioning of humanity or locating certain forms of racism in an unidentified elsewhere, habeas corpus, and the law in general, at least when it is not administering racial distinctions, tends to recognize the humanity of racialized subjects only in the restricted idiom of personhood-as-ownership. Bare life and biopolitics discourse not only misconstrues how profoundly race and racism shape the modern idea of the human, it also overlooks or perfunctorily writes off theorizations of race, subjection, and humanity found in black and ethnic studies, allowing bare life and biopolitics discourse to imagine an indivisible biological substance anterior to racialization. The idea of racializing assemblages, in contrast, construes race not as a biological or cultural classification but as a set of sociopolitical processes that discipline humanity into full humans, not-quite-humans, and nonhumans.

Habeas Viscus contains extended discussions of the weaknesses inherent in the specter of bare life and biopolitics discourse that haunts current scholarly debates in the Anglo-American humanities and social sciences.

However, this book's theoretical design owes much of its fuel to Hortense Spillers's and Sylvia Wynter's important mediations about the intellectual project of black studies vis-à-vis racialization and the category of the human in western modernity.[4] Wynter and Spillers configure black studies as an intellectual endeavor, even though acutely attuned to its institutional quirks, whose principal goal is to disrupt the governing conception of humanity as synonymous with western Man, while also supplying the analytic tools for thinking the deeply gendered and sexualized provenances of racializing assemblages. Moreover, I draw on Wynter's and Spillers's work in order to highlight and impede the precarious status of black feminism in the academy and beyond, since black feminism has sustained African American cultural theory at the same time as it has grounded the institutional existence of black studies for the last few decades but is nevertheless continually disavowed. According to Ann DuCille, black feminist theory is not conceived of as a serious field of inquiry by denying that black feminism represents "a discipline with a history and a body of rigorous scholarship and distinguished scholars underpinning it"; instead outsiders imagine it to be "an anybody-can-play pick-up game performed on a wide-open, untrammeled field."[5] My extensive exegeses of Spillers's and Wynter's "body of rigorous scholarship" in the pages that follow represent one way to counteract this methodical disremembering of the intellectual contributions black feminism has made to black studies and knowledge production in the academy tout court.

In addition, Wynter's and Spillers's reconceptualizations of race, subjection, and humanity provide indispensable correctives to Agamben's and Foucault's considerations of racism vis-à-vis biopolitics. In this vein, I argue that black studies and other formations of critical ethnic studies provide crucial viewpoints, often overlooked or actively neglected in bare life and biopolitics discourse, in the production of racialization as an object of knowledge, especially in its interfacing with political violence and (de)humanization. Rather than using biopolitics as a modality of analysis that supersedes or sidelines race, I stress that race be placed front and center in considerations of political violence, albeit not as a biological or cultural classification but as a set of sociopolitical processes of differentiation and hierarchization, which are projected onto the putatively biological human body. Even if distinctions among different groups of humans are based not on race but on nationality or religion, for instance, there exists no such thing as an absolute biopolitical substance, because those differentiations not only obey the procedural tenets of racializing assemblages but also very often are translated to visual phenomena. Racializing assemblages represent, among other things, the visual modalities in which dehumanization is practiced and lived. In this way, the conceptual tools of racialized minority discourse augment and reframe bare life and biopolitics discourse, because they focus on the nexus of differentiation, hierarchy, and the human, and ultimately on devising new forms of human life that are not constructed from the noxious concoction of racialization and/as political violence.

I am belaboring this point because Foucault's and Agamben's ideas are frequently invoked without scrutinizing the historical, philosophical, or political foundations upon which they are constructed, which bespeaks a broader tendency in which theoretical formulations by white European thinkers are granted a conceptual carte blanche, while those uttered from the purview of minority discourse that speak to the same questions are almost exclusively relegated to the jurisdiction of ethnographic locality. The challenges posed to the smooth operations of western Man since the 1960s by continental thought and minority discourse, though, as I discuss later, historically, conceptually, institutionally, and politically relational, still tend to be segregated, because minority discourses seemingly cannot inhabit the space of proper theoretical reflection. This applies especially to the critical conversations about bare life and biopolitics given that they revolve around racism, genocide, legal exclusion, torture, and humanity, for instance, topics which have been debated and theorized in black and critical ethnic studies for some time. The concepts of Foucault and Agamben are deemed transposable to a variety of spatiotemporal contexts because the authors do not speak from an explicitly racialized viewpoint (in contradistinction to nonwhite scholars who have written about racial slavery, colonialism, indigenous genocide, etc.), which lends their ideas more credibility and, once again, displaces minority discourse.[6] If I didn't know any better, I would suppose that scholars not working in minority discourse seem thrilled that they no longer have to consult the scholarship of nonwhite thinkers now that European master subjects have deigned to weigh in on these topics. As Junot Díaz remarks: "Women-of-color writers were raising questions about the world, about power, about philosophy, about politics, about history, about white supremacy, *because* of their raced, gendered, sexualized bodies; they were wielding a genius that had been cultivated *out of* their raced, gendered, sexualized subjectivities. . . . That these women are being forgotten, and their historical importance elided, says a lot about our particular moment and how real a threat these foundational sisters posed to the order of things."[7] Yet because women-of-color writers articulate their critiques as a result of and in relation to their identities, the knowledge they produce is often relegated to ethnographic locality within mainstream discourses.

Bare life and biopolitics discourse in particular is plagued by a strong "anti–identity politics" strain in the Anglo-American academy in its positioning of bare life and biopolitics as uncontaminated by and prior to reductive or essentialist political identities such as race or gender.[8] Supposing that analyses of race and racism are inherently essentialist where those concerning bare life and biopolitics are not—because they do not suitably resemble real-world identities—allows bare life and biopolitics to appear as unaffected by identitarian locality and thus as proper objects of knowledge. This occurs because the ideas of white European theorists are not regarded as affectable by a "critical consciousness" that would open them "up towards historical reality, toward society, toward human needs and interests, to point up those concrete instances drawn from everyday reality that lie outside or just beyond the interpretive area."[9] Traveling theories, particularly those supposedly transparent and universal soldiers in Man's philosophical army, should be exposed to and reconstructed not only according to the factors Edward Said mentions, but also in concordance with a critical consciousness that probes the conceptual constraints of these theories, especially as it pertains to the analytics of race and exhumes their historico-geographical affectability.[10] I am by no means contending that black and critical ethnic studies scholars should not engage the thought of Agamben and Foucault, nor am I emphasizing and bemoaning the exclusion of race from these conceptual apparatuses; rather I show how Foucault and Agamben, by placing racial difference in a field prior to and at a distance from conceptual contemplation, inscribe race as a "real object" or a "primitive notion."[11] In doing so, I want to underscore just how comprehensively the coloniality of Man suffuses the disciplinary and conceptual formations of knowledge we labor under, and how far we have yet to go in decolonizing these structures.[12] This is especially unfortunate, and perhaps a result of the fact that most of the recent innovative impulses in critical theory have been formulated within the context of (racialized) minority discourse (black and critical ethnic studies, postcolonial theory, queer theory, etc.).

Is this really new? ?

Since bare life and biopolitics discourse largely occludes race as a critical category of analysis, as do many other current articulations of critical theory, it cannot provide the methodological instruments for diagnosing the tight bonds between humanity and racializing assemblages in the modern era. The volatile rapport between race and the human is defined above all by two constellations: first, there exists no portion of the modern human that is not subject to racialization, which determines the hierarchical ordering of the Homo sapiens species into humans, not-quite-humans, and nonhumans; second, as a result, humanity has held a very different status for the traditions of the racially oppressed. Man will only be abolished "like a face drawn in sand at the edge of the sea" if we disarticulate the modern human (Man) from its twin: racializing assemblages.[13] My principal question, phrased plainly, is: what different modalities of the human come to light if we do not take the liberal humanist figure of Man as the master-subject but focus on how humanity has been imagined and lived by those subjects excluded from this domain? Some scholars associated with black and critical ethnic studies have begun to undertake the project of thinking humanity from perspectives beyond the liberal humanist subject, Man.[14] There humanity emerges as an object of knowledge, which offers the means of conceptualizing how the human materializes in the worlds of those subjects habitually not thought to define or belong to this field. The greatest contribution to critical thinking of black studies—and critical ethnic studies more generally— is the transformation of the human into a heuristic model and not an ontological fait accompli, which seems particularly important in our current historical moment.

Though the human as a secular entity of scientific and humanistic inquiry has functioned as a central topos of modernity since the Renaissance, questions of humanity have gained importance in the academy and beyond in the wake of recent technological developments, especially the advent of biotechnology and the proliferation of informational media. These discussions, which in critical discourses in the humanities and social sciences have relied heavily on the concepts of the cyborg and the posthuman, largely do not take into account race as a constitutive category in thinking about the parameters of humanity. Reading thinkers such as Jacques Derrida, Michel Foucault, or Louis Althusser today, one cannot help but notice the manifesto-like character of their writings, historicizing the western conception of Man (Foucault), providing a more scientific, nonhumanist version of Marxism (Althusser), or attempting to think at the limits of humanism while being aware that this just reinscribes the centrality of Man (Derrida). Going back further, the axial project of linguistic, anthropological, and literary structuralism that emerged in the aftermath of World War II was to displace a holistic notion of the human through various structural features that constitute, frame, and interpellate Man. We can also locate these tendencies in the German philosophical traditions that inspired a number of poststructuralist projects, or, for that matter, in the works of Sigmund Freud, Karl Marx, and Ferdinand de Saussure. These thinkers, however, are hardly regarded as posthumanist philosophers; instead they are classified as "antihumanist."[15]

Here we would do well to retrieve the deracination of post-structuralism once annexed by the U.S. academy in the 1970s and rechristened as "theory." As Pal Ahluwalia and Robert Young among others have shown, the Algerian war in particular, and decolonization in general, provided the impetus for a generation of French intellectuals (Jacques Derrida, Pierre Bourdieu, Hélène Cixous, and Jean-François Lyotard, for example, who would later be associated with post-structuralism), to dismantle western thought and subjectivity.[16] The nearly simultaneous eruptions of ethnic studies and post-structuralism in the American university system have been noted by critics such as Hortense Spillers and Wlad Godzich, yet these important convergences hardly register on the radar of mainstream debates.[17] That is to say that the challenges posed to the smooth operations of western Man since the 1960s by continental thought and minority discourse, though historically, conceptually, institutionally, and politically relational, tend to be segregated, because minority discourses seemingly cannot inhabit the space of proper theoretical reflection, which is why thinkers such as Foucault and Agamben need not reference the long traditions of thought in this domain that are directly relevant to biopolitics and bare life.

We also find this in current studies of posthumanism associated with theories of technological virtuality, as well as in the embryonic field of animal studies. In these modes of inquiry, Man interfaces with a plethora of informational technologies, or in the case of animal studies sheds its superiority complex vis-à-vis nonhuman animals, and enters into the space and time of the posthuman. Moreover, many invocations of posthumanism, whether in antihumanist post-structuralist theorizing or in current considerations of technology and animality, reinscribe the humanist subject (Man) as the

personification of the human by insisting that this is the category to be overcome, rarely considering cultural and political formations outside the world
of Man that might offer alternative versions of humanity.[18] Moreover, posthumanism and animal studies isomorphically yoke humanity to the limited
possessive individualism of Man, because these discourses also presume
that we have now entered a stage in human development where all subjects
have been granted equal access to western humanity and that this is, indeed,
what we all want to overcome. It is remarkable, for instance, how the (not
so) dreaded comparison between human and animal slavery is brandished
about in the field of animal studies and how black liberation struggles serve
as both the positive and negative foil for making a case for the sentience
and therefore emancipation of nonhuman beings.[19] This sleight of hand
comes easy to those critics attempting to achieve animal rights and is frequently articulated comparatively vis-à-vis black subjects' enslavement in
the Americas—"the moral and intellectual jujitsu that yielded the catachre-
sis, person-as-property."[20]

When I taught a graduate seminar on the human and animal a few years
ago, I was struck both by how frequently this comparison appeared in recent
critical texts associated with animal studies and how carelessly—and often
defensively—this comparative analogy was brandished about in this area
of inquiry. Here is one of the more spiteful instances of this current:

> In Toni Morrison's eloquent meditation . . . she argues that the hallmarks
> of the individualist imagination in the founding of United States cul-
> ture—"autonomy, authority, newness and difference, absolute power"—
> are all "made possible by, and shaped by, activated by a complex aware-
> ness and employment of a constituted Africanism," which in turn has
> as its material condition of possibility the white man's "absolute power
> over the lives of others" in the fact of slavery. My point here, however, . . .
> is to take Morrison very seriously at her word—and then some. For what
> does it mean when the aspiration of human freedom, extended to all,
> regardless of race or class or gender, has as its material condition of pos-
> sibility absolute control over the lives of nonhuman others?[21]

Given that Morrison mentions neither the subjugation nor liberation of
animals, it remains unclear why her ideas about blackness and chattel
slavery are summoned here, why the aspiration for human freedom would
ineludibly lead to the subjugation of nonhuman others, and why black

subjects—rather than, say, slave owners—must bear the burden of representing the final frontier of speciesism. In supposing that all human subjects occupy the space of humanity equally, post- and antihumanist discourses cannot conceptualize how "the transubstantiation of the captive into the volitional subject, chattel into proprietor, and the circumscribed body of blackness into the disembodied and abstract universal seems improbable, if not impossible."[22] Much post-1960s critical theorizing either assumes that black subjects have been fully assimilated into the human qua Man or continues to relegate the thought of nonwhite subjects to the ground of ethnographic specificity, yet as Aimé Césaire has so rightfully observed, "The West has never been further from being able to live a true humanism—a humanism made to the measure of the world."[23]

Turning to the problematic of black suffering in enslavement and beyond, I highlight how the universalization of exception disables thinking humanity creatively. Because black suffering figures in the domain of the mundane, it refuses the idiom of exception. Mobilizing suffering that results from political violence as a conduit to new forms of life, however, requires some spatial and emotional distance from comparativity and the exception, since both often contain trace elements of calculability that deem some forms of humanity more exceptional than others. Conversely, putting into play interpretive devices such as the example and relation unearths differential variants of humanity severed from the dangling participles of particularity and calculability. Moreover, because full access to legal personhood has been a systematic absence within racialized minority cultures, the analyses of political violence that arise from them tend to neither describe this brutality in the idiom of dehumanization nor make legal recognition the focal point of redress. The conjoining of flesh and habeas corpus in the compound *habeas viscus* brings into view an articulated assemblage of the human (viscus/flesh) borne of political violence, while at the same time not losing sight of the different ways the law pugnaciously adjudicates who is deserving of personhood and who is not (habeas).

That said, I am not making any claims about the desirability of flesh, the unmitigated agency it contains, or how it abolishes the violent political structures at its root, but rather I investigate the breaks, crevices, movements, languages, and such found in the zones between the flesh and the law. Finally, I am by no means endorsing political wounding as it appears in various human (and animal) rights discourses since the Enlightenment, where suffering becomes the defining feature of those subjects excluded from the law, national community, the human, and so on—while paradoxically also highlighting their equality with those ensconced firmly in the hegemonic sphere—insofar as it allows for recognition by the liberal state in order to assuage this pain and therefore claim to free the oppressed. Since the recognition of black humanity via the conduit of suffering before and subsequent to emancipation in the United States was used to subjugate black subjects in much more insidious and elaborate ways than de facto enslavement, the questions "Aren't I a Woman?" and "Am I not your brother?" lose, at the very least, some of their purchase.[24]

Habeas viscus suggests a technological assemblage of humanity, technology circumscribed here in the broadest sense as the application of knowledge to the practical aims of human life or to changing and manipulating the human environment. Consequently, the figuration of humanity found in the tradition of the oppressed represents a series of distinct assemblages of what it means to be human in the modern world. The particular assemblage of humanity under purview here is habeas viscus, which, in contrast to bare life, insists on the importance of miniscule movements, glimmers of hope, scraps of food, the interrupted dreams of freedom found in those spaces deemed devoid of full human life (Guantanamo Bay, internment camps, maximum security prisons, Indian reservations, concentration camps, slave plantations, or colonial outposts, for instance). Beyond the dominion of the law, biopolitics, and bare life they represent alternative critical, political, and poetic assemblages that are often hushed in these debates. Habeas viscus accents how race becomes pinioned to human physiology, exposing how the politicization of the biological always already represents a racializing assemblage. Taking leave from considering racial categorization as a mere ideological imposition of scientifically "wrong" phenomena, habeas viscus, as an idea, networks bodies, forces, velocities, intensities, institutions, interests, ideologies, and desires in racializing assemblages, which are simultaneously territorializing and deterritorializing.

Edouard Glissant describes relation as an open totality of movement, which "is the boundless effort of the world: to become realized in its totality, that is, to evade rest."[25] Relation is not a waste product of established components; rather, it epitomizes the constitutive potentiality of a totality that is structured in dominance and composed of the particular processes of bringing-into-relation, which offer spheres of interconnected existences that are in constant motion. Relationality provides a productive model for critical inquiry and political action within the context of black and critical ethnic studies, because it reveals the global and systemic dimensions of racialized, sexualized, and gendered subjugation, while not losing sight of the many ways political violence has given rise to ongoing practices of freedom within various traditions of the oppressed. As Richard Iton states, one of the principal goals of black politics has been "the always complicated struggle to make plain these denials of relationality and the commitment to thinking reflexively with regard to the extended problem space that is the modern/colonial matrix and to positively value discursive spaces in which black thoughts might occur."[26] Part of this project is to think the question of politically motivated acts of aggression in relational terms rather than through the passages of comparison, deviance, exception, or particularity, since they fail to adequately describe how specific instances of the relations that compose political violence realize articulations of an ontological totality: the constitutive potentiality of a totality structured in dominance composed of the particular processes of bringing-into-relation. More concretely, Lisa Lowe has suggested that we can no longer disarticulate "the study of slavery from immigration studies of Asians and Latinos or . . . separate the history of gender, sexuality, and women from these studies of 'race.' Native Caribbeans have been rendered invisible by both the histories that tell of their extermination in the sixteenth century and the subsequent racial classifications in which their survival is occluded."[27] While we should most definitely bring into focus the relays betwixt and between the genocide of indigenous populations in the Americas, the transatlantic slave trade, Asian American indentured servitude, and Latino immigration among many factors, we cannot do so in the grammar of comparison, since this will merely reaffirm Man's existent hierarchies rather than design novel assemblages of relation.

While thinking through the political and institutional dimensions of how certain forms of violence and suffering are monumentalized and others are relegated to the margins of history remains significant, their direct comparison tends to lead to hierarchization and foreclose further discussion. Comparativity frequently serves as a shibboleth that allows minoritized groups to gain recognition (and privileges, rights, etc.) from hegemonic powers (through the law, for instance) who, as a general rule, only grant a certain number of exceptions access to the spheres of full humanity, sentience, citizenship, and so on. This, in turn, feeds into a discourse of putative scarcity in which already subjugated groups compete for limited resources, leading to a strengthening of the very mechanisms that deem certain groups more disposable or not-quite-human than others. In the resulting oppression Olympics, white supremacy takes home all winning medals in every competition.[28] In other words, as long as numerous individuals and populations around the globe continue to be rendered disposable by the pernicious logics of racialization, and thus exposed to different forms of political violence on a daily basis, it seems futile to tabulate, measure, or calculate their/our suffering in the jargon of comparison.

Consequently, rather than assuming that suffering must always follow the path of wounded attachments in search of recognition from the liberal state, and therefore dismissing any form of politics that might arise from the undergoing of political violence as inherently essentialist, my thinking is more in line with a materialist reconceptualization of suffering.[29] Asma Abbas does not conscript minoritarian suffering to the realm of individual ressentiment used in the service of gaining liberal personhood but, instead, argues for an "understanding of suffering that allows us to honour the suffering and hope of others not because we are humbled by their impenetrability and unknowability, but because of how we see our sufferings and our labours as co-constitutive of the world we inhabit, however homelessly."[30] Once suffering that results from political violence severs its ties with liberal individualism, which would position this anguish in the realm of a dehumanizing exception, we can commence to think of suffering and enfleshment as integral to humanity. I emphasize the family ties between political violence and suffering not because they are nobler or more worthy than other forms of suffering, but because they usher us away from the liberal notion of wounding that is at the core of modern western politics and culture. Given the prominence of political violence within the histories of colonialism, indigenous genocide, racial slavery, internment, de jure segregation, and so on, black studies and other incarnations of racialized minority discourse offer pathways to distinctive understandings of suffering that serve as the speculative blueprint for new forms of humanity, which are defined above all by overdetermined conjurings of freedom. Overall, I am asking whether there exists freedom (not necessarily as a commonsensically positive category, but as a way to think what it makes possible) in this pain that most definitely cannot be reduced to mere recognition based on the alleviation of injury or redressed by the laws of the liberal state, and if said freedom might lead to other forms of emancipation, which can be imagined but not (yet) described.

Habeas Viscus is not intended to be comprehensive or exhaustive; rather it is purposefully written in an at times fragmentary and often suggestive style in order to launch alternate ways of understanding our uneven planetary conditions and imagine the other worlds these might make possible. I have found stylistic and conceptual inspiration in the extensive archive of collectively authored manifestos formulated by groups of modern racialized subjects:

The Combahee River Collective Statement (1977)

Trail of Broken Treaties: For Renewal of Contracts—Reconstruction of Indian Communities and Securing an Indian Future in America! (1972)

We Charge Genocide: The Historic Petition to the United Nations for Relief from a Crime of the United States Government against the Negro People (1951)

Alcatraz Proclamation: To the Great White Father and His People (1969)

Cannibal Manifesto (1928)

INCITE! Statement: Gender Violence and the Prison Industrial Complex (2001)

El Plan Espiritual de Aztlan (1969)

Declaration of the Rights of the Negro Peoples of the World: The Principles of the Universal Negro Improvement Association (1920)

Declaration on the Promotion of World Peace and Co-operation—Bandung Conference (1955)

Third World Women's Alliance, Black Woman's Manifesto (n.d.)

The Emergence of Yellow Power in America (1969)

To Determine the Destiny of Our Black Community: The Black Panther Party's Ten Point Platform and Program (1966)

Zapatista Manifesto (1993)[31]

Though articulated for different purposes across distinctive geographical terrains and historical coordinates, these credos point to a political, poetic, and philosophical jurisdiction that has as its aim, to summon Hortense Spillers's formulation, "try[ing] to open the way to responsible freedom."[32] As politico-theoretical reflections, these declarations of interdependence create alternate modalities of freedom in the interstices of the text, which while conjuring anterior futures also lay claim to and make demands in the here-and-NOW. Moreover, given that what constitutes a scholarly monograph but also the very basic notion of the book form (as opposed to a pamphlet, blog entry, a series of articles, and so on) has changed so radically over the last few years both inside and outside the academy, I wanted *Habeas Viscus* to reflect, refract, and address these shifts structurally.[33] But instead of looking primarily to contemporary technological changes in the creation, distribution, and publishing of textual artifacts, I turned to these earlier manifestos in order to imagine future forms of writing and/as freedom. As such, the manifestos mentioned above provide templates for the intermittently elliptical form of and disjunctive temporalities discussed in *Habeas Viscus*, because "the tenses of colonization are never conjugated with the verbs of an idyll."[34]

1 BLACKNESS: THE HUMAN

Now to talk to me about black studies as if it's something that concerned black people is an utter denial. This is the history of Western Civilization. I can't see it otherwise. This is the history that black people and white people and all serious students
of modern history and the history of the world have to know. To say it's some kind of
ethnic problem is a lot of nonsense.
—C. L. R. James

At first glance, C. L. R. James's 1969 proclamation in this chapter's epigraph
that thinking about black studies "as if it's something that concerned black
people is an utter denial" reads as at very least misguided if not wholly erroneous given that the relationship between black studies and black people
remains at the center of this interdiscipline.[1] Of course, James is far from
saying that black studies has no significance for black subjects; instead he
aims to underline the significance of black thought to western modernity
in toto: "all serious students of modern history and the history of the world
have to know." In order to come to a fuller understanding of the conceptual provenance of black studies, the assemblage of black people as the de
facto real object of black studies analytics, however, calls for closer scrutiny, albeit without completely disarticulating the two. In this vein, Hortense Spillers has called for black studies to define its disciplinary object

by virtue of "mov[ing] through a first step—to *become* a disciplinary object, or to undergo transformation of African American studies into an 'object of knowledge,' rather than a more or less elaborate repertory of performative gestures and utterances."[2] In the course of diagnosing this problematic's impact on the intellectual and institutional genesis of black studies, Spillers summons Althusser and Balibar's reconstruction of Karl Marx's critical epistemological intervention, especially with regard to intellectual production, since they "retrieve the 'object of knowledge,' concealed by a 'reading at sight' (RC, 16) and the 'empiricist conception of knowledge' (RC, 35), as a distinction to be made from the 'real object.' It seems to me that it is precisely that confusion, in one of its avatars, that persistently dogs African American sociocultural work as the hidden component of analysis" ("Crisis," 451).[3] Althusser and Balibar's structuralist reading of Marx clearly distinguishes Marx's project vis-à-vis the knowability of the object from the Kantian and Hegelian thought systems with the express aim of revealing the modes of production inherent in intellection. For Althusser, Balibar, and Spillers there exists no real object without the vehicular aid of particular modes of knowledge production. In fact, knowledge, now unlinked from the equivalency chain of ideology as false consciousness, represents a historically situated mode of production that transfigures real objects into objects of knowledge.

Thus, Spillers asks that black studies as such become an object of knowledge by virtue of recognizing itself in the mirror of a particular mode of knowledge production, which, in the process, "introduce[s] a new set of demands" ("Crisis," 451). Disarticulating the real object and the object of knowledge ("black people" and "blackness," for example) concocts a new set of demands for the black studies project that would emphasize its productive powers in the construction of the object.[4] And accenting these creative muscles demands "the knowledge of the complex articulation that makes the whole a whole," which moves away from "concrete co-presence" toward the "knowledge of the complexity of the object of knowledge."[5] Later, I consider racializing assemblages, insisting that understanding their overdetermined complexity will allow us to articulate, in both a limited and general sense, them as objects of knowledge within the conceptual domain of black studies. Instead of assuming that black studies reflects an already existent series of real objects, we need to draw attention to the complex ways this field of inquiry contributes to, or articulates, the creation of objects of knowledge such as the black community, black culture, and, indeed, black studies. Continuing to identify blackness as one of black studies's primary objects of knowledge with black people as real subjects (just as the human and Man appear as synonymous in western modernity) rather than an articulated object of knowledge accepts too easily that race is a given natural and/or cultural phenomenon and not an assemblage of forces that must continuously articulate nonwhite subjects as not-quite-human. Analogously, as an object of knowledge whiteness designates not actually existing groupings but a series of hierarchical power structures that apportion and delimit which members of the Homo sapiens species can lay claim to full human status. In short, insisting on black studies as a mode of knowledge production provides the conditions of possibility for viewing race as a set of articulated political relations or assemblages, and not a biological or cultural descriptor.[6]

In my opinion, the incipient promise that precipitated Spillers's injunction has yet to be fulfilled, leading to several disciplinary pitfalls that cannot but reticulate the structures of knowledge black studies initially sought to destroy. What is needed, then, is a more careful elaboration of black studies in order to map the field both within in its own institutional and intellectual genesis and in relation to other orders of knowledge. Yet this can be done only if the human emerges as a central object of knowledge in black studies and its intellectual enterprise is no longer conscripted to the realm of the particular, either by its practitioners or by critics outside the field. For the relegation of black thought to the confines of particularity only affirms the status of black subjects as beyond the grasp of the human.[7] Given the histories of slavery, colonialism, segregation, lynching, and so on, humanity has always been a principal question within black life and thought in the west; or, rather, in the moment in which blackness becomes apposite to humanity, Man's conditions of possibility lose their ontological thrust, because their limitations are rendered abundantly clear. Thus, the functioning of blackness as both inside and outside modernity sets the stage for a general theory of the human, and not its particular exception.

Spillers's focus is on the manifold tensions between black studies as an institutional and an intellectual project, especially as Harold Cruse, whose 1967 *Crisis of the Negro Intellectual* inspired her essay, was part of the disciplining of black studies and serves as the occasion for her thinking. Black studies, in its formation as an interdisciplinary department within the U.S.

university system since the 1960s and in earlier—but still existent—formations based in the traditional disciplines and located outside the university, has investigated the changing forms of racialization as they cut across history, ideology, politics, culture, economics, geography, social life, and so on. When W. E. B. Du Bois formulated a program for the study of the Negro at the turn of the twentieth century, based primarily in historiography and the then-nascent discipline of sociology, much of the data and analysis were concerned with how the category of the Negro qua Negro appeared on the stage of modern politics.[8] Rather than accepting as fact the assumed natural inferiority of black subjects, Du Bois interrogated systematically the historical genesis of the Negro while not losing sight of the multiple ways in which this category stood in relation to other contemporary racial groups (Southern whites or recent European immigrants, for example) and social structures. In this way, Du Bois devised a set of methodological and philosophical protocols that excavated the sedimented synchronic and diachronic relationality of the Negro—now transformed into a stated object of knowledge—so as to replace the Negro as a putatively given object of nature with the complex methods of racialization. In Du Bois's case these instruments include but are clearly not limited to the Negro's exclusion from institutions of higher learning, extremely limited labor choices in the urban North and even more constrained choices in the South, social segregation, Jim Crow, lynching, and sharecropping, as well as histories of enslavement and the systematic use of sexual violence. As an object of knowledge in the Du Boisian system of thought, the Negro appears not as a social Darwinist fait accompli but, rather, as the conglomerate effect of different racializing assemblages.

According to Ronald Judy, the systematic study of black life, which emerged at the end of the nineteenth century in the United States, is coterminous with the rise of the human sciences: "It is not mere coincidence that the earliest possibilities of such studies . . . emerge simultaneously with the human sciences, particularly the positivist sciences of sociology, history, and anthropology. These sciences were the means by which the Negro's humanity was to be determined once and for all."[9] In addition to establishing the black subject's humanity, as Judy and many other critics argue, black studies has also taken as its task the definition of the human itself. This is to say that, on the one hand, the human emerges as an object of knowledge as a by-product, so to speak, in the quest to ascertain black people's humanity because western humanity necessitates recalibration once black folks and other nonwhite subjects become part of its conceptual protectorate. On the other hand, black studies has also made humanity an avowed ideological and ontological battleground, since racializing assemblages are not autonomous, ethnographic categories but articulate how the human functions as a relational whole. And because the problematic of the human has held a pivotal place in various historical formations of black studies since its inception, this category needs to be foregrounded as a central object of knowledge of contemporary black studies and minority discourse so as to stave off the wholesale ingestion of black studies by the liberal multiculturalist morass defined by bioeconomic Man.[10] Consequently, we should deviate from the "descriptive and justificatory" models of intellectual practice with the purpose of embracing approaches that are "inventive . . . finding and exposing things that otherwise lie hidden beneath piety, heedlessness, or routine."[11]

In what follows, I use Sylvia Wynter's work to show how black studies provides a conceptual precipice, in the productionist vein of Spillers, Althusser, Said, and Massumi, from and through which to imagine new styles of humanity. Similar to Spillers, Wynter also seeks to specify the object of knowledge of black studies and modes of knowledge construction liminal to the western order of modernity more generally. Within the context of her work, it is the human—or different genres of the human—that materializes as the object of knowledge in the conceptual mirror of black studies.[12]

In recasting the human sciences, Wynter's commitment lies with disfiguring their real object, Man, through the incorporation of the colonial and racialist histories of the modern incantations of the human. This spot should be understood neither as an identitarian land claim concerned with particular borders of exclusion nor a universal terra nullius, but instead as a ceaselessly shifting relational assemblage that voyages in and out of the human. The cluster I am tracing here brings forth a "demonic ground" to versions of humanity unburdened by shackles of Man. Demonic ground is Sylvia Wynter's term for perspectives that reside in the liminal precincts of the current governing configurations of the human as Man in order to abolish this figuration and create other forms of life.[13] Consequently, the figuration of humanity found in black cultures forms an amalgamation of technologies— the application of knowledge—that have generally not been construed as central to, or even as part of, this category. These assemblages remain muf-

fled in mainstream critical thinking, which either consigns minority intellectuals or thought to the language of radical particularity or, conversely,
places them on the Olympus of the deracinated master subject, which, of
course, they cannot comfortably occupy.

Take, for instance, Judith Butler's passing reference to Wynter's oeuvre: "[Fanon's] project has been extended by contemporary scholars, including the literary critic Sylvia Wynter, to pertain to women of color and
to call into question the racist frameworks within which the category of the
human has been articulated."[14] While Fanon might not have been a cham-
pion of feminism as we have come to understand it—though one could
contest this, seeing how easy it has become to brush aside in a single sen-
tence Fanon's work on the basis of his androcentrism, although this does
not occur nearly as frequently in the case of Georg Wilhelm Friedrich Hegel
or Michel Foucault—it is not quite clear how his theorization of interior
colonies would not pertain to women of color, unless Butler were writing
under the presumption that black people such as Fanon and Wynter could
produce thought only for and about their particular identities as black men
and women. Viewing Wynter's colossal project, with which Butler does
not engage in any sustained way, both of critiquing the current western
instantiation of the human as coterminous with the white liberal subject
and of crafting a new humanism should not be reduced to observing the
historicity of this concept with the aim of showing how women of color and
other groups are excluded from its purview. Or to put it in Butlerian terms:
Wynter is interested in human trouble rather than "merely" woman-of-color
trouble, even while she deploys the liminal perspective of women of color
to imagine humanity otherwise.[15] In response to Butler and western feminism more generally, Wynter has stated on several occasions that her object
of knowledge is not gender but genre—genres of the human: "Our struggle
as Black women has to do with the destruction of the genre; with the displacement of the genre of the human of 'Man.'"[16] For Wynter, destroying
only western bourgeois conceptions of gender leaves intact the genre of the
human to which it is attached, and thus cannot serve as a harbinger of true
emancipation, which requires abolishing Man once and for all. It seems as
if we have yet to countermand the "unrecognized contradiction" which, as
Gayatri Spivak so fittingly diagnosed in 1988, "valorizes the concrete experience of the oppressed, while being so uncritical about [how] the historical
role of the intellectual is maintained by a verbal slippage."[17] Rather than

contending with Wynter's thinking as an intellectual project in the same manner as she does with Althusser, Hegel, or Irigaray, Butler privileges her concrete experience as a woman of color.[18]

In addition to rejecting gender as a category independent of other axes of subjugation, Wynter states that in her writings "'race' is really a code-word for 'genre.' Our issue is not the issue of 'race.' Our issue is the issue of the genre of 'Man.' It is this issue of the 'genre' of 'Man' that causes all the '-isms.' . . . Now when I speak at a feminist gathering and I come up with 'genre' and say 'gender' is a function of 'genre,' they don't want to hear that."[19] Thus, Wynter does not privilege race over gender as much as she insists that the master's tools (a universal notion of gender) cannot dismantle the master's house (Man), in Audre Lorde's formulation. Rather, Wynter's is a feminism typified by a critique of race and coloniality that focuses on the liberation of humans from all "-isms" versus only one specific form of subjection such as sexism, and it does not contradict the majority of women-of-color feminisms, which have not taken gender as an isolatable— or even primary—category of analysis but have instead highlighted the complex relationality between different forms of oppression.[20] Mainstream feminism in contrast sees itself "as an autonomized particularity, rather than as a particularity constitutive of a new non-middle class mode of universality."[21] For Wynter, a feminism that does not aspire to create a different code for what it means to be human merely sketches a different map of Man's territorializing assemblages; however, in order to abolish these assemblages feminism's insurrection must sabotage "its own prescribed role in the empirical articulation of its representations in effect by coming out of the closet, moving out of our assigned categories."[22] Hortense Spillers makes a similar point when she maintains, "we are less interested in joining the ranks of gendered femaleness than gaining the insurgent ground as female social subject."[23] In this context, "gendered femaleness" denotes gender as a "purely natural" and sovereign modality of difference while the revolt of a "female social subject" articulates gender as an integral component in the abolition of the human as Man. As phrased by one of the defining texts in the recent history of black feminism: "If Black women were free, it would mean that everyone else would have to be free since our freedom would necessitate the destruction of all the systems of oppression."[24] Moving away from discourses of inclusion and recognition, the Combahee River Collective dwells on the specific positions of black women within western modernity to launch global critiques, expansive theories, poetic tactics, and relational political projects that spurn the ethnographic encampment of Man's racializing assemblages.[25] Neither Wynter nor Spillers asks us to choose between race and gender but, instead, their thinking demands vigilance about how different forms of domination create both the conditions of possibility and the "semiosis of procedure" necessary to hierarchically distinguish full humans from not-quite-humans and nonhumans.[26] Spillers's and Wynter's ideas have been essential to formulating my arguments, because they represent systems of thought—both individually and taken together—that tackle notions of the human as it interfaces with gender, coloniality, slavery, racialization, and political violence without mapping these questions onto a mutually exclusive struggle between either the free-flowing terra nullius of the universally applicable or the terra cognitus of the ethnographically detained.

Wynter's large-scale intellectual project, which she has been pursuing in one form or another for the last thirty years, disentangles Man from the human in order to use the space of subjects placed beyond the grasp of this domain as a vital point from which to invent hitherto unavailable genres of the human.[27] According to this scheme in western modernity the religious conception of the self gave way to two modes of secularized being: first, the Cartesian "Rational Man," or homo politicus, and then beginning at the end of the eighteenth century, "Man as a selected being and natural organism . . . as the universal human, 'man as man.'"[28] The move from a supernatural conception of world and the self's place within this cosmos, however, does not signal the supersession of a primitive axiomatic with an enlightened and rarefied type of the human. Rather, one genre of the human (Judeo-Christian, religious) yields to another, just as provincial, version of the human, and, although both claim universality, neither genre fully represents the multiplicity of human life forms. In the context of the secular human, black subjects, along with indigenous populations, the colonized, the insane, the poor, the disabled, and so on serve as limit cases by which Man can demarcate himself as the universal human.[29] Thus, race, rather than representing accessory, comes to define the very essence of the modern human as "the code through which one not simply *knows* what human being is, but *experiences* being."[30] Accordingly, race makes its mark in the dominion of the ideological and physiological, or rather race scripts the elision of the former with the latter in the flesh.

In her latest writings, Wynter identifies homo politicus's successor in the long road from "theodicy" to "biodicy" as the liberal "bio-economic man."[31] The idea of "bio-economic man" marks the assumed naturalness that positions economic inequities, white supremacy, genocide, economic exploitation, gendered subjugation, colonialism, "natural selection," and concepts such as the free market not in the realm of divine design, as in previous religious orders of things, but beyond the reach of human intervention all the same. In both cases, this ensures that a particular humanly devised model of humanity remains isomorphic with the Homo sapiens species. Wynter's approach differs markedly from arguments that seek to include the oppressed within the already existing strictures of liberal humanism or, conversely, abolish humanism because of its racio-colonial baggage; instead Wynter views black studies and minority discourse as liminal spaces, simultaneously ensconced in and outside the world of Man, from which to construct new objects of knowledge and launch the reinvention of the human at the juncture of the culture and biology feedback loop.

Even though the genre of the human we currently inhabit in the west is intimately tied to the somatic order of things, for Wynter, the human cannot be understood in purely biological terms, whether this applies to the history of an individual organism (ontogenesis) or the development at the level of a species (phylogeny). This is where Fanon's important concept of sociogeny comes into play, offering Wynter an approach of thinking of the human—the "science in the social text," to echo Spillers's phrase—where culture and biology are not only not opposed to each other but in which their chemistry discharges mutually beneficial insights.[32] In this scenario, a symbolic register, consisting of discourse, language, culture, and so on (sociogeny) always already accompanies the genetic dimension of human action (ontogeny), and it is only in the imbrication of these two registers that we can understand the full scope of our being-in-the-world. Fanon's concept of sociogeny, arising from the inadequacy of traditional psychoanalytic models in the analysis of racialized colonialism, builds on Freud's appropriation of recapitulation theory.[33] Thus, according to Fanon, Freud breaks with the strict codes of Darwinism and social Darwinism (phylogenetic theory) in order to analyze the psyche of the modern individualized subject from an ontogenetic vantage point. While the ontogenetic technique yields, depending on your general sympathy for the now very antiquated protocols of Freudian psychoanalysis, abundant results when evaluating white subjects ensconced in the liberal nuclear family, it encounters a road-block when transplanted to the colonial settlement, which is why "the alien-ation of the black man is not an individual question. Alongside phylogeny and ontogeny, there is also sociogeny. . . . Society, unlike biochemical pro-cesses, does not escape human influence. Man is what brings society into being."[34] Why does the colonial situation specifically necessitate a reformu-lation of Freud's and Darwinism's procedural frame of reference?

Since colonial policies and discourse are frequently grounded in racial distinctions, the colonized subject cannot experience her or his nonbeing outside the particular ideology of western Man as synonymous with human, or, as Fanon writes, "not only must the black man be black; he must be black in relation to the white man."[35] The colonial encounter determines not just the black colonial subject's familial structure or social and physical mobility and such, but colors his or her very being as he-or-she-which-is-not-quite-human, as always already tardy in the rigged match of the survival of the fittest. Conversely, in this ontological face-off, the white colonial sub-ject encounters herself or himself as the "fullness and genericity of being human." However, he or she only does so in relation to the deficiency of the black subject and indigenous (Wynter, 40). To be precise, Fanon and Wynter locate racializing assemblages in the domain of being rather than the realm of epiphenomena, showing how humans create race for the benefit of some and the detriment of other humans. Yet because race is thought to rest in biology, it necessitates different analytic protocols than bare life and bio-politics, namely ones that draw on both ontogeny and sociogeny.

Whereas Fanon's mobilization of ontogeny remains rooted in the Freud-ian paradigm as pertaining to the individual subject, Wynter summons the explanatory apparatus of neurobiology to elucidate how racialization, de-spite its origins in sociogeny, is converted to the stuff of ontogenesis; this is what Wynter refers to as "sociogenetic."[36] Although human life has a bio-chemical core defined by a species-specific adaptive reward and punishment mechanism (poison = bad and food = good) that "determines the way in which each organism will perceive, classify, and categorize the world," it is "only through the mediation of the organism's experience of what feels good to the organism and what feels bad to it, and thereby of what it feels like to be that organism" that a repertoire of behaviors, which ensure the continued existence of the species, develops (Wynter, 50). For the human species, because it is defined by both organic and symbolic registers, this is complicated by the way culturally specific sociogenic principles such as what is good or bad work to trigger neurochemical reward and punishment processes, in the process "institut[ing] the human subject as a culture-specific and thereby verbally defined, if physiologically implemented, mode of being and sense of self. One, therefore, whose phenomenology . . . is as objectively, constructed as its physiology" (Wynter, 54).[37] Phenomenological perception must consequently don the extravagant drag of physiology in order to "turn theory into flesh, . . . [into] codings in the nervous system," so as to signal the extrahuman instantiation of humanity.[38]

Wynter's description of the autopoiesis of the human stretches Fanon's concept of sociogeny by grounding it in an, albeit false or artificial, physiological reality. In other words, Wynter summons neurobiology not in order to take refuge in a prelapsarian field anterior to the registers of culture and ideology, but to provide a transdisciplinary global approach to the study of human life that explains how sociogenic phenomena, particularly race, become anchored in the ontogenic flesh. Also, in contrast to treatments of racialization more squarely articulated from the disciplinary perspective of sociobiology, Wynter does not focus on the origins and adaptive evolution of race itself but rather on how sociogenic principles are anchored in the human neurochemical system, thus counteracting sociobiological explanations of race, which retrospectively project racial categories onto an evolutionary screen.[39] That is to say, Wynter interrogates the ontogenic functioning of race—the ways it serves as a physiologically resonant nominal and conceptual pseudonym for the specific genre of the human: Man—and not its role in human phylogeny.

Consequently, racialization figures as a master code within the genre of the human represented by western Man, because its law-like operations are yoked to species-sustaining physiological mechanisms in the form of a global color line—instituted by cultural laws so as to register in human neural networks—that clearly distinguishes the good/life/fully-human from the bad/death/not-quite-human. This, in turn, authorizes the conflation of racialization with mere biological life, which, on the one hand, enables white subjects to "see" themselves as transcending racialization due to their full embodiment of this particular genre of the human while responding antipathetically to nonwhite subjects as bearers of ontological cum biological lack, and, on the other hand, in those subjects on the other side of the color line, it creates sociogenically instituted physiological reactions against their own existence and reality.[40] Since the being of nonwhite subjects has been coded by the cultural laws in the world of Man as pure negativity, their subjectivity impresses punishment on the neurochemical reward system of all humans, or in the words of Frantz Fanon: "My body was returned to me spread-eagled, disjointed, redone, draped in mourning on this white winter's day. The Negro is an animal, the Negro is bad, the Negro is wicked, the Negro is ugly."[41] Political violence plays a crucial part in the baroque techniques of modern humanity, since it simultaneously serves to create not-quite-humans in specific acts of violence and supplies the symbolic source material for racialization.

For Wynter, the promise of black studies—and the numerous other ruptures precipitated by the 1960s—lies in its liminality, which contains potential exit strategies from the world of Man. However, we must first devise new objects of knowledge that facilitate "the calling in question of our present culture's purely biological definition of what it is to *be*, and therefore of what it is *like* to be, human."[42] We must do so because we cannot fully understand the present incarnation of the human from within the "biocentric and bourgeois" epistemic order that authorizes the biological selectedness of Man and, conversely, the creation of "dysgenic humans" (those who are evolutionarily dysselected), "a category comprised in the US of blacks, Latinos, Indians as well as the transracial group of the poor, the jobless, the homeless, the incarcerated," the disabled, and the transgendered.[43] Within our current episteme, these groups are constituted as aberrations from the ethnoclass of Man by being subjected to racializing assemblages that establish "natural" differences between the selected and dysselected. In other words, black, Latino, poor, incarcerated, indigenous, and so forth populations become real objects via the conduit of evolutionarily justified discourses and institutions, which, as a consequence, authorizes Man to view himself as naturally ordained to inhabit the space of full humanity. Thus, even though racializing assemblages commonly rely on phenotypical differences, their primary function is to create and maintain distinctions between different members of the Homo sapiens species that lend a suprahuman explanatory ground (religious or biological, for example) to these hierarchies. As Wynter explains, "all our present struggles with respect to race, class, gender, sexual orientation, ethnicity, struggles over the environment, global warming, severe climate change, the sharply unequal distribution of the earth resources . . . —these are all differing facets of the central ethnoclass

Man vs. Human struggle."[44] Wynter's oeuvre facilitates the analysis of the relay between different forms of subjugation, because in it the human operates as a relational ontological totality. Therefore, the Man versus Human battle does not dialectically sublate the specificity of the other struggles but articulates them in this open totality so as to abolish Man and liberate all of humanity rather than specific groups.

While I'm yet unsure of how far I'm willing to trail Wynter's pioneering inroads into the territory of the neurobiological, I believe strongly that her global approach to racialization and the human represents one of the most significant contributions to contemporary critical thought. It is important that Wynter formulates these ideas from the liminal standpoint of black studies—even more specifically from the Caribbean as the primal scene of the protracted modern colonization of the Americas—showing how racialization remains vital to the ways we experience our being-in-the-world. In addition, Wynter's model ushers us away from thinking race via the conduits of chromatism, which simply reaffirms the putatively biological basis of this category, or the radical particularity of black life and culture, which accepts too easily the unimpeachable reality of the "Man-as-human" episteme. By contrast, the insights reaped from the comparison of different black populations in recent formulations of black diaspora studies tend to reinforce exactly this particularity, thereby consenting to the current governing manifestation of the human as synonymous with western Man. Instead, Wynter constructs a model of black studies that has as its object of knowledge the role of racialization in shaping the modern human and that takes the resultant liminal vantage point as an occasion for the imagination of other forms of being and becoming human. Wynter's focus on racial coloniality vis-à-vis physiology is especially relevant today given the rising significance of genomic theories of race in science, industry, and public policy, and, conversely, the recent almost wholesale turn away from discussions about race and biology on the academic left, as well as the depoliticization of biology, especially physiology, frequently found in affect theory.[45] Wynter's and Spillers's thinking provides alternate genealogies for theorizing the ideological and physiological mechanics of the violently tiered categorization of the human species in western modernity, which stand counter to the universalizing but resolutely Europe-centered visions embodied by bare life and biopolitics. They do so—in stark contrast to Foucault and Agamben—without demoting race and gender to the rank of the ethnographically particular, instead exposing how these categories carve from the swamps of slavery and colonialism the very flesh and bones of modern Man.

Wynter's idea of black studies runs counter to the mobilization of black studies in the service of a discourse of black particularity established by the conventions of inter- or intraracial comparison. In Wynter's vocabulary, diaspora discourse, although containing the possibility of defacing one of Man's most significant instruments of subjection—the nation-state— tends to focus on the map rather than territory, thereby not challenging reigning conceptions of community. The recent prominence of diaspora discourse in black studies has supplanted the emphasis on African American identity that defined the field for some time with the interrogation of U.S. black life within and against the context of other diasporic groups. The nominal passage from black studies to African American studies and now diaspora studies sets some of the groundwork for querying the conceptual underpinnings of these developments.[46] Replacing the designation *black* with *African American* signals foremost a turn away from a primarily political category toward an identitarian marker of cultural and/or ethnic specificity; *diaspora* suggests a concurrent de-emphasizing of specificities in the embrace of transnational frames of reference and a return of said particularities via the comparison of black populations that differ in nationality.

The turn to the diaspora concept in the history of black studies and the coterminous reign of the transnational paradigm in American studies frequently position the nation as a dialectical stepping-stone toward a supranational sphere that appears as more desirable than its national shadow. Still, these discourses often replicate and reify the very nation form they are seeking to escape in their comparison of different national literatures, cultures, languages, and so on. Though at the outset it appears as if this approach seeks to present a "planetary imagination" of blackness that surpasses "African American hegemony and/or provinciality," diaspora studies's reliance on comparison frequently affirms the given instead of providing avenues for the conjuring of alternate possibilities.[47] By so determinedly stressing the disparities between these different nationally located communities, these inquiries run the risk of interpellating individual African diasporas, whether in Europe, the United States, or the Caribbean, as primordially constituted beacons of racial kinship. Instead of a transnational ethnic notion of peoplehood that unites all African-descended subjects around the globe, national boundaries, or linguistic differences that often help define the national ones, become the ultimate indicators of differentiation. In this process, national borders and/or linguistic differences are in danger of entering the discursive record as ontological absolutes, rather than as structures and institutions that have served again and again to relegate black subjects to the status of western modernity's nonhuman other, or, as Katherine McKittrick describes the dangers of diaspora discourse: "Diaspora has the potential to be a hegemonic geographic project, a renewed version of Man's classificatory-exclusionary-bourgeoisie-spaces-for-us-spaces-for-them (them-as-the-absolute-Other)—unless, I think, we fill it with human life, attend to its radical creolized potential, and continue to insist that mapping diaspora is an ethical and unresolved politic, a really human, human geography."[48]

My point is that the turn away from envisioning the African diaspora as a transcendental racial bond to series of radical differences can unwillingly lead to the importation of what Etienne Balibar calls the "nation form" into diaspora discourse. Balibar describes the process by which collectivities are transformed into "the people" in the following fashion: "Social formations . . . [are] represented in the past or in the future *as if* they formed a natural community, possessing of itself an identity of origins, culture and interests which transcends individuals and social conditions."[49] This "natural community" also constitutes a spectral grammar of current diaspora discourse. Given that peoplehood represents the foremost mode of imagining, (re)-producing, and legislating community, and thus managing inequality in the intertwined histories of capitalism and the nation-state, peoplehood sneaks in as the de facto actualization of diasporas in the national context, especially when we avoid specifying how black collectivity might be codified in the absence of this category. Thus, in the parlance of comparison, diasporic populations appear as real objects instead of objects of knowledge.

The particularities of national diasporic groupings occupy central positions in current diaspora discourse, and they do so through the lens of the comparative method. As a result, the empirical existence of national boundaries, or linguistic differences that often help define the national ones, become the ultimate indicators of differentiation and are in danger of entering the discursive record as transcendental truths, rather than as structures and institutions that have served repeatedly to relegate black subjects to the status of western modernity's nonhuman other. Blackness, however, cannot be defined as primarily empirical nor understood as the nonproperty of particular subjects, but should be understood as an integral structuring assemblage of the modern human. Once we take this into account, we can practice a politics, which, rather than succumbing to the brutal facticity of blackness, introduces invention into existence, as Frantz Fanon argues.[50] This is precisely what the insistence on the existent variations between nationally bound Afro-diasporic groups in diaspora studies jeopardizes: the entry of invention into the regions of blackness and, therefore, humanity.[51] The twinning of comparativity and specificity does not allow for the initiation of different humanities, particularly because it fails to probe the foundations upon which these particularities are put and kept in place. Instead, we might do well to conceive humanity as a relational ontological totality, however fractured this totality might be. Not doing so will extend the conflation of one genre of the human: western Man with a real object (extrahumanly instituted and based completely in physiology) instead of viewing humanity as a "complex and differentially articulated structure in dominance of the social totality that constitutes the social formation arising from a determinate mode of production."[52] Black studies can and should take up a pivotal position in this process, because analyses of racialization have the potential to disarticulate the human from Man, thus metamorphosing humanity into a relational object of knowledge.

———

To approach the social totality of the human as an object of knowledge we must understand the workings of the flesh.

2 BARE LIFE: THE FLESH

According to Agamben's influential theorization, modern sovereignty is haunted and shadowed by the figure of the "homo sacer."[1] The homo sacer, a human being that cannot be ritually offered, but whom one can kill without incurring the penalty of murder, first appears in the city-states of Roman antiquity. Taking this figure as his starting point, Agamben infuses it with Michel Foucault's concept of biopolitics, Walter Benjamin's concern with mere life, Carl Schmitt's thoughts on sovereignty and the state of exception, and Hannah Arendt's notion of statelessness. The homo sacer's ban from the political community facilitates a double movement that is contradictory but necessary: on the one hand, these subjects, by being barred from the category of the human, are relegated to bare or naked life, being both literally and symbolically stripped of all accoutrements associated with the liberalist subject. Conversely, this bare life stands at the center of the state's exercise of its biopower, its force of legislating life and death, which, in this framework, provides one of the central features of the modern nation-state.[2] As Agamben writes, "the syntagm homo sacer names something like the originary 'political' relation, which is to say, bare life insofar as it operates in an inclusive exclusion as the referent of the sovereign decision" (Homo Sacer, 85).[3] Thus, the incorporation, production, and politicization of zoe (mere biological life), as opposed to bios ("full" human existence) forms the core of political modernity and increasingly comes to define the scope of state power, particularly in the legal state of exception. Departing somewhat from Foucault, Agamben locates the political digestion of *zoe* in a generalized, quasi-ontological "zone of indistinction" in which the categories that segregate bare life and other modes of life become obsolete: "What characterizes modern politics is . . . that, together with the process by which the exception everywhere becomes the rule, the realm of bare life—which is originally situated at the margins of the political order—gradually begins to coincide with the political realm, and exclusion and inclusion, outside and inside, *bios* and *zoe*, right and fact, enter into a zone of irreducible indistinction" (*Homo Sacer*, 9). Agamben imagines the field of bare life as eradicating divisions among humans along the lines of race, religion, nationality, or gender, because it creates a substance that, albeit in its debasement, transcends traditional social and political markers. However, for Agamben, this zone of indistinction is both historically presaged and conceptually defined by the order of terror found in Nazi concentration camps, prompting the question: how can such an irreducibly indefinite space be so thoroughly engulfed by such a tremendous modality of mere life? Nazi death camps provide the ultimate incarnation of this arrangement not as a deviation but as the sine qua non of modern politics as sovereignty, one that resonates in various current biopolitical institutions such as refugee and detainment camps. The concentration camp and its progeny map a terrain in which the central aim of politics is the manufacture of bare life, and, according to Agamben, it is the politics in which we live. Still, we should proceed with caution here, since equating modern politics with the concentration camp, as Agamben does by calling these camps both the nomos (law, convention) and hidden matrix of politics, is surely not the same as saying that the camp forms an integral part of modernity, or even that bare life is an essential aspect of state power. By placing the severest version of the bare life at the core of contemporary politics, Agamben seeks to disentangle the Holocaust from its status as an ultimate yet historically discrete aberration of modernity. This, paradoxically, grounds the concentration camp in the deviant terrain Agamben desires to leave behind, while also placing under erasure the idea that bare life represents the sphere of modern politics in which differences (race, gender, nationality, religion, etc.) no longer matter. So, while these distinctions are used to fabricate bare life, their incantatory powers become null and void in the zone of indistinction, which is why "today there is no longer any one clear figure of the sacred man, . . . perhaps because we are all virtually *homines sacri*" (*Homo Sacer*, 115). If bare life embodies a potential dimension of contemporary politics as such, we might ask, then, why certain subjects are structurally more susceptible to personifying its actualization and why the concentration camp functions as the epitome of modern sovereignty for Agamben, especially considering that most instantiations of bare life do not necessarily entail physical mortality per se but other forms of political death.

Concentration camps shared an intimate history with different forms of colonialism and genocide before being transformed into the death camps of Nazi Germany. The *Encyclopædia Britannica* defines a concentration camp as "an internment centre for political prisoners and members of national or minority groups who are confined for reasons of state security, exploitation, or punishment, usually by executive decree or military order. Persons are placed in such camps often on the basis of identification with a particular ethnic or political group rather than as individuals and without benefit either of indictment or fair trial." Modern concentration camps were initially constructed in the 1830s in the southeastern United States as part of the campaign for "Indian removal" to detain 22,000 Cherokee (Gunter's Landing, Ross's Landing, and Fort Cass), and later during the Dakota War of 1862 a camp was constructed on Pike Island near Fort Snelling, Minnesota, in which 1,700 Dakota were interned.[4] So-called contraband camps, which existed during and immediately after the Civil War, were designed as temporary domiciles for "freed" slaves throughout the U.S. South. The conditions in these precarious holding zones at the crossroads of enslavement and freedom were defined by starvation and the outbreak of diseases, which lead to the death of thousands of black subjects.[5] In 1895 imperial Spain utilized concentration camps in Cuba to stop local uprisings, and the British first used the English-language term in 1900 to name similar efforts during the Boer War in South Africa. During the Philippine-American War (1901), the United States constructed an encampment in Batangas province.[6]

The German variant of the concentration camp is also the product of a colonial provenance, having its point of origin in German Southwest Africa at the turn of the twentieth century to detain the Herero and Namaqua and which was integral to the genocidal acts perpetrated by the German colonists against these groups from 1904 to 1907: "Whereas the prototype of settler violence in the history of modern colonialism is the near-extermination of Amerindians in the New World, the prototype of settler violence in the African colonies was the German annihilation of over 80 percent of the Herero population in the colony of German South West Africa in a single year, 1904."[7] In addition, Eugen Fischer and Theodor Mollison, who would be extremely influential to Nazi eugenics as Joseph Mengele's mentors and to the genocidal endeavors carried out in the death camps, undertook extensive medical experiments in the colonial camps located in German Southwest Africa.[8] Overall, a thick historical relation defines the rise of modern concentration camps in colonial contexts and their subsequent reconstitution as industrialized killing machines in Europe during the Third Reich.[9] Agamben briefly mentions the colonial prehistory of concentration camps, however, only to argue that the camps' true telic significance becomes apparent when they are annexed into the legal state of exception during the Third Reich.[10] Nevertheless, the effects of colonial eugenics carried out in Southwest Africa during Germany's colonial period were not confined to this locale, but, more crucially, helped establish German bourgeois society during colonialism and after,[11] in much the same way as they did other colonial metropoles, despite Germany's relatively brief stint as a colonial power (1885–1917).[12] Instead of advancing an ethos of historical determinism that would deem German colonial camps and those in the United States, Cuba, or the Philippines (or, alternately, early twentieth-century U.S. and European psychiatric wards and prisons) nascent versions of the more radical and all-encompassing Nazi concentration camps, I am interested in the crosscurrents and discontinuities of the irreducible relation at the heart of modern terror and encampment that gets lost in the shuffle between the state of exception and the zone of indistinction. In other words, the sociohistorical texture of relation that establishes the camp as a locus centralis of modern terror qua politics languishes in Agamben's universalization of the concentration camp. To be clear, I am not taking issue with the figuration of concentration camps in Agamben's argument per se, as much as I am questioning the projection of death camps onto an exceptional ontological screen (both as an end point and as a site of origin) rather than emphasizing their constitutive relationality in the modern world as well as the resultant displacement of racial slavery, colonialism, and indigenous genocide as nomoi of modern politics.

A number of critics have noted how different forms of enslavement, colonialism, genocide, immigration policies, racism, and the current U.S. prison system constitute integral components of modern terror and therefore politics.[13] Paul Gilroy, for instance, draws attention to both the conceptual contiguity of the plantation and the camp in their suspension of law in the name of the law, while also showing how the camp emerged from assorted forms of colonial domination. He writes, "Both [the slave plantation and the concentration camp] constituted exceptional spaces where normal juridical rules and procedures had been deliberately set aside. In both, the profit motive and its economic rationalities were practically qualified by the geopolitical imperatives of racialized hierarchy. It is easy to overlook how colonial societies and conflicts provided the context in which the concentration camp emerged as novel form of political administration, population management, warfare, and coerced labor."[14] Thus, the concentration camp, the colonial outpost, and slave plantation suggest three of many relay points in the weave of modern politics, which are neither exceptional nor comparable, but simply relational. Although racial slavery and the Holocaust exhibit the state of exception, they do so in different legal and political ways, since slavery's purpose was not to physically annihilate, at least not primarily, as much as to physiologically subdue and exploit, erasing the *bios* of those subjects that were subject to its workings.

Racial slavery, by virtue of spanning a much greater historical period than the Shoah, and, more importantly, by not seeming as great an abnormality both in its historical context and in the way it is retroactively narrativized, reveals the manifold modes in which extreme brutality and directed killing frequently and peacefully coexist with other forms of coercion and noncoercion within the scope of the normal juridico-political order. This is what invents the homo sacer as homo sacer, for bare life must be measured against something, otherwise it just appears as life; life stripped of its bareness, as it were. Though murdering slaves was punishable by law in many U.S. states, usually these edicts were not enforced, and the master could kill slaves with impunity since they were categorized as property.[15] Consequently, slavery conjures a different form of bare life than the concentration camp, since the more prevalent version of finitude in this context was what Orlando Patterson has referred to as "social death," the purging of all citizenship rights from slaves save their mere life.[16] Although Patterson provides the preliminary tools for thinking through the specific disjointed form of life inhabited by the enslaved, his notion of social death emphasizes mortality at the cost of sociality, no matter how curtailed it may be in this context, and it fails to incorporate in any significant manner the messy corporeality of bare life. In Patterson's thinking, social death does not produce "a zone of indistinction," but he falls prey to some of the same ruses as Agamben given that both thinkers tend to disembody the homo sacer figure. Hortense Spillers's distinction between body and flesh extends, while also offering a corrective to these approaches by highlighting the embodiment of those banished to the zone of indistinction and by showing how bare life is transmitted historically so as to become affixed to certain bodies. Which is to say, Spillers interrogates the visual, fleshly distinctions that comprise the nexus of racialization and/as bare life, which Agamben labors to render inoperable in this field, and Spillers does so because she deploys the middle passage and plantation slavery in the Americas as the nomoi of modern hierarchical governance. Thus, we could just as well assert that racial slavery represents the biopolitical nomos of modernity, particularly given its historically antecedent status vis-à-vis the Holocaust and the many different ways it highlights the continuous and nonexceptional modes of physiological and psychic violence exerted upon black subjects since the dawn of modernity, or in the phrasing of Edouard Glissant, "The plantation is one of the bellies of the world, not the only one, one among many others, but it has the advantage of being able to be studied with the utmost precision. . . . The place was closed, but the word derived from it remains open. This is one part, a limited part, of the lesson of the world."[17] The fact that the Middle Passage, plantation slavery, Jim Crow, and so on, are not included in most conceptualizations of this category, whether in scholarly discourse or by the United Nations, only highlights just how routine the brutalization of black flesh continues to be in the world of Man.[18] How would Foucault's and Agamben's theories of modern violence differ if they took the Middle Passage as their point of departure rather than remaining entrapped within the historiographical cum philosophical precincts of fortress Europe?

When asked in an interview by Saidiya Hartman about the continued significance of her path-breaking 1987 essay, "'Mama's Baby, Papa's Maybe': An American Grammar Book," what animated this intellectual project vis-à-vis feminism, Hortense Spillers responds thus:

What I saw happening was black people being treated as a kind of raw material. That the history of black people was something you could use as a note of inspiration but it was never anything that had anything to do with you—you could never use it to explain something in theoretical terms. There was no discourse that it generated, in terms of the mainstream academy that gave it a kind of recognition. And so my idea was to try to generate a discourse, or a vocabulary that would not just make it desirable, but would necessitate that black women be in the conversation.[19]

In line with my earlier discussion of the vexed status of racialized subjectivity in the recent history of theory, Spillers creates an intervention within the fields of black studies, feminist criticism, and critical theory in order to theorize some general dimensions of modern subjectivity from the vantage point of black women, which develops a grammar, creates a vocabulary that does not choose between addressing the specific location of black women, a broader theoretical register about what it means to be human during and in the aftermath of the transatlantic slave trade, and the imagination of liberation in the future anterior tense of the NOW.[20]

Spillers concentrates on the processes through which slaves are transformed into bare life/flesh and then subjected to the pleasure of the bodied subject, arguing, "before the 'body' there is 'flesh,' that zero degree of social conceptualization that does not escape concealment under the brush of discourse or the reflexes of iconography. . . . We regard this human and social irreparability as high crimes against the flesh, as the person of African females and males registered the wounding."[21] Flesh, while representing both a temporal and conceptual antecedent to the body, is not a biological occurrence seeing that its creation requires an elaborate apparatus consisting of "the calculated work of iron, whips, chains, knives, the canine patrol, the bullet" ("Mama's Baby," 207), among many other factors, including courts of law.[22] If the body represents legal personhood qua self-possession, then the flesh designates those dimensions of human life cleaved by the working together of depravation and deprivation. In order for this cruel ruse to succeed, however, subjects must be transformed into flesh before being granted the illusion of possessing a body. What Spillers refers to as the "hieroglyphics of the flesh" created by these instruments is transmitted to the succeeding generations of black subjects who have been "liberated" and granted body in the aftermath of de jure enslavement. The hieroglyphics of the flesh do not vanish once affixed to proper personhood (the body); rather they endure as a pesky potential vital to the maneuverings of "cultural seeing by skin color" ("Mama's Baby," 207). Racializing assemblages translate the lacerations left on the captive body by apparatuses of political violence to a domain rooted in the visual truth-value accorded to quasi-biological distinctions between different human groupings. Thus, rather than entering a clearing zone of indistinction, we are thrown into the vortex of hierarchical indicators: racializing assemblages. In the absence of kin, family, gender, belonging, language, personhood, property, and official records, among many other factors, what remains is the flesh, the living, speaking, thinking, feeling, and imagining flesh: the ether that holds together the world of Man while at the same time forming the condition of possibility for this world's demise. It's the end of the world—don't you know that yet?

While Wynter's resistance to the universalization of gendered categories associated with bourgeois whiteness in certain strands of feminism, which I discussed in chapter 1, is understandable, her genealogy of modernity, which sees a "mutational shift from the primacy of the anatomical model of sexual difference as the referential model of mimetic ordering, to that of the physiognomic model of racial/cultural difference" in the Renaissance, remains less convincing, because it leads to the repudiation of gender analytics as such.[23] This aspect of Wynter's thinking fails to persuade in the way the other elements of her global analytics of the human do, since it assumes that beginning with the colonization of the Americas, race (physiognomy) dislodges gender/sex (anatomy) as the systematizing principle according to which the Homo sapiens species is categorized into full humans, not-quite-humans, and nonhumans. The shift Wynter diagnoses, though surely present in the history of modernity, cannot be encompassed by the distinction between physiognomy and anatomy, even if not construed as either categorical or complete, because neither anatomy nor sexual difference recede like silhouettes sketched in the soil at the shores that delimit the Drexciyan waters of the Middle Passage.[24] Instead, sexual difference remains an intoxicating sociogenically instituted mode of mimetic structuring in modernity, though always tied to specific variants of (un)gendering. Wynter's dismissal of gender/sex as forceful indicators of the hierarchical ordering of our species thus seems to discard sexual difference with the proverbial bathwater; and it also largely leaves intact the morphological dimorphism upon which the modern west constructs gendered stratification. In this context, it is useful to distinguish between physiognomy as inferring from an individual's external appearance, particularly "a person's facial features or expression[, their] character or ethnic origin," while anatomy designates "the bodily structure of humans, animals, and other living organisms," and physiology analyzes how organisms or bodily parts (e.g., the brain) function and behave.[25] Wynter's statement assumes a substantial variance between physiognomy and anatomy, even though the former is unthinkable without some recourse to the latter, at the same time as it does not account for the many attempts at creating an isomorphic echo chamber between racial and anatomical difference, as was the case with Sarah Baartman, the so-called Venus Hottentot, for instance. Put differently, in the sphere of racial and sexual difference, anatomy and physiognomy form a continuum in a larger modern assemblage that requires the physiognomic territorialization of anatomic qualities.

Moreover, if, according to Wynter, there exists no universal instantiation of gender, then how can racial differentiation persist without being modulated by gender or sexuality? To be clear, I am not after an academic commonsense invocation of the necessary intersectionality of all "axes of subjugation" but of one that takes Wynter's insights about how race inflects human physiology in colonial modernity seriously, while still asking how, even if it is not the primary model of hierarchical differentiation, sexual difference might figure into this theory of the human. How do we think gender categories based upon the anatomical foundation of sexual distinction through the lens of racialization, and vice versa? How do we account for what Spillers calls "female flesh 'ungendered'" birthed by the Middle Passage ("Mama's Baby," 207), which continues to affect all black subjects?[26] As black feminist theorists Hazel Carby, Julia Oparah, Claudia Tate, Evelynn Hammonds, Patricia Hill Collins, Angela Davis, Darlene Clark Hine, and Cathy Cohen, among many others, have pointed out, black subjects' genders and sexualities operate differently from those found in the mainstream of the world of Man.[27] Namely, in the same way that black people appear as either nonhuman or magically hyperhuman within the universe of Man, black subjects are imbued with either a surplus (hyperfemininity or hypermasculinity) of gender and sexuality or a complete lack thereof (desexualization). However, regardless whether deficit or surplus, what remains significant is that the histories of racial slavery, colonialism, Jim Crow, the prison, and the like, which all represent different racializing assemblages in Man's extensive armory, have constitutively incapacitated black subjects' ability to conform to hegemonic gender and sexuality norms, and often excessively so. Drawing on examples from racial slavery and the more recent pathologization of the black family in the infamous Moynihan report, Cathy Cohen and Spillers ascertain how the prohibition of marriage among slaves and the complete erasure of traditional kinship arrangements during and subsequent to the Middle Passage underwrite the policing and disparaging of those black genders and sexualities "outside of heteronormative privilege, in particular those perceived as threatening systems of white supremacy, male domination, and capitalist advancement."[28]

Thus, circling back to Wynter's distrust of gender-focused inquiries, it is imperative to consider how the translation of sexual difference to de facto nonnormative genders and sexualities within black communities (the ungendered flesh) suggests a fundamental component in the barring of black people from the category of the human-as-Man. Which is to say that taking on the semblance of full humanity requires apposite gender and sexuality provisos that cannot be taken for granted in postslavery black cultures. Indeed, this is why I believe we need both Wynter and Spillers to come to a fuller understanding of how racializing assemblages operate, since the sociogenic anchoring of racial difference in physiology and the banning of black subjects from the domain of the human occur in and through gender and sexuality. Retrospectively describing the concept of the hieroglyphics of the flesh in the introduction to her 2003 collection of essays, Spillers maintains that she was attempting not only to pinpoint "one of diasporic slavery's technologies of violence through marking, but also to propose that 'beyond' the violating hand that laid on the stigmata of a recognition that was a misrecognition, or the regard that was disregard, there was a *semiosis* of procedure that had enabled such a moment in the first place." Spillers concludes, "The marking, the branding, the whipping—all Instruments of a terrorist regime—were more deeply that—to get in somebody's face in that way would have to be centuries in the making that would have had little to do, though it is difficult to believe, with the biochemistry of pigmentation, hair texture, lip thickness, and the indicial measure of the nostrils, but everything to do with those 'unacknowledged legislators' of a discursive and an economic discipline."[29] Despite having no real basis in biochemistry, the hieroglyphics of the flesh requires grounding in the biological sphere so as to facilitate—even as it conceals and because it masks—the political, economic, social, and cultural disciplining (semiosis of procedure) of the Homo sapiens species into assemblages of the human, not-quite-human, and nonhuman; this is what I am referring to as racialization. The "profitable 'atomizing' of the captive body" (and the bodies of the colonized, tortured, imprisoned, interned, etc.) puts into place the conditions of possibility for the creation and maintenance of racializing assemblages and most decidedly not the suspension of racialized divisions in a biopolitical zone of indistinction ("Mama's Baby," 208). As a result, the flesh epitomizes a central modern assemblage of racialization that highlights how bare life is not only a product of previously established distinctions but also, and more significantly, aids in the perpetuation of hierarchical categorizations along the lines of nationality, gender, religion, race, culture, sexuality, and so on.[30]

In its focus on both the genesis and the aftermath of zoe's specifically modern politicization, Spillers's conceptualization of the flesh shines a spotlight on slavery's alternate passages to the formation of bare life. In other words, the flesh is not an abject zone of exclusion that culminates in death but an alternate instantiation of humanity that does not rest on the mirage of western Man as the mirror image of human life as such. Analogously, Luce Irigaray argues that within phallogocentric structures, women, "as commodities, are a mirror of value of and for man."[31] Here the different groups excluded from the category of proper humanity encounter only a scopic echo of their deviance from—and therefore reinscribe—the superiority of western Man, reflecting their own value as ontological lack and western Man's value as properly human. Thus, as Spillers remarks, "[the black American woman] became instead the principal point of passage between the human and the non-human world. Her issue became the focus of a cunning difference—visually, psychologically, ontologically—as the route by which the dominant modes decided the distinction between humanity and 'other.' At this level of radical discontinuity in the 'great chain of being,' black is vestibular to culture."[32] And being vestibular to culture means that gendered blackness—though excluded from culture, and frequently violently so—is a passage to the human in western modernity because, in giving flesh to the word of Man, the flesh comes to define the phenomenology of Man, which is always already lived as unadulterated physiology. As a result, the flesh rests at that precarious threshold where the person metamorphoses into the group and "the individual-in-the-mass and the mass-in-the-individual mark an iconic thickness: a concerted function whose abiding centrality is embodied in the flesh," and which is why—as we shall see later—the flesh resists the legal idiom of personhood as property.[33]

For Maurice Merleau-Ponty, the flesh "is not matter, is not mind, is not substance"; rather, in his phenomenological theorization, the flesh functions as an integral component of being, which is "not a fact or a sum of facts, and yet adherent to location and to the now."[34] If the flesh represents an element in the vein of the classical quadfecta of earth, wind, (water,) and fire, it appears as a vital prop in the world of Man's dramaturgy of Being. Following Merleau-Ponty, Elizabeth Grosz holds that the relationality of the flesh—its nonsubstantive substance—materializes through "an inherent intertwining of subject and world," creating a "new ontology, one which supersedes the ontological distinction between the animate and the inanimate, between the animal and the human, . . . in ways that might also suit the interests of feminists," since the hierarchical differentiation between reason and enfleshment is "complicit with the hierarchy which positions one kind of subject (male, white, capitalist) in the position of superiority over others."[35] Conceptualized in this way, the flesh thus operates as a vestibular gash in the armor of Man, simultaneously a tool of dehumanization and a relational vestibule to alternate ways of being that do not possess the luxury of eliding phenomenology with biology. Not an aberration, yet excluded, not at the center of being but nevertheless constitutive of it, the flesh is "that ether, that shit that make your soul burn slow" as well as a modality of relation.[36] Though the meaning of ether, long thought to be one of the elements, has been redefined within the constellation of modern science, I want to keep in play both its ancient (medium/substance) and modern (anesthetic) significations to highlight how the flesh stands as both the cornerstone and potential ruin of the world of Man. If "the privilege granted to consciousness . . . is the ether of metaphysics, the element of our thought that is caught in the language of metaphysics," then the flesh represents nothing less than the ether of Man.[37] For the flesh provides a stepping stone toward new genres of human, in which we finally begin to honor the long-ago issued expiration date to the "materialized scene . . . of female flesh 'ungendered'" in its role as a deviation from Man and instead begin to concentrate on how the flesh "offers a praxis and a theory, a text for living and for dying, and a method for reading both through their diverse mediations" (Spillers, "Mama's Baby," 207).

———

To subsist in the force field of the flesh, then, might just be better than not existing at all.

3 ASSEMBLAGES: ARTICULATION

Assemblages (*agencement* in French, which translates literally to *arrangement*), in accordance with Deleuze and Guattari's thinking, constitute continuously shifting relational totalities comprised of spasmodic networks between different entities (content) and their articulation within "acts and statements" (expression).[1] Nonetheless, content does not antecede expression, or vice versa, as much as these two forces and their constituent components must enter into mutually coconstitutive machinic becomings that coalesce at certain points while seceding at others. That is to say that the differing elements articulated in an assemblage become components only in their relational connectivity with other factors. For Deleuze and Guattari, assemblages pivot on both a vertical and a horizontal axis. The horizontal line, consisting of content and expression, features "*machinic assemblages of bodies, actions and passions, an intermingling of bodies reacting to one another*" as well as "*collective assemblages of enunciation, of acts and statements, of incorporeal transformations of bodies,*" while the vertical dimension is marked by "*territorial sides, or reterritorialized sides, which stabilize it, and cutting edges of deterritorialization, which carry it away*" (*Plateaus*, 88). Assemblages are inherently productive, entering into polyvalent becomings to produce and give expression to previously nonexistent realities, thoughts, bodies, affects, spaces, actions, ideas, and so on. The fecundity of these becomings, what Deleuze and Guattari term *machinic*, however, ought not be cognized as unavoidably positive or liberating, particularly when set against putatively rigid structures such as race and colonialism, since assemblages transport potential territorializations as often if not more frequently than lines of flight: "The identity of any assemblage at any level of scale is always the product of a process (territorialization and, in some cases, coding) and it is always precarious, since other processes (deterritorialization and decoding) can destabilize it."[2] Because assemblages do not assume change to adhere in full, self-present, and coherent subjects, in addition to highlighting the double-pronged milieu of assemblages, Manuel DeLanda's concise account also demonstrates how these circumvent the structure versus agency problematic I mentioned in the introduction.

[I insert a methodological breather here to observe that taking on ideas from the toolbox of Deleuze and Guattari runs the risk of a descent into the quagmire of orthodox Deleuzianism, which insists on transforming Deleuze into a great thinker by reading him exclusively within the western European philosophical tradition but also by an intense concentration on Deleuze as a master thinker at the cost of folding his collaborative writings with Guattari into Deleuzianism. Judging from of the writings of Deleuzians, then, it seems that once you go D&G you never go back. Though I've learned much from doctrinaire Deleuzians, I have found more generative the work of Rosi Braidotti, Brian Massumi, Kara Keeling, Jasbir Puar, Elizabeth Grosz, and Manuel DeLanda, whose sustained deployment of concepts from the Deleuze (and Guattari) archive eschews rendering this usage the primary aim of their critical inquiry.[3] Rather, these thinkers productively rearticulate and reframe Deleuze and Guattari's thoughts, creating novel assemblages and insights that only become possible when these ideas are put to work in milieus (e.g., racialized minority discourse or queer theory as in the case of Puar) beyond the snowy masculinist precincts of European philosophy; these thinkers also heed Deleuze and Guattari's invitation to plunder their ideas in the service of producing new concepts and assemblages. In contrast to these heterodox Deleuzians, strict Deleuzianism keeps in place segregated and colonial structures of knowledge by insisting on a proper form of being Deleuzian, as can be gleaned from several chapters in the recent anthology *Deleuze and the Postcolonial*, which endeavor to prove erroneous Gayatri Spivak's discussion of Deleuze vis-à-vis subaltern subjectivity in "Can the Subaltern Speak?"; from the debate between Christopher

Miller and Eugene Holland about Deleuze and Guattari's indiscriminate deployment of nomadology and other concepts from anthropology; or from the fraught relationship of orthodox Deleuzians to feminism.[4] This is one of the reasons why I have found it necessary to create a conversation between theories of assemblage and articulation.]

We should remain cautious, as Barbara Christian, Stuart Hall, and Gayatri Spivak urge us to do, about the complete disavowal of subjectivity in theoretical discourse, because within the context of the Anglo-American academy more often than not an insistence on transcending limited notions of the subject or identity leads to the neglect of race as a critical category, as we have seen in scholars such as Judith Butler, and as I show shortly in my discussion of Foucault and Agamben.[5] In this context, Spivak's remarks concerning Deleuze and Guattari's refusal to contemplate the interactions between "desire, power and subjectivity" remain acutely relevant, because it "renders them incapable of articulating a theory of interests," and Foucault's emphasis on "'genealogical' speculation . . . has created an unfortunate resistance . . . to 'mere' ideological critique."[6] The opposition to ideology as a metaterritorializing category on the part of Foucault and Deleuze and Guattari is understandable within the context of post-1960s French thought given the then–au courant disenchantment with Marxism and grand narratives. Nevertheless, notions such as power, ideology, gender, coloniality, identity, and race jinglingly dawdle in the margins of Deleuze and Guattari's putatively asubjective and disinterested universes, since otherwise, as Stuart Hall remarks, "there is no reason why anything is or isn't potentially articulatable with anything," while the "critique of reductionism has apparently resulted in the notion of society as a totally open discursive field."[7] It should be noted that Hall and Spivak, two of the most significant contemporary Anglo-American theorists of cultural studies and deconstruction, are not simply rejecting post-structuralist tenets for their arbitrariness or relativism but are asking about the stakes of evacuating seemingly retrograde concepts such as identity, especially within the context of "societies structured in dominance."[8]

Stuart Hall's elaboration of the Marxian notion of articulation, which Marx referred to as *soziale Gliederung*, represents "the necessity of thinking unity and difference; difference in complex unity, without this becoming a hostage to the privileging of difference as such."[9] Hall's outline of articulation here emphasizes relational connectivity in much the same way as the

Deleuzo-Guattarian notion of assemblages while still retaining some of the political traction called for by Spivak and Hall. Hall is also careful to acknowledge the existence of "tendential combinations," which are "not prescribed in the fully determinist sense" but are nevertheless the "'preferred' combinations, sedimented and solidified by real historical development over time."[10] Preferred articulations insert historically sedimented power imbalances and ideological interests, which are crucial to understanding mobile structures of dominance such as race or gender, into the modus operandi of assemblages. Accordingly, a robust fusion of articulation and assemblage accents the productive ingredients of social formations while not silencing questions of power, reinstituting an innocent version of the subject, or neglecting the deterritorializing capabilities of power, ideology, and so on. Articulated assemblages such as racialization materialize as sets of complex relations of articulations that constitute an open articulating principle—territorializing and deterritorializing, interested and asubjective—structured in political, economic, social, racial, and heteropatriarchal dominance.

In one of the few passages in which Deleuze and Guattari explicitly address racial difference, they contend the "race-tribe exists only at the level of an oppressed race, and in the name of the oppression it suffers: there is no race but inferior, minoritarian; there is no dominant race," which intimates the rudiments of a political theory of racialization in its honing in on race as an assemblage of hierarchy and the deracination of the majoritarian. In the end, however, this theory flounders on Deleuze and Guattari's celebration of racial impurity: "A race is defined not by its purity but rather by the impurity conferred upon it by a system of domination. Bastard and mixed-blood are the true names of race" (*Plateaus*, 379). By asking neither how racialized impurity is articulated within a given sociohistorical totality (or what counts as racial hybridity and what does not) nor whose interests are served by the adjudication of racial categories, Deleuze and Guattari foreclose the conceptual reflection of the ways racialization and different axes of domination cooperate in founding racializing assemblages.[11] The one-drop rule, the Nuremberg laws, or the blood quantum laws have exposed how the juridico-political territorialization of racial hybridity frequently serves to solidify the ordering of humans along racial lines rather than heralding the suspension of racializing assemblages. The idea of racial admixture assumes the reality of distinctive races that are sublated in Deleuze and Guattari's deterritorialized "mixed-race bastard." For, in contrast to Glissant's notion of relation, which I discussed earlier and which takes as its point of departure the constitutive relatedness of the world, Deleuze and Guattari's exhalation of impurity must inevitably presuppose an erstwhile racial pureness, which territorializes the very notion of racial difference. Besides underscoring the necessity for ideology and articulation to be introduced into a theory of assemblages, the privileging of racial hybridity points to the limits of the Deleuzo-Guattarian model. If not, then Deleuze and Guattari's supposition of the actuality of races and their failure to explore how and why the impure represents the real faciality of race would go unchecked.[12] As a result, Deleuze and Guattari conjure a "self-proximate, if not self-identical, subject of the oppressed," only in this context the racially subjugated subject emerges as pristine via its hybridity.[13]

With regard to the category of race, racializing assemblages ascribe "incorporeal transformations . . . to bodies," etching abstract forces of power onto human physiology and flesh in order to create the appearance of a naturally expressive relationship between phenotype and sociopolitical status: the hieroglyphics of the flesh (*Plateaus*, 98). Or, in Colin Dayan's words: "Slavery . . . rendered material the conceptual, giving a body to what had been abstraction. . . . An idea of lineage thus evolved and turned the rule of descent into the transfer of pigmentation, which *fleshed out* in law the terms necessary to maintain the curse of color."[14] As a result, the legal and extralegal fictions of skin color and other visual markers obscure, and therefore facilitate, the continued existence and intergenerational transmission of the hieroglyphics of the flesh. Spillers adds to and recasts the concept of bare life by forcefully showing how, within the context of racial slavery, it gives birth to a cluster of classifying assemblages that stands at the center of modernity.

Deleuze and Guattari point to the productive components of assemblages in which "the material or machinic aspect of an assemblage relates not to the production of goods but rather to a precise state of intermingling of bodies in a society, including all the attractions and repulsions, sympathies and antipathies, alterations, amalgamations, penetrations, and expansions that affect bodies of all kinds in their relations to one another" (*Plateaus*, 90). Racializing assemblages articulate relational intensities between human physiology and flesh, producing racial categories, which are subsequently coded as natural substances, whether pure or impure, rather than as the territorializing articulations of these assemblages. By not thinking through race in any sustained or critical manner, Deleuze and Guattari leave the door open for the naturalization of this category. Race, however, should be viewed not as ideology or the erroneous ascription of social meaning to existent biological classifications, as Deleuze and Guattari do by giving preference to the hybrid, but, in the words of Dorothy Roberts, as "a political system that governs people by sorting them into social groupings based on invented biological demarcations. . . . Race is not a biological category that is politically charged. It is a political category that has been disguised as a biological one."[15] The flesh, although not synonymous with racialization in toto, represents one such racializing assemblage within the world of Man, and, consequently, it represents both a subject and an object of knowledge within black studies's intellectual topographies.

Though these viscous assemblages may not be equivalent to physicochemical indices such as skin pigmentation, according to Spillers the hieroglyphics of the flesh nevertheless touch the physiological register as the sociogenic institution through which "our culture-specific conceptions of being human (e.g., theory) are inscribed, turned into *flesh*."[16] Spillers's theorization of the flesh highlights one significant instance of this biocultural stigmatic apparatus in which ideas are literally and figuratively deformed into racialized assemblages of human flesh that invest human phenomenology with an aura of extrahuman physiology. The hieroglyphics of the flesh still dwell among us in the fissures of our current governing configuration of the human as Man; they are the ether that animates racializing assemblages, the ether that broadcasts slashes onto the scar tissue of succeeding generations, testifying to the truth-value of Zora Neale Hurston's proclamation, "the white man thinks in a written language and the Negro thinks in hieroglyphics."[17] We can say, then, by way of Karl Marx: race is a mysterious thing in that the social character of racializing assemblages appears as an objective character stamped upon humans, which is presented not in the form of sociopolitical relations between humans, but as hierarchically structured races. Taken together, these factors form the basis for racializing assemblages, which, although borne partially of political violence, cannot be reduced to it. Namely, instances of systemic political violence moored in the law and beyond not only herald the naissance of bare life and its racialized progeny but also produce a surplus, a line of flight in Deleuze and Guattari's and George Jackson's parlance, that evades capture, that refuses rest, that testifies to the impossibility of its own existence. Taking the workings of flesh seriously frees and sets in motion the deviances that lay dormant in the concept of bare life and that repudiate by their very existence the equation of domination and violence with the complete absence of subjectivity, life, enjoyment, hunger, and so on. Maurice Merleau-Ponty describes the general provenance of the flesh, which is not "a color or a thing, therefore, [but] a difference between things and colors, a momentary crystallization of colored being or of visibility. Between the alleged colors and visibles, we would find anew the tissue that lines them, sustains them, nourishes them, and which for its part is not a thing, but a possibility, a latency, and a flesh of things."[18] Once the flesh becomes a centrifugal factor in the theorization of political violence, racialization, and modern politics construed more broadly, we have the beginnings of habeas viscus, which, contrary to bare life and habeas corpus, does not have as its prerequisite the comparative tabulation of suffering, the suspension of racial caesuras in the state of exception, or the transcendence of the flesh.

———

There can never be an absolute biopolitical substance and racializing assemblages cannot escape the flesh.

4 RACISM: BIOPOLITICS

Over the course of Agamben's academic blockbuster homo sacer trilogy (*Homo Sacer, State of Exception,* and *Remnants of Auschwitz*), the idea of bare life accomplishes a conceptual feat that race as an analytical category cannot: it founds a biological sphere above and beyond reach of racial hierarchies. This becomes especially evident in the treatment of the Muselmann, who figures in *Remnants of Auschwitz* as the most absolute incarnation of modernity's politicization of *zoe*. The Muselmänner were a class or caste of Nazi concentration camp detainees so ravaged by chronic malnutrition and psychological exhaustion that they resembled phlegmatic but still living corpses.[1] Due to extreme emaciation, often accompanied by the disappearance of muscle tissue and brittle bones, the Muselmänner could no longer control basic human functions such as the discharge of feces and urine and the mechanics of walking, which they did by lifting their legs with their arms, or they performed "mechanical movements without purpose,"[2] leading the other inmates and later commentators to view becoming-Muselmann as a state of extreme passivity. Observers portray Muselmänner as apathetic, withdrawn, animallike, not-quite-human, unintelligible—in short, as ghostly revelations of the potential future fate that awaited the still functional inmates in an already utterly dehumanized space where everyone was exposed to chronic hunger and death. Being forced to occupy a phenomenological zone that could in no way be reconciled with possessive individualism, the Muselmänner exemplified another way of being human and were, in fact, likened by several observers to starving dogs.[3]

The term *Muselmann* (also *Muselmane* or *Muselman*)—an antiquated and now derogatory German language designator for Muslim men that was also applied to women—is derived from the Arabic word for a follower of Islam: *Muslim* and its cognates in Farsi (*musulmān*) or Turkish (*müslümān*).[4] Since World War II, the German *Muselmann* has referred specifically to the death camps and, although the derivation of the term within the camps is clouded by uncertainty, no one has been able to explain—not for lack of speculation—why it was this term and not another that came to be associated with this condition. Agamben believes it to reference the Arabic signification of Muslim, "the one who submits unconditionally to the will of Allah." However, this theological explanation does not appear in the testimonies collected by Polish sociologists Zdzislaw Ryn and Stanslav Klodzinski. In these testimonies, former inmates frequently mention Muselmänner wearing scarves around their heads or wrapping blankets around their bodies to keep warm as a likely explanation of the term's widespread utilization across different languages (besides German, similar Polish and French words were also used) in the camps.[5] Most scholars who write about the Muselmann do not pause to reflect on the name of this figure, thereby leaving intact the bonding of an abject process/status to a racio-religious label.[6]

While the derivation of the name *Muselmann* remains veiled, the figure nevertheless reveals the possibility "that there is still life in the most extreme degradation. And this new knowledge becomes the touchstone by which to judge and measure all morality and all dignity. The *Muselmann*, who is its most extreme expression, is the guard on the threshold of a new ethics of a form of life that begins where dignity ends" (*Remnants*, 69). Agamben's invocation of novelty and extremity vis-à-vis the Muselmann suggest that this incarnation of bare life had yet to appear in such a radical constellation before the invention of Nazi death camps and that it shadows any notion of ethics in the historical aftermath of the Third Reich. However, it is only because Agamben codifies the Muselmann as an apolitical *(Un)Mensch* that he can state the following: "At the point in which Häftling becomes a Muselmann, the biopolitics of racism so to speak transcends race, penetrating into a threshold in which it is no longer possible to establish caesuras"

(*Remnants*, 85). It is neither transparent how the biopolitics of racism supersedes race, nor what particular properties of racism are unleashed through the Muselmann that allow for the transcendence of race. More simply, how can racism—biopolitical or otherwise—exist without race? Agamben believes the Muselmann to coincide with "the emergence of something like an *absolute biological substance* that cannot be assigned to a particular bearer or subject, or divided by another caesura" (*Remnants*, 85; emphasis added). So the fallen biopolitical flesh of the Muselmann gives birth to a desubjectified and quasi-ontological domain, which transcends race, and hence its indissolubility by caesuras. This, in turn, leads to a fuller comprehension of the definitive goal of Nazi biopolitical genocide, the death camps, since these "are not merely the place of death and extermination; they are also, and above all, the site of the production of the Muselmann, the *final biopolitical substance* to be isolated in the biological continuum" (*Remnants*, 85; emphasis added). Summoning the orderly tools of teleology, Agamben positions the Muselmann as indicative of bare life tout court and as exemplifying the final frontier of biopolitics. As an exemplary limit case for biopolitics, racism, humanity, bare life, and sovereignty, the Muselmann must shoulder a very heavy burden in Agamben's typology of bare life. In order for the Muselmann to function as the most radical paradigm of bare life, Agamben must insist on the indivisibility of this state so that it does not resemble traditional racial identities. And, despite being the product of racialization, the Muselmann represents the indivisible endpoint of modern politics' conscription of human biological matter. In fact, for Agamben, the advent of the Muselmann in Nazi death camps represents a completely unique event in its ethical and biopolitical radicality. Yet the death camps not only were aimed at extermination, they also produced a surplus, an excess, not just "an absolute biopolitical substance" but the Muselmann as a racial category; this is how racializing assemblages work, plain and simple. Far from exceeding race, then, the Muselmann represents an intense and excessive instantiation thereof, penetrating every crevice of political racialization; how else to explain the very name Muselmann, a racial slur for Muslims?[7]

If we follow Ruth Wilson Gilmore's definition of racism as not resting on phenotype or culture, but as "the state-sanctioned and/or extra-legal production and exploitation of group-differentiated vulnerabilities to premature death," what, then, is racism if not the political exploitation and (re)production of race?[8] Which is to say that the biopolitical function of race is racism; it is the establishment and maintenance of caesuras, not their abolition. Clearly, racism cannot erase race in the force field of the political, whether state sanctioned (legal) or not. This is what Agamben desires of the Muselmann: his or her transcendence of race, and therefore politics, via the sublatory powers of a radical post-Holocaust ethics. The ethical shrouds the politics that rest in becoming-Muselmann as one, albeit extreme, version of the systematic and hierarchical susceptibility to premature death that marks modern sovereignty's assemblages of racialization. This is why racialization ("group-differentiated vulnerabilities to premature death") operates simultaneously as the nomos and matrix of modern politics. And, in this way, Agamben departs from Foucault, who shows how biopolitics authorizes caesuras "within the biological continuum addressed by biopower" and how it creates a decidedly modern mode of "racism [that] justifies the death-function in the economy of biopower by appealing to the principle that the death of others makes one biologically stronger insofar as one is a member of a race or a population, insofar as one is an element in a unitary living plurality."[9] Accordingly, the existence of the Muselmann flows back into the economy of racialization qua "unitary living plurality" as the annihilated element that makes the Aryan race stronger and purer.

In contrast to Agamben's disavowal of racialization, racism plays a crucial role in Foucault's genealogy of biopolitics. At least it does so in the lectures that compose Society Must Be Defended (1975–76), since racism and colonialism do not figure prominently in the remainder of Foucault's extensive oeuvre, neither in the works published during his lifetime nor in the eight volumes of posthumously issued lectures that were given at the Collège de France from 1973–84. Though the absence of these concerns is especially glaring in The Order of Things, which charts how Man became an object of knowledge within the modern episteme without contemplating how racialization or colonialism were and still remain fundamental to this enterprise, virtually all of Foucault's work exhibits this truancy.[10] With regard to the series of lectures published after Foucault's lifetime, in Abnormal (1974–75) Foucault treats what he calls "ethnic racism" as a negative point of comparison for biopolitics in much the same way he does in Society Must Be Defended. In Security, Territory, Population (1977–78) he alludes to colonialism only in passing, while in The Birth of Biopolitics (1978–79) Foucault briefly acknowledges racism but merely as a phenomenon during the time period in which he delivered the lectures.[11] I introduce Foucault's other writings in order to highlight the singular place occupied by Society in terms of its explicit and extended analysis of racism and, conversely, to register the lacunae of racism as an object of knowledge in the majority of his work.

In the Society lectures Foucault defines biopolitics as the power of the European state to "make live and let die," which begins to shatter the hitherto unitary body politic of European nations at the end of the eighteenth century and comes to fully engulf these societies that must be defended throughout the nineteenth century.[12] This is the moment in which politics takes hold of the biological and the biological health of the national population defines the exercise of state power; and, according to Foucault, it produces a "racism that society will direct against itself, against its own elements, and its own products. This is the internal racism of permanent purification, and it will become one of the basic dimensions of social normalization" (Society, 60). Careful to establish that racism preexists this moment, even though both its quality and primary function shift, Foucault shows how racism "had already been in existence for a very long time. But I think it functioned elsewhere [Je ne veux pas dire du tout que le racisme a été inventé à cette époque. Il existait depuis bien longtemps. Mais je crois qu'il fonctionnait ailleurs]" (Society, 254/214). Racism, which up to this point had led a peaceful conceptual and historical life in an unspecified terra incognita, thus journeys from the uncharted periphery into the heart of the modern European nation-state. Yet despite locating the naissance of modern racism in "colonization, or in other words, with colonizing genocide" (Society, 257), for Foucault, in a reversal of colonial modernity's teleology that locates the temporal origin of all things in the west, racism only attains relevance once it penetrates the borders of fortress Europe. Even though the originating leap of racism can be found in the colonized "rest," only its biopolitical rearticulation in the west imbues it with the magical aura of conceptual value. Because Foucault does not describe this ailleurs or even mention it again in the text, it materializes as a primitive topography, operating as a constitutive outside for his theory of biopolitics throughout these lectures. In logic, primitive terms or notions, also referred to as axioms or postulates, name instantly understandable terms that are used without elucidating their signification. The meanings of all other concepts in a logical system are determined by these primitive terms and by previously established expressions. Over the course of his argument about the genesis of biopolitics in the lectures, Foucault will continue to distinguish European state racism and biopolitics from those primeval forms of racism that linger in the aforementioned philosophical, geographical, and political quicksands of an unspecified elsewhere; at least, this is what we are asked to infer as a consequence of Foucault's taciturnity about the reach and afterlife of those other modalities of racialization. In another context, Foucault defends the recurrent dearth of geographical specification in his oeuvre thus: "I don't specify the space of reference more narrowly than that since it would be *as warranted to say 'I am speaking only of France' as to say 'I am talking about all of Europe.'* There is indeed a task to be done of making the space in question precise, saying where a certain process stops, what are the limits beyond which one could say 'something different happens'—though this would have to be a collective undertaking."[13] Alas, this collective undertaking has yet to be realized and it continues to be reproduced in contemporary biopolitics and bare life discourse.

In several of the 1975–76 lectures Foucault also employs the term *colonization* figuratively in order to ask whether there "isn't a danger that they [our genealogical fragments] will be recoded, recolonized by these unitary discourses" (*Society*, 11), to explain how madness and sexuality were "colonized and supported by global mechanisms and, finally, by the entire system of the State" (33), to demonstrate how "normalizing procedures are increasingly colonizing the procedures of the law" (38–39), to argue that the Hegelian dialectic "be understood as philosophy and right's colonization and authoritarian colonization of a historico-political discourse that was both a statement of fact, a proclamation, and a practice of social warfare" (58), and to show how the discourse of war was "restricted, colonized, settled, scattered, civilized if you like, and up to a point pacified" (215) within historical discourse at the close of the eighteenth century. The slippage between colonialism as a historical phenomenon and colonization as a synonym for hegemonic appropriation or annexation underscores the primitiveness of this concept in Foucault's system of thought, in much the same way as the idea of ethnic racism, which I discuss shortly. That is, despite the fact that the histories of colonialism and racism secure Foucault's definition of biopolitics, for Foucault the meaning of colonization and ethnic racism are immediately understandable, and as such they are exploited without the peripheral benefits of explication.

More generally, Foucault positions biopolitics against rather simplified definitions of, on the one hand, an "ordinary racism . . . that takes the traditional form of mutual contempt or hatred between races" and, on the other, racism as an "ideological operation that allows States, or a class, to displace the hostility that is directed toward them . . . onto a mythical adversary" (*Society*, 258). In its place, modern European racism provides a deeper domain, because it supplies the conditions of possibility for biopolitics, and although Foucault sees modern racism as originating in colonialism, he ultimately uses the Third Reich to illustrate the full reach of biopower when he writes, "of course, no state could have more disciplinary power than the Nazi regime. Nor was there any other State in which the biological was so tightly, so insistently, regulated" (*Society*, 259).[14] We should remain vigilant about not acquiescing to these monumentalizing protocols (and Agamben's) because, more often than not, they achieve their aggrandizing effect by not taking into account the historical relationality and conceptual contiguity between Nazi racism and the other forms of biopolitics I discussed earlier, those perfected in colonialism, indigenous genocide, racialized indentured servitude, and racial slavery, for instance.[15] They also discount discussions of those racializing assemblages that Foucault and Agamben consign to a theoretico-geographical no-Man's-land. Moreover, given Foucault's principal point about the overall pervasiness of biopolitics in Europe, why must its most severe incarnation bear the heavy burden of paradigmatic exemplariness, just as it does in Agamben? Why not simply examine the biopolitics of Nazi racism qua Nazi racism? Why must this form of racism necessarily figure as the apex in the telos of modern racializing assemblages?

Even when considering modes of biopolitical racialization in the socialist state, Foucault's interpretation hinges on setting it apart from a narrow definition of racism: "Quite naturally, we find that racism—*not a truly ethnic racism [le racisme proprement ethnique]* but racism of the evolutionist kind, biological racism—is fully operational in the way socialist States (of the Soviet Union type) deal with the mentally ill, criminals, political adversaries, and so on" (*Society*, 261–62/222). Initially, the caesura Foucault places between ethnic and biological racism seems to productively counteract some of his foregoing remarks about this question; at closer look, however, the distinction exposes the shortcomings of Foucault's approach to race and racism. Because Foucault fails to probe the decidedly undemonic ground of his argument, he uncritically embraces an ontological differentiation between ethnic and biopolitical racism, leaving the door open for the naturalization of racial categories and the existence of a biological sphere that is not always already subject to ethnic racism. However, all modern racism is biological, first, because it maintains the believed natural—often evolutionary—inferiority of the targeted subjects and, second, because racialization is instituted, as elucidated by Wynter, in the realm of human physiology as the sociogenic selection of one specific group in the name of embodying all humanity. So rather than dysselecting phenotypically nonwhite or Jewish subjects, socialist biopower racializes sets of humans (criminals, dissidents, etc.) that are not distinctive in Man's racial epidermal schema but are nevertheless classified as deviating from full (socialist) humans according to a preestablished pecking order that is deemed beyond the authority of human culture or politics.[16] Put bluntly, there exists no significant difference between ethnic and biological racism in the way Foucault imagines, since both rely on the same tools of trade: racializing assemblages. Nevertheless, it appears as if Foucault can only authenticate the uniqueness and novelty of European biopolitical racism by conjuring the antithetical spirits of racisms always already situated in a primitive elsewhere.

Foucault concedes that the idea of race has no stable anchor in the biological; rather it names "a certain historico-political divide" in which "two races exist whenever one writes the history of two groups which do not, at least to begin with, have the same language or, in many cases, the same religion" (Society, 77). If divergences in language and religion between different humans serve as the markers for racial difference within the confines of Europe, this passage cannot explain how the operations of race differ constitutively from those of nationalism, to name one obvious example. Foucault, then, moves quite swiftly to explain that races "exist when there are two groups which, although they coexist, have not become mixed because of the differences, dissymmetries, and barriers created by privileges, customs and rights, the distribution of wealth, or the way in which power is exercised" (Society, 77). Here, Foucault supplies so broad a definition of racism that it could be applied to any number of categories that have been brandished to create caesuras among different humans: economic and social class, nationality, gender, for instance. We are confronted with these resulting questions: How does this definition of race diverge from ethnic racism? Are the racialized classes in ethnic racism not segregated as a result of the distribution of wealth or the deployment of power? Moreover, Foucault does not explain how these groups come to exist as different. How are we to understand the distinction between coexistence and mixing, or what their particular mixing might entail, and so on? Hence, in a fashion similar to Deleuze and Guattari, Foucault positions hybridity as a panacea for racial difference without querying the foundation upon which the idea of racial differences among humans is built.

Ultimately, Foucault, despite stressing the importance of racism to the machinations of biopolitics, restrains its full conceptual reverberations, because he relies on a commonsensical notion of racism as his primitive straw man, and because he remains confined to a version of nineteenth-century Europe oddly unscathed by colonialism and ethnic racism. Of course colonial configurations in the late eighteenth and early nineteenth centuries would at least partially derive from the intramural tensions within and between European nations given that these tensions were exported to the colonies elsewhere around the globe. As a result, colonization unavoidably reflects the racializing assemblages interior to Europe, while techniques that discipline humanity into full humans, not-quite-humans, and nonhumans developed in the colonies inflect those at home, and which Foucault, following Hannah Arendt, terms the *boomerang-effect* of colonialism.[17] The fundamental problem, then, is not that Foucault largely omits colonialism and the non-western world from the province of his discussion of racism, but, to be more precise, that he and some of his followers assume there to be substantial inconsistency between a "confrontation of two alien races" and the "bifurcation within Europe's social fabric," which demarcates the inadequate and limiting theoretical parameters of Foucault's conception of racism.[18] Though Foucault does not deploy the term *alien races*, his insistence on the spatiotemporal disjuncture between the race from "here" and the race that came from "another place" as well as the reemergence of the race from the past within it cannot but echo colonialist tropes and "recapitulation theory": "The other race is basically not the race that came from *elsewhere* . . . but . . . it is a race that is permanently, ceaselessly infiltrating the social body. . . . What we see . . . as a binary rift within society is not a clash between two distinct races. It is the splitting of a single race into a superrace and a subrace. To put it a different way, it is the reappearance, within a single race, of the past of that race" (*Society*, 61). Within this context, alien races—Ann Stoler's very unfortunate rephrasing of Foucault's ethnic racism, to be sure—dodge the brush of discourse, dwelling in a speculative state of organic truth. This line of reasoning rests on the presumptions that such a thing as alien races exist, that the confrontation between them (ethnic racism) need not be explained, and that Europe—remember it is immaterial whether this signifies France or Europe as a whole—was internally cohesive, because racism dwelled elsewhere prior to the ascent of biopolitics in the late eighteenth and early nineteenth centuries. Therefore, in Foucault's schema race and racism, insofar as they have yet to achieve proper biopolitical credentials, take on the shape of an inevitable clash between unacquainted civilizations.

There lies a vast gulf between an argument that explores the particular techniques of racialization which appeared in Europe over the course of the eighteenth and nineteenth centuries and one that attests to some form of cultural, social, or ontological anteriority of alien races. Put simply, Foucault never interrogates the bare existence of racial difference and those hierarchies fabricated upon this primordial notion and, as a result, reinscribes racial difference as natural. Because ethnic racism is based on preestablished variances among different ethnicities, it evidently demands no further elaboration in Foucault's genealogical deduction of modern racializing assemblages, and thus emerges as a fixed category rather than as the biopolitical apparatus it actually is. Conversely, the fission that appears within Europe's autochthonous population in this period assumes the fragmentation of a formerly cohesive body politic: the proliferation of biopower produces the hierarchical differentiation of internal groups as races, whereas the caesuras between European and alien races exist outside the vicissitudes of biopolitics. In Foucault's model, race and ethnicity remain always already beyond the administrative, ideological, and conceptual precincts of Europe; they function *as and in* an unnamed elsewhere.[19] The elision and active disavowal of *racism, colonization,* and *ethnic racism* in these lectures and beyond become even more pronounced if we bear in mind the unacknowledged influence of the Black Panther Party (BPP), especially the thinking of George Jackson and Angela Davis, on Foucault's work in this period.

According to Brady Heiner and Joy James, Foucault was familiar with Davis's and Jackson's thinking through his affiliation with Groupe d'Information sur les Prisons, an antiprison group Foucault helped found, and which translated Davis's and Jackson's writings and published a pamphlet about the assassination of George Jackson in France. In addition to tracing historical lines between Foucault and the BPP, persuasively showing just how much Foucault's ideas about incarceration, state racism, and disciplinary power owe to Davis and Jackson, Heiner asks, "Given the formative role that black power plays in Foucault's elaboration of the concepts

of power-knowledge, genealogy and biopower, why is it that the enuncia-
tive force of black power is met with social, civil and biological death while
that of power-knowledge is subject to canonization in a host of academic
disciplines?"[20] The short answer to this important question would insist
on the many different ways white supremacy and coloniality still form the
glue for the institutional and intellectual disciplinarity of western critical
thought. Since the ideas of the BPP are limited to concerns with ethnic racism elsewhere, they do not register as thought qua thought, and can thus
be exploited by and elevated to universality only in the hands of European
thinkers such as Foucault, albeit without receiving any credit. [Dear reader,
if this reminds you of the colonial expropriation of natural resources, you
would be neither wrong nor alone in making such an assumption. In the
words of Kanye West: that shit cray.]

In a trenchant and timely essay, Achille Mbembe offers an extensive
contextualization for the many reasons that the history of colonialism and
postcolonial studies have made so little impact on French thought since the
1960s. This lacuna represents a marked departure from Sartre's conversation with Negritude or the relays between surrealism and anticolonialism,
to name only a few of the most obvious instances of earlier white French
intellectual discussions of these thematics.[21] Though Mbembe writes specifically about France, most western European nations exhibit the same sort
of popular cultural and intellectual amnesia regarding (post)coloniality;
whither, for instance, coloniality in Jürgen Habermas's or Antonio Negri's
thinking? Not only does the systematic neglect of race and coloniality as
analytic topoi in much of western European critical thought since the 1960s
accent the poverty of theory in the European context, it also enables the disavowal of these questions in the U.S. variant of critical theory. Ironically,
despite—and most likely because of—the provinciality of post-1960s French
and western European thought with regard to questions of coloniality and
race, it continues to enjoy great success in the Anglo-American academy,
which, in turn, authorizes the ongoing acts of active disremembering such
as Foucault's. Thus, while French president François Hollande may now
acknowledge the presence of "Niggas in Paris," Mbembé offers a more
somber and radical diagnosis of this dilemma: "For such a critical thought
to have a future at all, we must first turn our backs on that form of anachro-
nism we have come to know as Parisianism."[22] Perhaps, then, the time has
come to bid adieu to Foucault's metropolitan *territoire d'outre-mer*.[23]

Agamben has even less to say about racism, colonialism, and the world beyond fortress Europe.[24] The passage about the Muselmann discussed earlier represents one of the few instances that reference racism throughout the major texts in which Agamben develops his theory of bare life. And, as with Foucault, in both cases theories of racism and/or race appear almost exclusively in conjunction with the extremity of Nazism: "The link between politics and life instituted by [Nazism] is not (as is maintained by a common and completely inadequate interpretation of racism) a merely instrumental relationship, as if race were a simple natural given that had merely to be safeguarded" (Homo Sacer, 147–48). In a vein similar to Foucault's brushing aside of ethnic racism, Agamben perfunctorily dismisses the instrumental definition of racism without explicating its historical or conceptual provenances. What is more, as untenable as an instrumental form of racism might be, does this disqualify all other analyses of race and racism, and, if so, on what grounds? If Agamben and Foucault are to be believed, all interpretations of race, ethnicity, and racism that are not immediately tied to Nazism or concerned with caesuras among European populations are crude, simplistic, prehistorical, and undeserving of sustained critical attention, which, as a consequence, naturalizes traditional racial and/or ethnic delimiters. Writing about the proliferation and internal contradictions of "biopolitics and bare life discourse," David Scott asks, "Why should we be obliged to submit to the semiotic inflation that makes the Holocaust the primal scene of the original crime, and the extermination camp the fundamental paradigm, of modern western power? What western anxiety—what desire—drives this philosophico-political exorbitance? What complex of powers produce—and reproduce so relentlessly—the shock effect of that particular instance of historical violence? There is an uncanny epistemological totalization at work here that is at odds with the exemplary political critique of totalitarianism it seeks to enact."[25] Similarly, while Foucault and Agamben render biopolitical racism as an object of knowledge, that is, an object constituted by particular modes of knowledge production, racism that is based on ethnic difference, because it is camouflaged by a reading at sight, acts as a real object against which their proper objects of knowledge—biopolitics and bare life—are gauged. This is why we cannot cede speaking of race in terms of biology or ontology to either the proponents' "bare life and biopolitics discourse" or those who would conflate race with nature, now frequently done in the language of genetics rather than phenotype.

Viewed in this light, the transcendence of race Agamben ascribes to the Muselmann rests on the philosophical *unseeing of racializing assemblages*. For, pace Agamben, the Muselmann names not only the conditions of possibility for violent exclusions but also serves as the foundation for policing the borders between bare life, life, and death. As a result, the pure organic essence borne of the biopolitics of racism is a form of racial classification and most definitely not its supersession. There can be no absolute biological substance, because in the history of modernity this field always already appears in the form of racializing assemblages. In order to illustrate this destructive racializing assemblage at the heart of modern humanity, I turn my attention to an instructive example culled from popular culture.

The short film accompanying the song "Born Free" by British and Sri Lankan Tamil musician M.I.A. (Maya Arulpragasam), a collaboration with Romain Gavras, was released in April 2010 and immediately banned from YouTube. Arulpragasam herself is no stranger to controversy, since she has often drawn attention to the violence perpetrated against the Tamil minority in Sri Lanka and has shown sympathy for the militant Tamil organization Liberation Tigers of Tamil Eelam, considered a terrorist organization by some. In addition, M.I.A.'s music and accompanying visual work is replete with references to different forms of political violence and identification with non-western persecuted populations, such as the looped sounds of gunshots and cash registers heard on her best-known record, "Paper Planes," or the artwork for Arulpragasam's first album, *Arular* (2005), which prominently features tanks, machine guns, and bombs (fig. 4.1).

As one of the few (female) artists in contemporary popular music that fuse explicit political content with cutting-edge sonics, Arulpragasam has often been accused of merely toying with radical chic and being politically naive, rather than being seen as part of a long tradition of women-of-color musical iconoclasts that ranges from Betty Davis, Polly Styrene, Debora Lyall, and Grace Jones to Nicolette, Erykah Badu, and Ebony Bones. M.I.A. extends this lineage by infusing her artistic practice with sights, sounds, and politics from the Global South, deploying these not as fountains of premodern authenticity but as thoroughly enmeshed in the globe and spanning technological flows of bodies, capital, and ideas so that they cease to play the role of a nondescript elsewhere. The entanglements between "the west and the rest" become legible and audible in M.I.A.'s work via the mixological putting-into-relation of putatively incongruent components like, for in-

4.1 M.I.A., *Arular* (2005).

stance, the photo on the background of her Twitter page that shows M.I.A. donning a niqab adorned with Scarlett Johansson's face.

Born Free, set in the southwestern United States, begins with a shot of a SWAT (special weapons and tactics) police unit in an armored vehicle, which corresponds to the increasing—if not complete—militarization of the urban police and criminalization of black life in the U.S. carceral state. The deployment of paramilitary SWAT units for domestic policing was pioneered by the Los Angeles Police Department. SWAT teams were initially deployed in the state's fight against radical political organizations such as the United Farm Workers in Delano, California, and the LA chapter of the BPP in 1969.[26] In the video, the team in search of a suspect then forcibly enters a residential building, brutally beating the tenants they encounter.

Once the officers locate and apprehend the man they have been hunting, he is transferred to a prison bus occupied only by red-haired men and boys. As the bus drives through deserted streets, we see a mural depicting three red-haired men in camouflage gear holding machine guns above their heads, accompanied by the caption "Our Day Will Come" (fig. 4.2).

Next, the film cuts to several red-haired men—wearing keffiyehs to disguise their faces—throwing rocks at the bus. Ultimately, the "gingers" are taken to the desert, where the SWAT team forces them to exit the bus and commands the men to run over a plot of land swimming with land mines. When the gingers refuse to comply, one of the officers shoots a small boy, an event shown in graphic detail (fig. 4.3).[27] Finally, the remaining men run into the desert, where they are either executed by the members of the SWAT team or blown to pieces by the land mines.

In contrast to traditional music videos that only feature songs as soundtracks, Born Free also includes a menacing electronic score, as well as spoken dialogue and sound effects relating to the plot. Within the context of the film, the song intensifies the violence in the images. Instead of the song playing for the duration of the film, the other sounds interrupt the song proper, allowing it to function as an unsettling sonic accent, and, although the lyrics seemingly bear no relation to the plot of the video, they too focalize important plot points as, for example, when we hear the words "we were born free" during the depiction of an arrest. The song, composed almost entirely from a cacophonous bass line (a sample of synth punk pioneers Suicide's 1978 recording "Ghost Rider"), martial drumming, and M.I.A.'s highly distorted voice, intensifies the violent assault of the images, generating an affective surplus in which "the life of the individual gives way to an impersonal and yet singular life that releases a pure event freed from . . . the subjectivity and objectivity of what happens."[28] This is why much of the commentary about the video, which focuses on the metaphorics of how Arulpragasam, as a female artist of color, imagines the racially motivated extermination of whites, misses the point. For Born Free does not swap gingers (nonreal) for an actually oppressed nonwhite group (real) in a revanchist manner. If anything, it uses the hypothetical persecution of red-haired men as a visual tool that places an affective spotlight on the global operations of racializing assemblages. Reading this work as metaphoric substitution not only denies the nimble mutability of racial taxonomies but also too readily accepts our current racializing order of things as inevitable rather than

4.2–4.3 M.I.A., *Born Free*, dir. Romain Gavras (2010).

as a set of sedimented political relations: racializing assemblages. *Born Free* makes sense only within modern assemblages of racialization, which veil political processes of subjugation through natal markers (hair color, skin pigmentation, etc.) of biological selectedness; otherwise, the film's central gambit of placing gingers in the victim role would be unremarkable. While the video recasts the familiar bonds between state-sponsored persecution and historical subjects and objects, it maintains the relentlessly biovisual basis of the distinction between human life worthy of protection (eugenic), and that which is not (dysgenic).

Furthermore, the song's title evokes Joy Adamson's 1960 best-seller *Born Free: A Lioness of Two Worlds*, which chronicles how Adamson and her husband raised the first female lion in captivity while working as game wardens in Kenya, the 1966 film based on Adamson's story, as well as the film's popular theme song recorded by several artists, including Frank Sinatra.[29] Echoing the settler/colonialist underpinnings of Adamson's narrative, M.I.A.'s Born Free video depicts once-free subjects that are captured and subsequently released back into "the wild," only here the gingers die due to a calculated system of racialized political violence and not of natural causes, as was the case with the lioness Elsa once the Adamsons set her free.

By using a visually distinctive group of white people, who have faced discrimination, albeit in less severe form than depicted in the video, Born Free illustrates the techniques by which bare life is affixed to the bodies of specific Homo sapiens so that their expulsion from humanity appears to spring from their biological inferiority and appears, therefore, warranted. The killing of the gingers not only serves the purpose of targeted eradication—the purification of the nonginger body politic—it also functions to distinguish red-haired, phenotypically white men from the rest of the population, to scopically brand them as dysselected within the racial order portrayed in the video. Born Free refuses to compare the gingers with a racially identifiable antagonist, since the nongingers depicted do not conform to any typologies of our current racializing assemblages. The (seemingly white) SWAT officers are by virtue of their black uniforms, body armor, shields, black masks, helmets, and gas masks virtually indistinguishable from one another, with one exception: an ostensibly black man who commands the gingers to exit the prison bus when they arrive in the desert (figs. 4.4–4.6). The poor (white and Latino) inhabitants of the apartment building raided by the SWAT team at the beginning of the video also do not exhibit phenotypical features that would classify them racially in the world of Man. The SWAT team does not discriminate among the civilians it encounters, handling all of these subjects in a less than gingerly fashion. In the end, the SWAT team is the sole group—besides the gingers—unified by external signifiers so as to form a visually distinct entity, a group racialized not through biological signifiers but through the chromatic and textural uniformity of its armor as well as the vested power of the genocidal state. That the gingers and the SWAT team's passageways to racialization might appear as radically incommensurable, or that the latter do not even form a racial grouping, both highlight some central features of modern racializing assemblages. In creating an alternate racializing logic, which produces different racial subjects and objects, Born Free deterritorializes Man's racializing assemblage and exposes its abstract daily operations: the manifold

4.4–4.6 M.I.A., *Born Free*, dir. Romain Gavras (2010).

techniques by which sociopolitical hierarchies are camouflaged by the natural features of the human body.

In excess of the optical component of establishing caesuras, the very idea that there is an ontological difference between skin tone, hair color, and such, on the one hand, and uniforms, masks, and so on, on the other, which is of course not simply a logical distinction, conveys the deepness of sociogenic ideas about racial difference, which is precisely what Foucault and Agamben take for granted. Although certain nonbiological visual traits have been used in the service of signifying "natural" differences among human populations such the yellow star, the hijab, the pink triangle, the turban, or non-gender-conforming clothing, by and large racial assemblages have relied on permanent fixtures on and in the human body. As Ronald Judy ~~physical?~~ remarks somewhat counterintuitively, "there are amazing resemblances between the Muslim population that emerges in twentieth-century Europe and the Negro population of late nineteenth- and early twentieth-century America. I mean precisely their constitution as an essential disposable population."[30] How can a clearly identifiable racial/ethnic group (Negro) populate the same political space as a community of belief that exhibits no unifying physical or even cultural attributes given that Muslims belong to numerous ethnic/racial categories?

What connects the classifications *Negro* and *Muslim*, then, is not biology per se but their conscription to a set of political relations that necessitates inventing new caesuras in order for Man to remain interchangeable with the human and that these relations are sociogenically imprinted to generate hieroglyphics of the flesh. In the United States the Negro came into being when the slave no longer accomplished the required labor of distinguishing black from white subjects so as to ensure the continued superiority of Man with its attendant class privilege, at the same time as *Muslim* became necessary as a racialized category in Europe when it threatened to dislodge the until then unchallenged advantages of whiteness, Europeanness, and Protestant secularism of the autochthonous population.[31] Similarly, the visual indices exhibited by the SWAT team register as unmarked because they signal a position of power and privilege within the universe portrayed by *Born Free*, which would not be the case if the relationship between the officers and the gingers were upturned. This is to say, contra Agamben, racialized political violence always possesses a function beyond its mere exercise, which is the façade of race as an absolute biological substance that enforces existent categories while also producing new ones. All in all, *Born Free* brilliantly stages how the idea of human life is intimately bound to processes of racialization in which scopic differentiation forms an integral link in the great chain of human life according to racializing assemblages. Ruth Wilson Gilmore highlights the missing component in Foucault's and Agamben's analyses of racism: "Racism is the ordinary means through which dehumanization achieves ideological normality, while, at the same time, the practice of dehumanizing people produces racial categories. . . . This culture, in turn, is based on the modern secular state's dependence on classification, combined with militarism as a means through which classification maintains coherence."[32] Since homo sacerization commonly goes hand in hand with racialization, homines sacri not only legally and ideologically reside beyond the scope of the political community, even while they represent an integral part of said group's functioning, but their alterity is also visually marked, rendering the homo sacer's ban logical within the constraints of Man's racializing assemblages. After all, Jews had to be racialized as non–white/ Aryan in order to be excommunicated from the German national and ethnic community during the Third Reich, and the theologico-political appellation of the Muselmänner relegated them to a dimension that banned them from Judaism at the same time as it segregated these subjects from functional inmates and the guards in the death camps. Accordingly, the hieroglyphics of the flesh in the current system of racializing assemblages must clearly demarcate the selected from the dysselected.

The flesh is nothing less than the ethereal social (after) life of bare existence. The point to be made here does not concern replacing the camp with the plantation as the nomos and hidden matrix of current politics but that it is necessary to think through the commonalities and disparities between these two spaces without awakening the demon of comparison. Setting Agamben's ideas afoot in the plantation and its remnants requires an understanding of the life support systems that sustain terror and bare life, which frequently appear in more benign forms of political control, as well as the functioning of social life alongside exceptional incidents of violence and (social) death. The barring of subjects that belong to the Homo sapiens species from the jurisdiction of humanity depends upon the workings of racialization (differentiation) and racism (hierarchization and exclusion); in fact the two are often indistinguishable. Bare life and biopolitics are but alternative terms for racism, though a designation that attempts to conjure a sphere more fundamental to the human than race. Agamben's description of the Muselmann, who represents the most extreme incarnation of bare life, as the production of an absolute biological substance reaches out to a territory that seemingly precedes racialization in its insistence on the absolute and the biological, yet, as we have seen, the assemblages by which human beings are transmuted into bare life are scripted onto the bodies of the dysgenic so that their expulsion appears both deserved and natural. We might say, then, paraphrasing Agamben: the novelty of modern racializing assemblages lies in the fact that the biological given is as such immediately racialized, and the political is as such immediately the racialized given: Man.[33] Thus, in the next chapter, I concentrate on the role of the U.S. juridical apparatus (including the use of habeas corpus by minoritized subjects) in the formation of racializing assemblages by equating the human, on the one hand, with property ownership, and, on the other hand, with a legal status that can be granted and annulled by the court.

———

The articulation of the flesh as a racializing assemblage in the world of Man cannot be apprehended by legal recognition and inclusion.

how is this the conclusion of this chapter?

5 LAW: PROPERTY

Nuruddin Farah's *Variations on the Theme of an African Dictatorship* trilogy is set in 1970s Mogadishu during the socialist heyday of Somali dictator Siad Barre's reign, which ended in 1991 and triggered twenty years of civil war. Barre is only referred to as "The General" in the trilogy, allowing Farah to develop a fictional universe that focuses simultaneously on the specificities of Somalia in the 1970s and on the defining role of charismatic leaders such as Barre, Muammar Gaddafi, Idi Amin, or Jomo Kenyatta in African postcolonial history. Farah, however, is not primarily concerned with understanding why all these figures became increasingly autocratic or the spectacular forms of violence that are endemic to dictatorial governmentality but with describing how these changes in postcolonial rule affected the everyday lives of citizens.

The second volume in the trilogy, *Sardines* (1981), concentrates on clitoridectomy and the politically motivated rape of women in order to chart how, in the wake of colonialism, these traditional forms of gendered subjugation exist on a continuum with modern modes of postcolonial dictatorial domination. To this end, a telling interchange between the main character, Medina, a western-educated Somali woman, and Atta, an African American visitor to Somalia, occurs in medias res, during which Atta makes an argument about the racial specificity of pain and the form of its remembrance: "One doesn't forget centuries of suffering. My race remembers this suffering, my race hasn't forgotten it. I remember this suffering, this pain. *Therefore I am.*" For Atta, black suffering represents a political site of collective memory of racial subjectivity. In response, Medina delivers the following monologue:

> In Auschwitz it was humanity which suffered, not a particular race. . . . The same is happening in Palestine, in the US, in South Africa and other places. And when some blacks are suffering, rest assured that others are doing as well. You suffer because you are a human being, not because you are who you are, not *because you are black.* And if it were my own people making others suffer, I would suffer too. . . . I suffer this humiliation, this inhumane subjugation of circumcision; you can never know how painful it is unless you've undergone the operation yourself. But must every woman in the world suffer this act of barbarism in order to know the suffering it entails . . . ? It's not racial. Suffering is human.[1]

Even though it would be fairly easy to dismiss one position, either the traditionally humanist (suffering is human) or the racially particularistic (suffering is experienced only by those groups upon which it is inflicted), in favor of the other, both these stances rely on the same logic that deems one incompatible with the other, since the humanist brand would erase particularities in favor of a universalist sweep and the particularistic variant insists on its irreducibility by excluding all nonmembers from the group's affliction. Rather than urging us to choose sides, Farah's juxtaposition of these viewpoints draws attention to the ways racialized and gendered suffering at the hands of political brutalization are always already imbricated in the construction of modern humanity.

Suffering, especially when caused by political violence, has long functioned as the hallmark of both humane sentience and of inhuman brutality. Frequently, suffering becomes the defining feature of those subjects excluded from the law, the national community, humanity, and so on due to the political violence inflicted upon them even as it, paradoxically, grants them access to inclusion and equality. In western human rights discourse, for instance, the physical and psychic residues of political violence enable victims to be recognized as belonging to the "brotherhood of Man." Too often, this tendency not only leaves intact hegemonic ideas of humanity as indistinguishable from western Man but demands comparing different forms of subjugation in order to adjudicate who warrants recognition and belonging. As W. E. B. Du Bois asked in 1944, if the Universal Declaration of Human Rights did not offer provisions for ending world colonialism or legal segregation in the United States, "Why then call it the Declaration of Human Rights?"[2]

Wendy Brown maintains, "politicized identity" operates "only by entrenching, restating, dramatizing, and inscribing its pain in politics; it can hold out no future . . . that triumphs over this pain."[3] Brown suggests replacing the identitarian declaration "I am," which merely confirms and solidifies what already exists, with the desiring proclamation "I want," which offers a Nietzschean politics of overcoming pain instead of clinging to suffering as an immutable feature of identity politics. While I recognize Brown's effort to formulate a form of minority politics not beholden to the aura of wounded attachments and fixated almost fetishistically on the state as the site of change, we do well to recall that many of the political agendas based on identity (the suffragette movement, the movement for the equality of same-sex marriages, or the various movements for the full civil rights of racialized minority subjects, for instance) are less concerned with claiming their suffering per se (I am) than they are with using wounding as a stepping stone in the quest (I want) for rights equal to those of full citizens. Liberal governing bodies, whether in the form of nation-states or supranational entities such as the United Nations or the International Criminal Court make particular forms of wounding the precondition for entry into the hallowed halls of full personhood, only acknowledging certain types of physical violence. For instance, while the United Nations High Commissioner for Refugees passed a resolution in 2008 that includes rape and other forms of sexual violence in the category of war crimes, there are many forms of sexual violence that do not fall into this purview, and thus bar victims from claiming legal injury and/or personhood.[4]

Even more generally, the acknowledgment and granting of full personhood of those excluded from its precincts requires the overcoming of physical violence, while epistemic and economic brutalities remain outside the scope of the law. Congruently, much of the politics constructed around the effects of political violence, especially within the context of international human rights but also with regard to minority politics in the United States, is constructed from the shaky foundation of surmounting or desiring to leave behind physical suffering so as to take on the ghostly semblance of possessing one's personhood. Then and only then will previously minoritized subjects be granted their humanity as a legal status. Hence, the glitch Brown diagnoses in identity politics is less a product of the minority subject's desire to desperately cling to his or her pain but a consequence of the state's dogged insistence on suffering as the only price of entry to proper personhood, what Samera Esmeir has referred to as a "juridical humanity" that bestows and rescinds humanity as an individualized legal status in the vein of property.[5] Apportioning personhood in this way maintains the world of Man and its attendant racializing assemblages, which means in essence that the entry fee for legal recognition is the acceptance of categories based on white supremacy and colonialism, as well as normative genders and sexualities.

[handwritten margin note: Brown's point exactly.]

We need only to consult the history of habeas corpus, the "great" writ of liberty, which is anchored in the U.S. Constitution (Article 1, Section 9), to see that this type of reasoning leads to reducing inclusion and personhood to ownership.[6] The Latin phrase *habeas corpus* means "You shall have the body," and a writ thereof requires the government to present prisoners before a judge so as to provide a lawful justification for their continued imprisonment. This writ has been considered a pivotal safeguard against the misuse of political power in the modern west. Even though the Military Commissions Act of 2006, which denied habeas corpus to "unlawful enemy combatants" imprisoned in Guantanamo Bay, remains noteworthy and alarming, habeas corpus has been used both by and frequently against racialized groups throughout U.S. history, as was the case when habeas corpus was suspended during World War II, allowing for the internment of Japanese Americans. The writ has also led to gains for minoritized subjects as, for instance, in the well-known *Amistad* case (1839), in which abolitionists used a habeas corpus petition to free the "illegally" captured Africans who had staged a mutiny against their abductors. Likewise, when Ponca tribal leader Standing Bear was jailed as a result of protesting the forcible removal of his people to Indian Territory in 1879, the writ of habeas corpus affected his release from incarceration as well as the judge's recognition that, as a general rule, Indians were persons before U.S. law, even though Native Americans were not considered full U.S. citizens until 1924.[7]

Nevertheless, the benefits accrued through the juridical acknowledgment of racialized subjects as fully human often exacts a steep entry price, because inclusion hinges on accepting the codification of personhood as property, which is, in turn, based on the comparative distinction between groups, as in one of the best-known court cases in U.S. history: the Dred Scott case. In 1857, the Supreme Court invalidated Dred Scott's habeas corpus, since, as an escaped slave, Scott could not be a legal person. According to Chief Justice Taney: "Dred Scott is not a citizen of the State of Missouri, as alleged in his declaration, because he is a negro of African descent; his ancestors were of pure African blood, and were brought into this country and sold as negro slaves."⁸ In order to justify withdrawing Dred Scott's legal right to ownership of self, Chief Justice Taney's opinion in the decision contrasts the status of black subjects with the legal position of Native Americans vis-à-vis the possibility of U.S. citizenship and personhood: "The situation of [the negro] population was altogether unlike that of the Indian race. These Indian Governments were regarded and treated as foreign Governments. . . . [Indians] may, without doubt, like the subjects of any other foreign Government, be naturalized . . . and become citizens of a State, and of the United States; and if an individual should leave his nation or tribe, and take up his abode among the white population, he would be entitled to all the rights and privileges which would belong to an emigrant from any other foreign people."⁹ While slaves were not accorded the status of being humans that belonged to a different nation, Indians could theoretically overcome their lawful foreignness, but only if they renounced previous forms of personhood and citizenship. Hence, the tabula rasa of whiteness—which all groups but blacks can access—serves as the prerequisite for the law's magical transubstantiation of a thing to be possessed into a property-owning subject.¹⁰

The judge's comparison underscores the dangers of ceding definitions of personhood to the law and of comparing different forms of political subjugation, since hypothetical Indian personhood in the law rests on attaining whiteness and the violent denial of said status to black subjects. Additionally, while the court conceded limited capabilities of personhood to indigenous subjects if they chose to convert to whiteness, it did not prevent the U.S. government from instituting various genocidal measures to ensure that American Indians would become white and therefore no longer exist as Indians. In other words, the legal conception of personhood comes with a steep price, as in this instance where being seemingly granted rights laid the groundwork for the U.S. government's genocidal policies against Native Americans, since the "racialization of indigenous peoples, especially through the use of blood quantum classification, in particular follows . . . 'genocidal logic,' rather than simply a logic of subordination or discrimination," and as a result "whiteness constitutes a project of disappearance for Native peoples rather than signifying privilege."[11] Beginning in the nineteenth century the U.S. government instituted a program in which Native American children were forcibly removed from their families and placed in Christian day and boarding schools, and which sought to civilize children by "killing the Indian to save the man," representing one of the most significant examples of the violent and legal enforced assimilation of Native Americans into U.S. whiteness.[12] Though there is no clear causal relationship between Taney's arguments in the Scott decision and the boarding school initiative, both establish that legal personhood is available to indigenous subjects only if the Indian can be killed—either literally or figuratively—in order to save the world of Man (in this case settler colonialism and white supremacy). Furthermore, the denial of personhood qua whiteness to African American subjects does not stand in opposition to the genocidal wages of whiteness bequeathed to indigenous subjects but rather represents different properties of the same racializing juridical assemblage that differentially produces both black and native subjects as aberrations from Man and thus not-quite-human. The writ of habeas corpus—and the law more generally—anoints those individualized subjects who are deemed deserving with bodies even while this assemblage continually enlists new and/or different groups to exclude, banish, or exterminate from the world of Man. In the end, the law, whether bound by national borders or spanning the globe, establishes an international division of humanity, which grants previously excluded subjects limited access to personhood as property at the same time as it fortifies the supremacy of Man.[13]

The cruel irony of this fact is nowhere more pronounced than in the case of Henrietta Lacks, who died destitute after enduring great pain, but whose cervical cancer provided one of the first immortal cell lines to be successfully cultivated outside the biological jurisdiction of the human body. As such, even though they were not patented, the HeLa cells have served as the basis for not only scientific progress but also financial gain. The scientific and economic immortality of the HeLa cells, as they are known, stands in stark contrast to Henrietta Lacks's susceptibility to premature death at the age of thirty-one in 1951 and her family's continued poverty.[14] If Henrietta Lacks's story and the ongoing narrative of the eternal life of the HeLa cells prove anything, it is that the hieroglyphics of the flesh subsists even in death, and that it has now been transposed from the outwardly detectable to the microscopic interior of the human, since it "can be invaded at any given and arbitrary moment by the property relations" (Spillers, "Mama's Baby," 218). It would seem that persistence of the twin phantoms of racialization and property relations unsettle the promise of a subepidermal and cellular humanity as an absolute biological substance.[15]

More recently, as a result of his treatment for hairy cell leukemia at the UCLA Medical Center, John Moore's cancer cells were grown into a highly profitable immortal cell line (MO) patented by the University of California in 1984 without his knowledge. Subsequently, Moore sued the UC Regents, and in 1990 the California Supreme Court ruled that the law could not grant proprietorship over biological matter, at least not to those individuals from whom this zoe is expropriated. Though Moore was not granted even partial proprietary ownership of the patented cell line derived from his spleen, the court did rule "that the case was one of a breach of fiduciary duty and a lack of informed consent," since the doctors who patented the cell line had not informed Moore of their maneuvers.[16] The court was faced with determining whether the cell line belonged to the jurisdiction of Moore's body and, thus, "related to his rights of self-possession" or whether it represented "something different and artificial, belonging to its scientific makers. The court chose the latter, clearly influenced by the after-the-fact nature of the quandary."[17] Rather than outlawing the proprietary ownership of cell lines derived from humans outright, however, the opinion of one judge in this ruling absolves the court of responsibility: "Whether . . . cells should be treated as property susceptible to conversion is not, in my view, ours to decide."[18] Though the law has no problem adjudicating who can possess a body, and therefore full humanity, the highest legal authority in the United States cedes the field to corporate interests when confronted with "choices . . . that define our essence."[19]

Paradoxically, the particular biological material in question remains the property, at least nominally, of all humanity and is not proper to Moore the individual person: "Lymphokines, unlike a name or a face, have the same molecular structure in every human being and the same, important functions in every human being's immune system. Moreover, the particular genetic material which is responsible for the natural production of lymphokines, and which defendants use to manufacture lymphokines in the laboratory, is also the same in every person; it is no more unique to Moore than the number of vertebrae in the spine or the chemical formula of hemoglobin."[20] So, while the court grants personhood to human subjects in an individualized fashion that is based on comparatively distinguishing between different humans, when biological material clashes with the interests of capital, the court appeals to the indivisible biological sameness of the Homo sapiens species. Since the court's ruling does not place this slice of human flesh in the commons for all humans to share, it tacitly grants corporations the capability of legally possessing this material with the express aim of generating monetary profit. Considering that corporations enjoy the benefits of limited personhood and the ability to live forever under U.S. law, corporate entities are entrusted with securing the immortal life of biological matter, while human persons are denied ownership of their supposed essence.[21] My interest here lies not in claiming inalienable ownership rights for cells derived from human bodies such as Lacks's and Moore's but to draw attention to how thoroughly the very core of pure biological matter is framed by neoliberal market logics and by liberal ideas of personhood as property.

We are in dire need of alternatives to the legal conception of personhood that dominates our world, and, in addition, to not lose sight of what remains outside the law, what the law cannot capture, what it cannot magically transform into the fantastic form of property ownership. Writing about the connections between transgender politics and other forms of identity-based activism that respond to structural inequalities, legal scholar Dean Spade shows how the focus on inclusion, recognition, and equality based on a narrow legal framework (especially as it pertains to antidiscrimination and hate crime laws) not only hinders the eradication of violence against trans people and other vulnerable populations but actually creates the condition of possibility for the continued unequal "distribution of life chances."[22] If demanding recognition and inclusion remains at the center of minority politics, it will lead only to a delimited notion of personhood as property that zeroes in comparatively on only one form of subjugation at the expense of others, thus allowing for the continued existence of hierarchical differences between full humans, not-quite-humans, and nonhumans. This can be gleaned from the "successes" of the mainstream feminist, civil rights, and lesbian-gay rights movements, which facilitate the incorporation of a privileged minority into the ethnoclass of Man at the cost of the still and/or newly criminalized and disposable populations (women of color, the black poor, trans people, the incarcerated, etc.).[23] To make claims for inclusion and humanity via the U.S. juridical assemblage removes from view that the law itself has been thoroughly violent in its endorsement of racial slavery, indigenous genocide, Jim Crow, the prison-industrial complex, domestic and international warfare, and so on, and that it continues to be one of the chief instruments in creating and maintaining the racializing assemblages in the world of Man. Instead of appealing to legal recognition, Julia Oparah suggests counteracting the "racialized (trans)gender entrapment" within the prison-industrial complex and beyond with practices of "maroon abolition" (in reference to the long history of escaped slave contraband settlements in the Americas) to "foreground the ways in which often overlooked African diasporic cultural and political legacies inform and undergird anti-prison work," while also providing strategies and life worlds not exclusively centered on reforming the law.[24] Relatedly, Spade calls for a radical politics articulated from the "'impossible' worldview of trans political existence," which redefines "the insistence of government agencies, social service providers, media, and many nontrans activists and nonprofiteers that the existence of trans people is impossible."[25] A relational maroon abolitionism beholden to the practices of black radicalism and that arises from the incompatibility of black trans existence with the world of Man serves as one example of how putatively abject modes of being need not be redeployed within hegemonic frameworks but can be operationalized as variable liminal territories or articulated assemblages in movements to abolish the grounds upon which all forms of subjugation are administered.

The idea of bare life as espoused by Giorgio Agamben and his followers discursively duplicates the very violence it describes without offering any compelling theoretical or political alternatives to our current order. Paradoxically, by insisting on a limited notion of the law at the cost of neglecting so many other facets that flow into the creation of bare life, Agamben preempts a rigorous and imaginative thinking of the political imaginary that rests in the tradition of the oppressed. Agamben's impoverished conception of the political comes into view most clearly in the lack of current or past alternatives it offers to our current order and when we consult the fleshly testimonies of and about subjects that inhabit the sphere of mere life (the enslaved, political prisoners, concentration camp detainees, for instance). Still, these voices should not be construed as fountains of suffering authenticity but as instantiations of a radically different political imaginary, which refuses to only see, feel, hear, smell, and taste bare life in the subjectivity of the oppressed.

Even though it is one of Agamben's avowed goals to disassociate law from life, and vice versa, he is seemingly possessed by the law. For instance, in *State of Exception* Agamben envisions the redemptive aspect of the homo sacer project thus: "to show law in its nonrelation to life and life in its non-relation to law means to open a space between them for human action, which once claimed for itself the name of 'politics.'"[26] Yet Agamben opens this space of human action only insofar as he hones in on the ways in which law has completely engulfed life in modern politics—and he should be lauded for doing so in such an obsessive manner. Which is to say that, for Agamben, there exists no space beyond the law in our current historical moment because it is now synonymous with the state of exception and the production of bare life, and what once existed under the heading of politics, which should not be confused with the political, is suspended in an indeterminate futurity rather than in the Benjaminian "Jetztzeit."[27] Moreover, in this cosmology, the present and past are always already completely engulfed by law and sovereignty, while any pause or social life in the anthropological machine takes place in the future. Antonio Negri makes a similar point regarding Agamben's absolute "pessimism": "Everything that happens in the world today seems to have been fixed onto a totalitarian and static horizon, as under 'Nazism.' But things are different: if we live in a state of exception it is because we live through a ferocious and permanent 'civil war,' where the positive and the negative clash: their antagonistic power can under no circumstance be flattened onto indifference."[28] This tension between the utter contamination of the present (bare life) and a mystical redemption located in an indeterminate tomorrow (form-of-life) defines Agamben's thinking in toto, and also does not leave room for any sort of poetics or politics that might shift the current order of things.[29] To put it in the terms of Frantz Fanon and Sylvia Wynter, Agamben fails to introduce any sort of invention into existence, since these two forces always occupy separate spheres of orbit in his philosophy, and for him invention can occur only after the abolition of present life.[30]

One reason for the numinous futurity of life outside the purview of the law is Agamben's insistence on the state of exception and bare life as exclusively legal categories, which is precisely what Walter Benjamin sought to undo through his invocation of a "pure violence" (*reine Gewalt*) that abolishes law. In his 1921 essay "Critique of Violence," Benjamin holds that mere life is not manufactured by the law, but marks the precise moment in which "the rule of law over the living ceases."[31] Benjamin's essay, written in response to the use of state-sponsored violence against communists in the quelling of the Spartacist uprising (Berlin, January 1919), considers the possibility of nonbloody revolutionary violence in the form of the proletarian general strike, which, directed against the state, suspends the law without summoning the force of violence.[32] Benjamin writes that with the "abolition of state power, a new historical epoch is founded. If the rule of myth is broken occasionally in the present age, the coming age is not so unimaginably remote that an attack on law is altogether futile. But if the existence of violence outside the law, as pure immediate violence, is assured, this furnishes proof that revolutionary violence, the highest manifestation of unalloyed violence by man, is possible, and shows by what means."[33] Thus, for Benjamin, the elimination of state power and suspension of the law represents a potentiality of the current political constellation brought about by the revolutionary forces of a proletarian general strike. In other words, the radical shift in the political horizon is premised on the existing situation of the tradition of the oppressed and on the desire to create alternatives rather than an indeterminate future.

Instead of unleashing the potentiality of the tradition of the oppressed's complicated connection to the law and violence, its extrajudicial *Bewegungsgesetz* (law of motion), if you will, Agamben chooses to yoke this category to Carl Schmitt's legal "state of exception" by arguing, "even the criterion of 'purity' violence will therefore lie in its relation to law" (*State of Exception*, 61).[34] Nevertheless, the purity of this interpretation conflates a relation to the law with the wholesale colonization of contemporary life by the juridical apparatus. As a general rule, the primary lenses through which Agamben understands Benjamin are either as an interlocutor of Carl Schmitt or as a messianic figure in the tradition of the Pauline letters; the intensity with which Agamben at times labors to make Benjamin's thinking fit into these templates lends his interpretations an almost comical dimension.[35] Witness, for instance, the treatment of the "scandalous" Benjamin/Schmitt dossier in *State of Exception*, which insists that Schmitt's *Political Theology* was a response to Benjamin's "Critique of Violence," because Schmitt, as a regular reader of *Archiv für Sozialwissenschaften und Sozialpolitik* (the journal in which "Critique of Violence" was published in 1921) must have taken note of Benjamin's essay.[36] The dossier is scandalous because Carl Schmitt was not only a Nazi sympathizer and anti-Semite, but participated prominently in the party, and these activities are clearly reflected in his writings from the period. The actual dossier Agamben refers to consists of one letter Benjamin wrote directly to Schmitt in 1930, alerting him to the publication of his book *The Origin of German Tragic Drama* and one favorable mention of Schmitt in a 1923 letter to a friend.

Because the dossier is so limited in scope and in order to bring Benjamin into the Schmittian fold, Agamben takes it upon himself to revise the text of *Origin* as it appears in the German edition of Benjamin's collected works: "An unfortunate emendation in the text of the *Gesammelte Schriften* has prevented all the implications of this shift from being assessed. Where Benjamin's text read, *Es gibt eine barocke Eschatologie*, 'there is a baroque eschatology,' the editors, with a singular disregard for all philological care, have corrected it to read: *Es gibt keine* . . . 'there is no baroque eschatology'" (*State of Exception*, 56). According to Rolf Tiedemann, the editor of Benjamin's *Gesammelte Schriften*, this particular amendment is based on contextual conjecture, as are other editorial changes, since Benjamin states at several other points in the text that the German baroque was characterized by an absence of eschatology, for instance: "the baroque knows no eschatology" and "the rejection of the eschatology of the religious dramas is characteristic of the new drama throughout Europe."[37] The problem lies not so much in Agamben's linking of Schmitt's and Benjamin's ideas, but rather in the alacrity with which he postulates direct historical connections between these two thinkers. These philological canards become indicative of Agamben's overall appropriation of Benjamin, which has at its goal the annexing—by any means necessary—of Benjamin into the mainstream at the cost of disregarding Benjamin's liminal status in Germany during his lifetime; it also downplays both the Marxist elements, as fractured as they may have been, and those aspects regarding the revolutionary potentiality of the oppressed in Benjamin's philosophy. As a result, the homo sacer's social death appears as the only feature of his or her subjectivity. Taking in other instantiations of mere life such as colonialism, racial slavery, or indigenous genocide opens up a sociopolitical sphere in which different modalities of life and death, power and oppression, pain and pleasure, inclusion and exclusion form a continuum that embody the hidden and not-so-veiled matrices of contemporary sovereignty. Agamben's dogmatic insistence on a stringently juridical instantiation of the state of exception reinstitutes the Holocaust as the most severe and paradigmatic manifestation of bare life (here bolstered by a legal rather than moral frame of reference), and this argument also neglects forms of bare life that take place within the jurisdiction of the normal legal order.

This reliance on a dogmatic conception of not only the state of exception but law in general materializes in Agamben's discussion of incarceration. Contra Foucault, Agamben excludes the prison from the state of exception, and thus the production of bare life, because it forms a part of penal law and not martial law (the state of exception) and is therefore legally within "the normal order." The camp, on the other hand, represents the absolute space of exception, which is "topologically different from a simple space of confinement" (*Homo Sacer*, 20).[38] But as Angela Davis and Colin Dayan, among others, have shown, the violent practices in U.S. prisons neither deviate significantly from Agamben's description of bare life vis-à-vis the suspension of law nor are mere spaces of detention.[39] Dayan explicitly addresses the continuities between slavery, imprisonment, and the torture in the Abu Ghraib prison through an excavation of the various interpretations of the Eighth Amendment to the U.S. Constitution, especially the phrase "cruel and unusual punishment," which has been evacuated of its meaning by locating its significance solely in relation to the intent of the perpetrator.[40] In Angela Davis's observation, torture suffuses everyday life in the United States and abroad: "The military detention center as a site of torture and repression does not, therefore, displace domestic supermaximum security prison. . . . My point is that the normalization of torture, the *everydayness* of torture that is characteristic of the supermax may have a longer staying power than the outlaw military prison."[41] Slavery, imprisonment, and torture, in U.S. prisons and abroad, are legal in the strict sense and very much part of the "normal order." Still they display many of the same features Agamben ascribes to the camp as the definitive site for the production of bare life.

If we take into account the racial dimensions of the U.S. penal system, imprisonment, and torture in their full juridical and cultural normalness, it would seem that racial violence is always already beyond the law under a constant state of siege. In other words, the normal order is differentially and hierarchically structured and does not necessitate a legal state of exception in order to fabricate the mere life of those subjects already marked for violent exclusion; in fact, we might even say that this is its end goal. In the contemporary United States, the prison-industrial complex functions as a racializing assemblage that dysselects black and Latino subjects, branding them with the hieroglyphics of the flesh. In this way, blackness and racism figure as major zones of indistinction: blackness as a vital (nonlegal) state of exception in the domain of modern humanity. Which is to say, the judicial machine is instantiated differentially according to various hierarchical structures and frequently abandons numerous subjects, making them susceptible to premature death within the scope of the normal order, which, in turn, aids in the creation and maintenance of caesura among humans. Instead of being seduced by the supposed omniscience of the law, we should ask, as Dayan does, "what does the law mask?" to underscore what remains "rotten at the core of the law" (Benjamin) or its "bare-faced two-facedness" (Spillers), especially for the oppressed. Agamben goes to great lengths to show that the political tools of subjection developed during the Holocaust were not simply blunders in the progressive march of western modernity.

The Holocaust provides such an apt formation for Agamben's theorization of modern politics precisely because the Third Reich as a whole took place in a legal state of exception after the suspension of regular German law in 1933.[42] After Hitler had been appointed chancellor on January 30, 1933, the Verordnung des Reichspräsidenten zum Schutz von Volk und Staat and the Ermächtigungsgesetz (Enabling Act) were issued in February and March 1933 respectively, withdrawing most civil liberties from German citizens while granting the Nationalsozialistische Deutsche Arbeiterpartei (NSDAP) leadership almost unlimited powers in legislative, judicial, and executive matters. Since these edicts were not repealed until 1945, they established martial law (the state of exception) in effect for the duration of the Third Reich. Carl Schmitt has famously defined the sovereign as "he who decides on the state of exception," which Agamben takes as his starting point for thinking about the field of politics.[43] Even though he claims that the state of exception cannot be conceptualized solely in legal terms, since it represents the juridical suspension of the law, Agamben insists, "a theory of the state of exception is the preliminary condition for any definition of the relation that binds and, at the same time, abandons the living being to law" (State of Exception, 1). Nevertheless, as several critics have noted, the state of exception does not apply equally to all, since the exclusion of and violence perpetrated against some groups is anchored in the law. In a salient piece about planetary violence and the emergence of disposable populations, Ronald Judy states, "They [cannot] be explained in terms of exception, because the conditions of their existence know no temporal limits nor result from crises of sovereignty. . . . The occurrence of violence associated with disposable populations is symptomatic of the irrelevance of the entire discourse of sovereignty to the current arrangements of power, except when it operates as a means of 'effecting control over mortality' and as 'a way of exercising the right to kill.'"[44] As opposed to the temporally bound state of exception espoused by Agamben and Schmitt that revokes the legal entitlements of all citizens, here different populations—often racialized—are suspended in a perpetual state of emergency in which legal rituals stain dysselected individuals and groups with the hieroglyphics of the flesh. And, as evidenced in the prison-industrial complex, the pretense of juridical equality rarely abolishes selective legal insouciance or genocidal acts against those who have been touched by racializing assemblages of the flesh.

———

Disarticulating the flesh and the law occasions
the redeployment of depravation.

6 DEPRAVATION: PORNOTROPES

In *What Is a Thing?* Martin Heidegger states, "To question historically means to set free and into motion the happening [*das Geschehen*] which rests and is bound [*gefesselt*] in the question."[1] *Habeas Viscus* is concerned with freeing and putting in motion what Saidiya Hartman has identified as "the history that hurts—the still-unfolding narrative of captivity, dispossession, and domination that engenders the black subject in the Americas."[2] As opposed to being confined to a particular historical period, echoes of New World slavery rest in many contemporary spaces, for, as Heidegger explains, "it is a setting into motion [*in Gang zu bringen*] the initial happening of this question according to its simplest characteristic moves [*Bewegungszügen*], which have been congealed in a quiescence. This happening does not lie somewhere remote from us in the muted and distant past but is here in each analytic proposition and in all everyday opinions, in every single approach to things [*Dinge*]."[3] Heidegger's conjoining of historicity with bounded subjection and the thing opens a particular aspect encased in the tradition of the oppressed and asks how the unleashing of its happening contributes to the conceptualization of modern politics; or, what are the sexual dimensions of objectification (*Ver-gegen-ständlichung*) in slavery and other forms of extreme political and social domination?[4]

Spillers has referred to the enactment of black suffering for a shocked and titillated audience as "pornotroping": "This profound intimacy of interlocking detail is disrupted, however, by externally imposed meanings and uses: (1) the captive body as the source of an irresistible, destructive sensuality; (2) at the same time—in stunning contradiction—it is reduced to a thing, to *being* for the captor; (3) in this distance *from* a subject position, the captured sexualities provide a physical and biological expression of 'otherness'; (4) as a category of 'otherness,' the captive body translates into a potential for pornotroping and embodies sheer physical powerlessness that slides into a more general 'powerlessness'" ("Mama's Baby," 206). Spillers directs our seeing to several facets of the body/flesh, human/not-quite-human, sovereign/bare life, and so on pas des deux in her insistence on the simultaneous thingness and sensuality of the slave, which lays bare the extralegal components of this volatile *Ding*. Pornotroping unconceals the literally bare, naked, and denuded dimensions of bare life, underscoring how political domination frequently produces a sexual dimension that cannot be controlled by the forces that (re)produce it. As Daphne Brooks remarks, "born out of diasporic plight and subject to pornotroping," black flesh has "countenanced a 'powerful stillness.'"[5] The hieroglyphics of the flesh, embodied here by pornotroping, circumnavigate the connubial abyss of subjection and freedom, displaying at once the physical powerlessness of the dysselected slave subject and the untainted power of the selected master subject.

In order to better follow Spillers's brilliant coarticulation of *porno* and *trope*, a brief etymological detour is in order. Originally *porno* signified "prostitute" and in the ancient Greek context whence it sprang, the term referred to female slaves that were sold expressly for prostitution. Also a derivation from Greek, *trope*, according to Hayden White, refers to "turn" and "way" or "manner"; later, by way of Latin, *trope* is aligned with "figure of speech." White states the following of the palimpsestic structure of this word: "Tropes are deviations from literal, conventional, or 'proper' language use. . . . It is not only a deviation *from* one possible, proper, meaning, but also a deviation *towards* another meaning."[6] In pornotroping, the double rotation White identifies at the heart of the trope figures the remainder of law and violence linguistically, staging the simultaneous sexualization and brutalization of the (female) slave, yet—and this marks its complexity—it remains unclear whether the turn or deviation is toward violence or sexuality.[7]

Pornotroping, then, names the becoming-flesh of the (black) body and forms a primary component in the processes by which human beings are converted into bare life. In the words of Saidiya Hartman, it marks "the means by which the wanton use of and the violence directed towards the black body come to be identified as its pleasure and dangers—that is, the expectations of slave property are ontologized as the innate capacities and inner feelings of the enslaved, and moreover, the ascription of excess and enjoyment to the African effaces the violence perpetrated against the enslaved."[8] The violence inflicted upon the enslaved body becomes synonymous with the projected surplus pleasure that always already moves in excess of the sovereign subject's *jouissance*; pleasure (rapture) and violence (bondage) deviate from and toward each other, setting in motion the historical happening of the slave thing: a potential for pornotroping.[9] In Christina Sharpe's words, the black body and flesh "become the bearers (through violence, regulation, transmission, etc.) of the knowledge of certain subjection as well as the placeholders of freedom for those who would claim freedom as their rightful yield."[10] How does the historical question of violent political domination activate a surplus and excess of sexuality that simultaneously sustains and disfigures said brutality? Or what are the sexual dimensions of objectification in slavery and other forms of extreme political and social domination? My argument is not about erotics per se but dwells in the juxtaposition of violence as the antithesis of the human(e) (bondage) and "normal" sexuality (rapture) as the apposite property of this figure.[11] Once again, I am bracketing questions of agency and resistance, since they obfuscate—and not in a productive way—the textures of enfleshment, that is, the modes of being which outlive the dusk of the law and the dawn of political violence.

Let's set in motion two notable beginnings. First, Saidiya Hartman's *Scenes of Subjection* commences with a refusal to reproduce Aunt Hester's whipping at the beginning of Frederick Douglass's 1845 *Narrative of the Life of Frederick Douglass*, the locus classicus and primal scene of black female subjection, "in order to call attention to the ease with which such scenes are routinely reiterated, the casualness with which they are circulated, and the consequences of this display of the slave's ravaged body . . . especially because they reinforce the spectacular character of black suffering."[12] Second, Fred Moten's *In the Break* starts by redoubling Hartman's beginning performative gesture—which is never really a refusal, since Hartman cites many other violent incidents in the text and the scene is so familiar that it need not be presented in full, but a conceptual caesura that endeavors to disarticulate the commonsensical twinning of physical agony and enjoyment through the conduit of the black female body—by counterposing Aunt Hester's "heart-rending shrieks" with the equally well-known scene in Douglass about the spirituals—in terms of the apposition of pleasure and pain that Hartman seeks to submerge.[13] Moten questions Hartman's foreclosure of "the possibility of pain and pleasure mixing" and locates the conditions of possibility for the black subject and black culture in the space "where shriek turns speech turns song."[14] Aunt Hester, who as a female slave is marked by several asymmetrical burdens with regard to the category of humanity, epitomizes an (exceptional) example among many others. As opposed to negating humanity, then, the line of questioning initiated by Aunt Hester, Hartman, Moten, and others embraces the specificity of the subaltern body in pain as a (de)tour, a relational passage to a version of the human unburdened by shackles of Man.

Resting in the conceptual clearing ignited by Hartman's and Moten's thinking (and Hortense Spillers's, as will become evident), which locates Aunt Hester's scene of subjection as the originating leap (Ur-Sprung) of the modern (black) subject, I want to return to Aunt Hester, considering the prospect of shriek not transmogrifying into speech or song per se, or rather, the syntactical phrasing of the shriek itself and the way it is rendered by Douglass:

> I have often been awakened at the dawn of day by the most heart-rending shrieks. . . . I remember the first time I ever witnessed this horrible exhibition. I was quite a child, but I well remember it. . . . Aunt Hester had not only disobeyed his [the overseer Plummer] orders in going out, but had been found in the company of Lloyd's Ned; which circumstance, I found, from what he said while whipping her, was the chief offense. Had he been a man of pure morals himself, he might have been thought interested in protecting the innocence of my aunt; but those who know him will not suspect him of any such virtue. Before he commenced whipping Aunt Hester he took her into the kitchen, and stripped her from neck to waist, leaving her neck, shoulders, and back entirely naked. He then told her to cross her hands, calling her at the same time a d—d b—h. After crossing her hands, he tied them with strong rope, and led her to a stool

under a large hook in the joist, put in for the purpose. He made her get upon the stool, and tied her hands to the hook. She now stood fair for his infernal purpose. Her arms were stretched up at their full length, so that she stood upon the ends of her toes. He then said to her, "Now, you d—d b—h, I'll learn you how to disobey my orders!" and after rolling up his sleeves, he commenced to lay on the heavy cowskin, and soon the warm, red blood (amid heart-rending shrieks from her, and horrid oaths from him) came dripping to the floor. I was so terrified and horror-stricken at the sight, that I hid myself in a closet, and dared not venture out till long after the bloody transaction was over.[15]

This passage, which stands almost at the beginning of Douglass's *Narrative*, contains many of the hallmarks of what Hortense Spillers calls "a potential for pornotroping" that persistently adheres to the black subject during and subsequent to enslavement, and which forms an integral component of the great tolerance for black suffering evoked by Jesse Jackson in the aftermath of Hurricane Katrina. Most prominent in this "bloody transaction" is the liaison between political violence and sexuality, which appears here both in the references to Ned's loose morals and in the spec(tac)ular, partially denuded figuration of how the lick of the whip touches Aunt Hester. If this scene were an isolated case, then perhaps we could conclude by remaining at the crossroads of Hartman's, Moten's, and Douglass's openings.[16] However, since Aunt Hester's descendants, whether in literary, filmic, or televisual texts, habitually appear dressed in the same grammar as the one who inaugurated this tradition, it is tantamount to conjecture how, in the words of Édouard Glissant, "the cry of the plantation" was "transfigured into the [shriek] of the world."[17]

Before proceeding, I want to highlight how scholarly engagements with Douglass's *Narrative* such as Hartman's and Moten's—in particular, which passages critics choose to focus on—have become an emblem of generational shifts in black American literary and cultural theory in order to ascertain what this reveals about the gendering and sexualization of racializing assemblages. Following the canonization of slave narratives as literary texts rather than as historical documents in the 1970s, a process in which *Narrative of the Life* played a pivotal role, most interpretations concentrated on the scene depicting Douglass's struggle with Covey, especially the way this melee facilitates Douglass's transition from slave to man. Aunt Hester, however, was rarely mentioned in the initial conversations about Douglass's text as a literary object of knowledge.[18] Addressing the hegemonic place of Douglass and the prioritization of his heroic masculinity within African American literary criticism in 1991, Deborah McDowell holds that "the cultural function of the slave narrative as genre and its relations to the inscription of gendered ideologies of masculinity and femininity represents a reordering of priorities in Afro-American literary study."[19] Since McDowell wrote these lines, we can see this transferal very clearly in the recent prominence of Aunt Hester's whipping as the primary locus for scholarly debates about Douglass's Narrative in African American literary studies, which along with Harriet Jacobs's "loophole of retreat" has become representative of our particular postfeminist moment in black literary and cultural studies.[20] I say postfeminist not because we have ventured beyond feminism but insofar as the questions about gender, subjection, voyeurism, and sexualized violence discussed by Hartman, Moten, and others were made possible by earlier black feminist interventions, McDowell's and Spillers's, for instance.[21] As a result, the previous critical obscurity and current renown of Aunt Hester's flagellation within the context of feminist inquiry have not merely displaced the masculinist tenor of the debates surrounding how Douglass's physical strength in overcoming the overseer Covey allows him to inhabit a normative heteromasculinity, but have also largely jettisoned from scholarly view the passage that recounts this battle itself, which has led to the neglect of how the Covey section of Narrative specifically stages the "scaled inequalities," which forcefully "complement the commanding terms of the dehumanizing, ungendering, and defacing project of African persons" (Spillers, "Mama's Baby," 214). With this in mind, it is worth revisiting Douglass's Hegelian confrontation with his overseer, albeit not to abandon Aunt Hester or to reclaim Douglass's fierce heteromasculinity but, instead, to ascertain how we might apply the insights of black feminist theory to this passage in Narrative of the Life.

Covey makes many appearances in this text; even so his presence is most palpably felt in the tenth chapter of Douglass's Narrative. And although the chapter culminates in the struggle that reveals to readers "how a slave was made a man," Douglass conveys throughout that his dealings with Covey are defined by violence—frequently traversed by the libidinal—in all respects, and thus intimately trussed to the workings of the flesh. To that end, Douglass narrates several instances of spectacular enfleshment before arriving at the denouement. In the first occasion, having been at his new residence for only a week, Covey administers a brutal lashing, which cuts Douglass's back, Douglass says, "causing the blood to run, and raising ridges on my flesh as large as my little finger" (Narrative, 58). In the next encounter, Covey commands Douglass to strip off his clothing in order to brutalize him with a switch from a gum tree. When Douglass refuses to undress, Covey dashes toward him, Douglas writes, "with the fierceness of a tiger, tore off my clothes, and lashed me till he had worn out his switches, cutting me so savagely as to leave the marks visible for a long time after" (Narrative, 59–60). Though the sexualization of this interaction may not seem as clear-cut as Aunt Hester's blood-stained gate, we should nonetheless pause and note that Douglass's refusal to disrobe and Covey's desire for his denuded flesh initiate the savage beating. As we shall see shortly, stripped flesh, particularly in concurrence with brutality, represents a primary aspect of pornotroping in slavery and beyond.

In the well-known climactic episode of Narrative, Douglass's description of the battle with Covey continues to cast their interactions in a pornotropic light by emphasizing its homoerotic physicality:

> Mr. Covey entered the stable with a long rope; . . . he caught hold of my legs, and was about tying me. As soon as I found what he was up to, I gave a sudden spring, and as I did so, he holding to my legs, *I was brought sprawling on the stable floor.* Mr. Covey seemed now *to think he had me, and could do what he pleased*; but at this moment—from whence came the spirit I don't know—I resolved to fight; and . . . I seized Covey hard by the throat; and *as I did so, I rose. He held on to me, and I to him.* My resistance was so unexpected that Covey seemed taken all aback. He trembled like a leaf. . . . This battle with Mr. Covey was the turning point in my career as a slave. It rekindled the few expiring embers of freedom, and revived within me *a sense of my own manhood.* (Narrative, 71–72; emphases added)[22]

Initially Covey subjects Douglass to the subordinate position, believing that young Frederick is his to assail. Nonetheless, Douglass manages to wrest dominance from his overseer when they lock in a fraught embrace of sorts. The shift from subjection, which narratalogically recapitulates Aunt Hester's earlier pornotropic descent into the flesh, to subjectivity occurs spatially— Douglass ascends from the barn floor to face Covey—as much as it stages the shift in gendered power relations: moving from feminized prostration to upright and masculinized prowess.[23] Still, Douglass cannot scale the pecking order of heteromasculinity comfortably given his status as a slave, as I discussed in chapter 2, due to black subjects' vexed relationship to Man's nomoi of gender and sexuality. While some critics have written about this scene in juxtaposition to the depiction of Aunt Hester, often reading the latter as a gendered displacement of Douglass's own ensuing scene of enfleshment, far fewer critics have summoned Douglass's encounter with overseer Covey as a sadomasochistic moment of same-sex violence, which uncovers "the entwinement of desire and coercion that typifies the master–slave relationship," thus continuing to yoke enfleshment to ungendered black female subjects.[24] Not noting the pornotropic contours of Douglass's clash with Covey obscures that it represents a primal scene of the many ways that blackness, even the heroic masculine version embodied by Douglass, remains antithetical to the heteronormative. Thus, placing Douglass's and Aunt Hester's sexualized subjugation side by side reveals the continuum of ungendering that is unleashed by racial slavery's violence/sexuality matrix (pornotroping), and which has come to define sexuality in modernity.

For Douglass's battle with Covey only appears as less libidinally charged than Mr. Plummer's whipping of Aunt Hester if we suppose: (a) that sexuality is determined first and foremost by object choice and identity, that is, the master desires Aunt Hester because he is a man and she is a woman, where Covey cannot possibly desire Douglass given that both are biological men, and, (b) that libidinousness and political violence are mutually exclusive, particularly when they interface with normative masculinity. According to Spillers, within the defacing properties of enslavement "the gendered female *exists* for the male," while "the ungendered female—in an amazing stroke of pansexual potential—might be invaded/raided by another woman or man" ("Mama's Baby," 222). I would like to dwell in this space of the pansexual potential for a moment to test how reading the Covey scene through the black feminist lens usually applied to Aunt Hester allows us to ask how the ungendered male becomes possible in this context, if, as we have seen, he can also be conquered by another man or woman. Exerting some pressure on Spillers's text, we can register that in addition to the unremitting possibility of familial bonds rupturing as a result of their equation with property relations, the hieroglyphics of the flesh also throw a wrench into any steadfast divisions between property, gender, violence, and sexuality; not only can family structures be invaded by property relations at any given moment in this American grammar book of the flesh, but property circulates in a thoroughly libidinal economy. In other words, those defacing assemblages of the flesh ought to be recognized as putting under erasure the pronouns *she* and *he* as well as their attendant gender-sexuated baggage claims at the same time as they kindle a pansexual, or rather a queer, potential within this field. I am using the term *queer* here not exclusively as a designator for same-sex desires, acts, or identities but instead as a shorthand for the interruption of the violence that attends to the enforcement of gender and sexual norms, especially as it pertains to blackness. Ergo, pornotroping reveals spectacularly how racial slavery and its afterlives in the form of the hieroglyphics of the flesh intimately bind blackness to queering and ungendering. Supposing there to be no such thing as the "ahistorical Stoff of sexuality" located in the noumenal ether, then the racialized and spatialized power imbalance in the foregoing scene cannot *not* be interpreted as sexualized.[25] An erotic charge accrues to this violent imbroglio, because the phenomenon of modern sexuality, its very historical Stoff, largely comes into being through the roots and routes of the pornotropic lexicons of slavery and colonialism, which is evidenced in, among many other things, the sheer amount of visual data devoted to exploring the nexus of political violence and sexuality. Or, as Frantz Fanon states, "We know how much of sexuality there is in all cruelties, tortures, beatings."[26]

Instances of pornotroping feature prominently in literary and visual conjurings of slavery, the Holocaust, colonialism, and the images from the Abu Ghraib prison as well as from the aftermath of Hurricane Katrina.[27] In fact, it seems that no cinematic imagining of slavery exists without at least one obligatory scene of gratuitous whipping, branding, boiling, and so on. Besides the films I discuss here, other examples include *Roots*, *Beloved*, *Drum*, *The Legend of Nigger Charley*, *Amistad*, and *The Middle Passage*, giving credence to Gayl Jones's observation, "They make even that some kind of sex show, all them beatings and killings wasn't nothing but sex circuses."[28] Usually these scenes are presented in the form of flashbacks and feature nubile black bodies in pain. Pornotroping is very much at the heart of mainstream imaginings of slavery at least from Douglass's *Narrative* onward, while it only represents the fringe of how the Holocaust is projected, which is perhaps due to the fact that in the aftermath of the Shoah, Jews are primarily figured as hyperhuman, where black people are consigned to either this realm or the domains of the not-quite-human, an oscillation that *Sankofa* and *Man-*

Is aggression tied only to racialized sexuality? I think not.

Why is the Douglass scene with Mr. Covey only racialized?

dingo visualize quite extensively. In addition, pornotropes appear in a strand of Italian art films from the 1970s, and there exists a whole genre of Nazi sexploitation films also primarily produced during the same period in Italy (Pier Paolo Pasolini's *Salo, or The 120 Days of Sodom*, Lina Wertmüller's *Seven Beauties*, Tinto Brass's *Salon Kitty*, Liliana Cavani's *Nightporter*, and Luchino Visconti's *The Damned*). While not set in a concentration camp, the s/m relationship between Nazi sympathizer Hendrik Höffgens and Afro-German Juliette in Klaus Mann's novel *Mephisto* (1936) and its Oscar-winning 1981 film version is also pertinent here. Another important text in this tradition is Franz Kafka's *In the Penal Colony*, which shines a spotlight on the pornotropic modalities of colonial bare life in its extended, sexualized description of torture.[29] Overall, cinema enables the production of bare life as a politico-sexual form of life, wherein the remainder that is effected but cannot be contained by the legal order is disseminated in the visual realm.

With this in mind, I would like to turn my attention to two cinematic texts that present naked life qua pornotroping within the peculiar institution in very different ways. Since cinema cannot give a first-person account of the horror of torture, its testimony remains suspended between the cinematic apparatus and the tortured body, which, in turn, when it encounters slavery, produces a sexual surplus: pornotroping. I focus on those moments in the two films that stage the extreme violence inflicted upon slave bodies, because they highlight different aspects of pornotroping: the spectacular and mundane. The first is Heile Gerima's 1993 film *Sankofa*, and the second *Mandingo*, a 1975 potboiler sexploitation film based on the popular 1957 Kyle Onstott novel. Even though both films are concerned with racial slavery and its evils, they could not be more different in their content and production styles. While *Mandingo* was created under the auspices of a major Hollywood studio and luridly explores the sexual economy of plantation slavery, *Sankofa* was independently produced and distributed by esteemed black filmmaker Gerima and styles itself as an antidote to the public amnesia about slavery in the United States. That is, *Sankofa* traffics in political consciousness raising and *Mandingo* seemingly uses slavery as a titillating backdrop for a variety of sexual encounters, which generally crisscross the color line. Yet I want to resist rehearsing the preordained differences between the two films that would yield only commonsensical insights about *Sankofa*'s positive images and its negative flipside projected by *Mandingo*. I want to consider instead what these scenes reveal about the logic of the pornotrope in the cinema of slavery when applied to both female and male flesh. How does the cinema of slavery project the continued enfleshment and ungendering of black subjects?

Where Mandingo configures slaves as mere apparitions of their white masters' desire, in Sankofa they appear as noble and righteous subjects who, upholding their native African traditions, fight the institution of slavery in any way that they can. In this sense, Sankofa understands itself as recovering the lost subjectivity of slaves—their bodies in Spillers's terminology—rather than exploiting their flesh, but the film cannot resist making pornotroping an integral part of its allegorical visualization of transatlantic racial slavery. Indeed, viewed in relation to Mandingo, Gerima's film is noteworthy for the conspicuous absence of nude flesh, with a few notable exceptions, and the surplus of pornotroping given that most scenes of subjection and the recurring images of the master raping the main character, Mona/Shola, involve at least partially clad bodies.

Sankofa opens with images of an African American fashion model, Mona, on a photo shoot at Elmina Castle on the Atlantic coast of Ghana, one of the places where slaves were gathered before embarking on the Middle Passage, now a popular tourist destination. As Mona writhes on the beach in a blond wig and a leopard-print bathing suit (fig. 6.1), white tourists inspect the castle in the background of the frame. Later, when Mona enters the dungeon beneath the castle, the voice of a tour guide recedes and is replaced by the presence of chained slaves awaiting the Middle Passage as she is teleported back in time (fig. 6.2). Then Mona becomes the slave Shola despite her protests that she is not African but American. The remainder of Sankofa depicts Shola's experiences on the Lafayette plantation in Louisiana. When she returns to Ghana at the end of the film after being a slave and having been symbolically reprimanded and punished for her inauthentic blackness, the plot produces a reformed Mona, who epitomizes all African Americans that have neglected and/or forgotten the history of slavery and their ties to Africa.

We literally see Mona's body transmuting into Shola's flesh as she attempts to tell the slave traders that she is American and not African. The camera pans across Shola's bare breasts, resting there, as her body is seared and ripped apart by the branding iron of the slave traders. Everything rotates around, intensifying its spectacular shock value: the setting, the camera work, the lighting, the positioning of the characters, Mona's screams, the musical soundtrack, and the martyrological, Christlike iconography of

6.1 Model Mona during photo shoot at Elmina Castle
(*Sankofa*, dir. Haile Gerima, 1993).

6.2 Unnamed slaves in the dungeon of Elmina Castle
(*Sankofa*, dir. Haile Gerima, 1993).

6.3 Mona transforms into slave Shola
(*Sankofa*, dir. Haile Gerima, 1993).

Mona's body (fig. 6.3). The extradiegetic soundtrack features Aretha Franklin's recording of Thomas Dorsey's "Take My Hand, Precious Lord." The recording itself is very sparse, functioning primarily as a showcase for Franklin's rough vocal prowess accompanied only by a piano, and had, by the time *Sankofa* appeared, already accrued a significant political cachet. Mahalia Jackson performed the song at Martin Luther King Jr.'s funeral, and Aretha Franklin sang it at Lyndon B. Johnson's memorial service. The version used in the film was one of Franklin's first releases and was recorded live in her father's Detroit church in 1956. Here, the difference between the version used in *Sankofa* and the later, much better-known one found on Franklin's 1972 album, *Amazing Grace*, released after she had become a pop star and was returning to her gospel roots, is significant. Franklin's voice is far less dramatic and the production much more polished on the later recording, amplifying how Gerima exploits the 1956 version to signal an untainted authenticity and soulfulness. In this way, Mona reverses Franklin's journey from authenticity to commodification. The song and scene come to a climax around Franklin's melismatic stretching of the line "at the river I stand," which grows progressively louder and in the end completely displaces

Mona's screams on the soundtrack. Using the nondiegetic soundtrack, especially expressive black female voices, so prominently in moments of extreme violence is a common practice in the cinema of slavery and operates as an index of the severity of both the cruelty and ensuing pain. Here, the black singing voice signals both a radical alterity by pointing to the aspects of slavery that cannot be represented visually and stands as a marker for knowability, since it assumes that the black voice can encode the horrors of slavery aurally. And, while the religious dimension of the words does not take center stage, the prominence of the song and Franklin's delivery coupled with the visual aspects on the screen, however, make abundantly clear that we are witnessing a spiritual rebirth, a baptism of blood.

Furthermore, the grammar of the pornotrope—the cross-fertilization of violence and sexuality—is enacted by the camera's deviation toward the female slave's breasts and the turn away from the branding iron cauterizing her flesh. This scene dramatizes nothing less than the primal scene of the African diaspora, the natal alienation of the slave, with the added twist that the person undergoing this procedure is a present-day U.S. citizen, which is key to the allegorical working of Mona's conversion because it emphasizes the gulf between body (free U.S. citizen) and flesh (slave). When Mona goes back in time she encounters a group of mute, chained slaves that serve both as her historical unconscious and as the witnesses of her homo sacerization. As opposed to the slaves, Mona appears as a person, a full subject by law, a body, which renders this pornotroping more scandalous. When the slaves first hold out their hands to welcome Mona to the fold, she runs away in fear, and the camera focuses on the slaves as a mass in long and medium shots. In the process of Mona's branding, however, we see extreme close-ups of their faces and then the camera zeroes in further on the slaves' eyes. Finally, after Mona has become Shola, the film uses a tilt shot from her point of view, visually signifying Shola's membership in the group and the forced introjection of her status as flesh. Correspondingly, the slaves' positioning as witness-spectators enacts Mona's inability, as a late twentieth-century U.S. citizen, to bear witness to her own becoming-flesh. At this point Mona's body registers the wounding but cannot give account of it on screen and sees the slaves only as naked life. However, once Mona's subjection as Shola is completed, the point-of-view shot allows her, and by extension the spectator, to testify to the presence of the slaves as more than bare life. Pornotroping operates as the conduit for Mona's transformation from human to subhuman, American to African, subject to slave; it translates the abolition of her body and its rebirth as flesh into an ocular language.

In a later scene, Shola's master strings her up naked and the local Catholic priest exorcizes her, while the light-skinned overseer watches. The priest douses Shola in holy water and thrusts a large crucifix against her breasts so that the tools of subjection, like the branding iron, once again rupture her flesh, this time in a (meta)physical sense. Where the earlier sequence refused to disclose the iron searing Shola's skin, here the camera deviates to the corporeal mechanics of her enfleshment. Nevertheless, the film cuts to an image of a full moon when Shola is whipped so that we hear her heart-rending shrieks, but we are not granted visual access to the cruelty, dramatizing the scopic deviation from violence toward sexuality that makes pornotroping such a powerful (American) grammar book. Far from gratuitous, these two sequences are indispensable to both the logic of pornotroping and Gerima's film, because the first converts Mona into Shola as part of a group of slaves—deindividuated flesh—while the second, in an individuating gesture, shows Mona to have been fully engulfed by Shola.

The abjection, brutalization, and sexualization in slavery redeem Mona, unleashing her ideal alter ego, Shola, whom Mona introjects into her newer and better self at the close of the film when she reemerges stark naked from the dark dungeon into the bright daylight of Elmina Castle (figs. 6.4–6.5). Now Mona's renaissance is complete, and even if one essential aspect of pornotroping (violence) has gone missing, Mona's nudity, which in Sankofa has until this point always been coupled with brutalization, reminds viewers that a potential for pornotroping refuses to dissipate.

Overall, Gerima's film relies heavily on the fallen flesh/redeemed spirit typology, which is enacted in Mona's transformation from an inauthentic western black female subject into a noble slave that transcends her material conditions: her transubstantiation from human (Mona) to subhuman (Shola) to hyperhuman (Mona after Shola).[30] Here, Mona surfaces as a newly fangled Christlike figure; just as Christ suffered and died for our sins, Gerima uses Mona/Shola's flesh as a conduit for her and the viewers' salvation.[31] That is, Mona's seeming integration into the world of Man requires the film to dramatize her dysselection—both through the process of becoming an enfleshed slave and in the figure of Shola—so that she may rise above her abjection. Similarly, in Agamben the Muselmann becomes inhuman only insofar as he or she can be redeemed by testifying to the im-

6.4 Mona's return to Elmina Castle (*Sankofa*, dir. Haile Gerima, 1993).

6.5 Mona's rebirth (*Sankofa*, dir. Haile Gerima, 1993).

possibility of witnessing and as a model for a novel post-Holocaust ethics. And despite Agamben's hesitancy in using the term *Holocaust* because of its biblical origin, which figures Christ's sacrifice as the apex of this term and inaugurates Christian anti-Semitism, the Muselmann's abjection and redemption strongly echo the fallen flesh/redeemed spirit typology (*Remnants*, 28–31). *Sankofa*'s attempt to counteract previous negative representations of slavery operates, as Kara Keeling has so brilliantly shown, under the logic of a commonsense black nationalism, noting that the version of Mona who appears at the close of the film "is a masculine diasporic African cleansed of the impurities deposited by colonization and slavery, especially any form of sexuality that would align the Black with the 'genital.'"[32] Mona's masculine subjectivity also eerily echoes Douglass's transubtantiation from slave to man. Mona/Shola's sanitization—just like Douglass's—occurs via waters of pornotroping, which, in this case, eroticizes her for the viewer at the cost of not granting Mona/Shola any sexual agency within the diegetic universe of the film. Nevertheless, as Mona/Shola's repeated eroticization when under the duress of physical torture makes clear, the film cannot contain the deviance of the pornotrope. As hard as the film tries to idealize Mona/Shola, erase her sexuality and femininity, her ungendered flesh and its attendant pornotroping will not be moved; it remains a naggingly pained and eroticized presence that suffuses *Sankofa*'s narrative and visual grammar in toto, which, in turn, sets in motion the bare life that slumbers in the permanent state of exception, especially the libidinal charge that accrues to the slave.

In *Mandingo*, naked bodies are everywhere; thus pornotroping is the rule that proves the (state of) exception, and redemption is not on the horizon. In contrast to *Sankofa*, *Mandingo* is a gender-agnostic offender with regard to pornotroping, because the film ungenders while also sexualizing male and female slaves, though masculine flesh occupies more screen time and is more integral to the film's narrative. There is hardly a scene that does not prominently feature slaves in varying degrees of undress, though I should add that naked and semiclad white bodies also populate the screen often. Since most of the sex presented on screen is interracial, *Mandingo*, in contrast to *Sankofa*, focuses primarily not on slaves but on the masters' and mistresses' desire for black flesh. Essentially, the white characters are the only ones that do not engage in "homoracial" sexual acts over the course of the film's narrative, incest and prostitution notwithstanding. Accordingly,

Mandingo presents whiteness qua Man as a cannibalistic desiring machine that expropriates the putative surplus carnality and sexuality of black flesh ungendered in order to fuel its workings.

After engaging in sexual intercourse with his virginal slave mistress, we see *Mandingo*'s protagonist, Hammond Maxwell, instructing a slave on how to best administer a beating to fellow slave Agamemnon with a paddle—he is punished for acquiring literacy—while a slave child looks on in bemusement as a naked Agamemnon hangs upside down from the barn ceiling (figs. 6.6–6.8). Even though Agamemnon is positioned at the center of the frame, viewers are literally barred from seeing his enfleshment once his beating begins, since the wooden bars in the barn partially conceal his nudity and the pain engendered by the torture.[33]

Yet Agamemnon's "heartrending shrieks," just like Shola's, are foregrounded on the soundtrack, dramatizing once more the fractional deviation from the visual toward the auditory in the operations of the cinematic pornotrope. The matter-of-factness with which this sequence materializes positions these acts of violence at the heart of the normal order. The presence of the slave child further underscores the banality of the violence onscreen insofar as the child serves as a placeholder for the spectator as witness. Disgusted and disturbed by Agamemnon's muffled screams, Hammond removes himself from the scene until his cousin Charles arrives and begins "properly" punishing Agamemnon. Thus, the slave child and the master enact two different modes of spectatorship and, combined with Agamemnon's placement, concurrently split and form the fractured whole of the scene's testimony. Agamemnon's absent presence as the visual and sonic focal point of the scene, the slave child's amusement, and Hammond's repulsion project an inverse world in which nothing operates as it should and what should be exceptional is mundane, and vice versa. A child and his master witness Agamemnon, as opposed to Frederick Douglass's younger autobiographical self; however, this child cannot muster scandalization or amazement. Perhaps he knows something that we do not.

Mandingo and *Sankofa* draw on the model of pornotroping inaugurated by Douglass—in his depiction of both Aunt Hester's whipping and his fight with Covey—in their emphasis on the aural materiality of the screech and the cohabitation of the sexual and the violent; they also insist on the importance of the witness to the machinations of pornotroping. In *Sankofa* Mona/Shola undergoes pornotroping while a group of slaves in the dungeon of

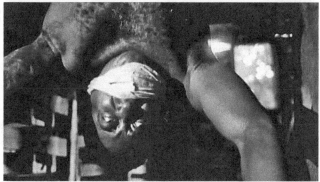

6.6 Slave beats Agamemnon while master Hammond Maxwell watches (*Mandingo*, dir. Richard Fleischer, 1975).

6.7 Agamemnon's muffled shrieks (*Mandingo*, dir. Richard Fleischer, 1975).

6.8 Slave child as witness (*Mandingo*, dir. Richard Fleischer, 1975).

Elmina Castle looks on and, later, during her second baptism, the film places the light-skinned overseer at the scene of her subjection. As opposed to *Sankofa*, however, *Mandingo* shocks in its visualization of routinized sexualized violence during racial slavery, its sheer unspectacular ordinariness. Put differently, where *Sankofa* endeavors to transcend the pornotrope so as to present a heroic black subject with full agency, *Mandingo* embraces the nexus of political violence, enslavement, and sexuality, and therefore unearths the pivotal role the sexualized ungendering of the black subject plays in modernity. Because *Sankofa* assumes that the dehumanization of slaves was simply a product of false consciousness that can be ameliorated by positive counternarratives that restore agency and full humanity (disembodied, nonsexual, and hyperhuman) to the black subject, it paradoxically reinscribes the very racializing assemblages it seeks to leave behind. It also takes for granted that black people have been fully integrated into the world of Man. The sociogenic dysselection encapsulated by the hieroglyphics of the flesh beg to differ, however.

Although the deviance from violence toward sexuality passes into actuality more frequently in the context of slavery than other forms of sovereign coercion, the idea of pornotroping must also be understood as conceptually igniting the im/potential libidinal currents that slumber in all acts of political domination and as part and parcel of modern sexuality as such—why else does sadomasochism shadow Agamben's *Homo Sacer* and *Remnants of Auschwitz*? In a brief passage in *Homo Sacer*, Agamben notes the fundamental codependency of sadomasochism and bare life: "The growing importance of sadomasochism in modernity has its root in the exchange [between the sovereign and the homo sacer]. Sadomasochism is precisely the technique of sexuality by which the bare life of a sexual partner is brought to light" (134). Agamben's version of sadomasochism differs from pornotroping, since in pornotroping the political acts as the primary technology—at least nominally—producing a sexual remainder that feeds back into the power dynamic. Sadomasochism is political for Agamben only insofar as it reflects sovereignty, but the political itself seems resistant to the touch of sadomasochism and sexuality in general, which is precisely what pornotroping offers as a heuristic model: the contamination of the political.

Remnants contains a fuller argument about the vicissitudes of (sado)masochism than *Homo Sacer*; in fact, Agamben tenders a theory of the subject that arises out of the discussion of (sado)masochism and shame (*Remnants*,

107–9). According to Agamben, in sadomasochism "discipline and apprenticeship, teacher and pupil, master and slave become wholly indistinguishable. The indistinction of discipline and enjoyment, in which the two subjects momentarily coincide, is precisely shame" (108–9).[34] Why does the commingling of discipline and pleasure result in shame, and not simply pleasure? In what sense are these lines applicable to the Muselmann as a cipher for absolute passivity at the border of life and death; does he or she feel shame? If so, is it shame due to the convergence of discipline and pleasure? The Muselmann and masochism appear as relational only via their spatial proximity within the confines of Agamben's book, but no reason for this juxtaposition is tendered. Since Agamben does not connect his analysis of masochism to the Muselmann, the reader is left wondering why they share the same textual space, especially since putatively abnormal sexuality appears in quite a few analyses of fascism.

Far from being diametrically opposed, erotics and fascism have always contaminated each other and pathologically deviant sexuality has frequently been summoned either to explain the appeal of fascism for its followers or the violent excesses of fascist politicians—the work of Wilhelm Reich, Herbert Marcuse, Klaus Theweleit, and Susan Sontag's essay "Fascinating Fascism" are perhaps the most prominent examples.[35] In many of these writings, recourse to sexuality in the vortex of fascism primarily serves to prop up the difference between the normal order and the state of exception. Rather than conceptualizing sadomasochism's bond with modern sovereignty as pornotroping—the catachrestic figuration of the sphere where political brutality bleeds into sexuality—Agamben's theory of biopolitics wields deviance, if only obliquely, as a way of locating both abnormal sexuality and fascism *elsewhere*. Agamben either keeps pornotroping at bay by not explicitly thinking sadomasochism together with the status of the Muselmann (completely outside politics), or he configures it as a biomimetic introjection of sovereignty (utterly engulfed and corrupted by politics). In a more recent piece, Agamben discusses the foreclosed potential of pornography for profanation, which is found in the transposition of carnal acts to a realm where they are no longer bound to representation but signify a new form of life: "the human capacity to let erotic behaviors idle, to profane them, by detaching them from their immediate ends. But while these behaviors thus open themselves to a different possible use, which concerns not so much the pleasure of the partner as a new collective use of sexuality, pornography intervenes at this point to block and divert the profanatory intention. The solitary and desperate consumption of the pornographic image thus replaces the promise of a new use."[36] As with the assessments of sadomasochism in *Homo Sacer* and *Remnants of Auschwitz*, Agamben abstracts sexuality from its immediate ends so as to redeem it from base enfleshment without considering the pornotropic dimensions of the acts as such; he attempts to erase their genitality, in Keeling's and Fanon's words. Put differently, the political facets of pornography and sexuality in the NOW are of less interest to Agamben than how they could be recast in an unspecified future. Instead of pornotroping, Agamben resorts to sovereignty, shame, and profanation, categories that are very much located on "the continent of man," in Walter Benjamin's phrasing.[37] Slavery and its afterlives do not allow for such an easy disentangling of political domination and sexuality. While deviant sexuality is often summoned as a reason for fascism, it rarely appears as a motivating factor for racial slavery, precisely because pornotroping is such an integral component of the intimacies at the very center of slavery's history that hurts, which, in the process, disenables the locating of both deviant sexuality and slavery beyond the reach of liberal democracy. As a component in the workings of habeas viscus, pornotroping mobilizes the happening bound by the question that rests in slave flesh. As such, it inches away from a space of pure negativity defined above all by the total privation of agency and subjectivity and toward something more elusive.

In sum, instead of emerging as an ontological condition, flesh comes into view as a series of desubjectivations, which are always already subjectivations, that hail the slave and the spectator in order to engrave upon him or her the hypervisible yet also illegible hieroglyphics of the flesh. The exception is that, here, Louis A.'s "Hey you" is replaced by whips, paddles, dungeons, chains, branding irons, large pots of boiling water, and other such instruments of torture. Perhaps, then, rather than exclusively serving as painful and exploitative illustrations of a forgotten past, these scenes of subjection in *Mandingo* and *Sankofa*, bearing witness to the processes of the black body becoming-flesh, stand as stark reminders of what covertly underpins modern political formations, namely visual instantiations of naked life or the hieroglyphics of flesh. Pornotroping is thus not a mere by-product of an already existing state but integral to the creation of the flesh. Both films also powerfully highlight the stubbornly scopic nature of pornotroping as a racializing assemblage, because, on the one hand, the dysselection of the black subject as not-quite-human requires visible inscriptions on the flesh and in the field of vision (lacerations, nakedness, black skin, etc.) while, on the other hand, desire must remain invisible. The happening of desire takes place off the screen, off the map, off the charts, off the books, which is what renders the symbols etched into and written by the flesh indecipherable to the extent that they do not appear as desire.

To this end, the white characters in *Mandingo* voice the declarative phrase, "I craves," so much that it acts as the film's diacritical mantra or refrain. Hammond and the other white characters crave blackness, sex, the subjection of slaves, life, and so on; in other words, they desire the flesh: the flesh that they, as selected master subjects, supposedly transcend and can therefore not inhabit. While carnality plays a significant role in this craving, there exists also within this hunger an immense longing for a different form of freedom, which, within the system of plantation slavery—seen as a miniature version of the world of Man—can only be articulated by white subjects in the form of social and sexual domination; to such an extent, in fact, that the very being of the white characters in *Mandingo* consists of alternatingly wanting and subjugating the flesh of slaves. Thus, the white I, synonymous with Man, is birthed through the labors of the desire encrypted in the regionally accented expression "I craves," which inaugurates this subject. In doing so, *Mandingo* draws our attention not only to the patently seeable subjection of black subjects but also to the usually tightly bound and gagged question of desire and its purpose in the creation of Man as the human. As a performative chant, "I craves" lends quasi-decipherability to the hieroglyphics of the flesh, decrypting the master code of "cultural seeing by skin color" (Spillers, "Mama's Baby," 207). Although the actual differentiation between desiring and conquering the flesh might not stretch further than the small tract of land located between nonexistent and very slight, it is nonetheless important to notice this ever-so-slight vacillation, because it gestures toward a conceptual galaxy—one not quite so far away as that other one—in which the flesh embodies both more and less, but above all something other, than it does in the world of Man.

The differently signified flesh is habeas viscus, for in the world of Man, the hieroglyphics of the flesh are translated to the jargons of negativity, lack, the subhuman, and so on. Given the systematic use of torture as a political tool of "democratic" governments—now legalized in the united states of exception—and the simultaneous sexualization of its medial images in our contemporary moment, how might we go about viewing and thinking these depictions not as deviations from the normal order, since that would only affirm the putative externality of pornotroping from the center stage of culture and politics?[38] A potential for pornotroping, however, is far from abnormal given that it shadows so many aspects of modern politics, culture, and sexuality. What the pornotrope contributes to the theorization of modern sociopolitical subjectivity is its freeing and setting in motion of the viscous deviances—the detours, digressions, and shortcuts that authorize violence as a vital layer in the attires of modern sovereignty—that lay dormant in bare life and social death, whether these are found in current practices of torture in U.S. domestic and foreign prisons, or the hauntological histories of the Holocaust, slavery, and colonialism. Because liberal democracy abandons the enfleshed silhouette of political violence, it returns in the form of deviance rather than as habeas viscus. Put simply, pornotroping is the historical Stoff of modern sexuality—its fleshy ether—and to experience the flesh, then, might just allow us to relate to the world differently. But, as I discuss shortly, cravings, just like leaves, humans, numbers, ghosts, species, and stars can manifest in radically different guises; we just have to recognize them as such, even if they dwell among us in the physiological and metaphysical hunger exhibited by C. L. R. James, Harriet Jacobs, and former Muselmänner.

———

Habeas viscus: because to fully inhabit the flesh might lead to a different modality of existence.

Desire as freedom?

7 DEPRIVATION: HUNGER

Where the first six chapters have for the most part inhabited the dominion of subjection, and chapter 6 set the stage for theorizing political violence in a different register, the remaining two chapters zero in on the equally important constructive dimensions of this topography. Put simply, they bring to the fore those transformative assemblages of the flesh that acknowledge the social life found in those bottomless circles and circles of sorrow around political violence. In contrast to bare life, biopolitics, and so on, habeas viscus incorporates the violent racializing assemblages that facilitate the continued conflation of Man with human while also pumping up the volume on the insurgent praxes of humanity composed in the hieroglyphics of the flesh. Besides trying to appreciate the creative politicopoetic contours of the flesh, I enter this territory with the following questions: How can C. L. R. James's hunger strike while he is detained on Ellis Island and the Muselmänner's apparitions of food teach us to mouth "I craves" in a tongue as of yet nonexistent in the world of Man? How might we read the scripture of the flesh, which abides among us "in every single approach to things," but too often lingers in the passing quicksands of indecipherability, otherwise? What does hunger outside the world of Man feel like? Is it a different hunger, or just the same as the famines created by racializing assemblages that render the human isomorphic with Man? How do we describe the sweetness that reclines in the hunger for survival? How is the craving for life sweetened by the sugary textures, smells, and tastes of freedom? What tastes does "the joy of being human" in and beyond "a land of freedom" proffer?[1] Will every cook finally be able to govern once we leave Man by the wayside? Can we practice an ontological politics that starves Man's fever but feeds the cold that will eventually spell his ruin?

In 1952 C. L. R. James was detained—imprisoned as he insists on calling it—for four months (June–September) on Ellis Island by the U.S. Immigration and Naturalization Service (INS) in order to be deported. James had been in the United States since 1938 on a tourist visa and in 1948 the INS ordered that he be deported. The hearings for James's case took place over the next two years, during which James delivered a series of lectures about American literature—in the hopes that this would sway the U.S. authorities to cease the deportation proceedings—that would later serve as the basis for his 1953 text, *Mariners, Renegades, and Castaways: The Story of Herman Melville and the World We Live In*, which uses Herman Melville's *Moby-Dick* to allegorize capitalism, totalitarianism, and the ascent of U.S. empire. James wrote and, with the help of friends, self-published *Mariners* while waiting for the state to repeal his order of deportation, and sent the book to all U.S. congresspersons and others who might speak on his behalf in the deportation proceedings.[2] Since his presence on Ellis Island resulted directly from the 1952 Immigration and Nationality Act, also known as the McCarran-Walter Act, James was a political prisoner.[3] James's legal indeterminacy and experience highlight some more general features of Man's juridical apparatus. While it removed race and gender as impediments to immigration and naturalization, the McCarran-Walter Act allowed the U.S. government to deport immigrants or naturalized citizens suspected of engaging in "subversive" activities and bar alleged subversives from entering the United States; it was also the first immigration act to codify terrorist activity as a national threat. According to Donald Pease, James's precarious legal position arose because when "the government agents cited the McCarran Act as warrant for . . . reclassif[ying] James as an illegal alien and transporting him to Ellis Island," they "removed from James the power to speak in his own name. The state's pronouncement that he was a foreign subversive had disallowed the possibility that James would ever be brought to give testimony before a congressional committee. The testifying phrases of an alien subversive were defined by the state as void of truth-value. As a consequence of this classification, James was denied the legal rights of due process and habeas corpus."[4] Thus James occupied a juridical state of indeterminacy in which, on the one hand, he could not testify on his own behalf, because as an alien subversive he was not a person before U.S. law and therefore had no recourse to habeas corpus, and, on the other hand, he was subject to U.S. law through his internment and pending deportation.

In the final chapter of *Mariners*, titled "A Natural but Necessary Conclusion," which was until recently excised from all editions of this text subsequent to the first printing, James steps away from his pathbreaking interpretation of *Moby-Dick* to offer a detailed analysis of his internment, his legal troubles, and life on Ellis Island, including his two-month-long stint under police supervision in the Stapleton Hospital on Staten Island in October–November 1952 due to problems with a duodenal ulcer. James states, "My chief trouble was the food."[5] He was unable to digest the local cuisine and ate only one meal a week and, as a result, suffered from extreme ulcer pains (137). Initially, James was determined to consume the food but after three weeks he simply could not take it any longer and only took a mouthful or nothing at all (135). After being transferred to the infirmary, where the culinary offering was the same, James subsisted on milk and the inside of rolls with a bit of butter and only took one full meal during a four-week period (137). Then James relocated from Ellis Island to the hospital on Staten Island, initially thinking that he was once again "within the boundaries of civilization" (140), but later when confronted with "inhuman and barbarous" treatment (141), he realized that he had no human rights (141).

In another passage, James reveals the response he received from the district director of the INS to his attorney's request for immediate intervention given the deterioration of his health: "I could always leave and go to Trinidad, where I was born, and drink my papaya juice" (138). Even though papayas are generally conducive to the workings of the human digestive tract—they are, in fact, frequently used as a dietary supplement for precisely this reason—the manner in which the director expelled James from the ideological borders of the United States underscores the political dimensions of James's digestive troubles. After weeks of no proper nourishment on Ellis island, James was severely weakened and experienced constant retching fits when confronted with the victuals, reflecting the political nature of his disgust: "I expect if I had been on a desert island after some shipwreck, I would have managed much better. To a man in my condition, there was added not only the sense of unwarranted inhuman persecution but a never-ceasing battle to put an end to it" (138). Although the site of James's imprisonment, his homeland, and the scenario he envisions are all islands, these landmasses diverge sharply in their political resonances. Trinidad, at least as envisaged by the INS official, imprisons James within a national particularity and locates him in a culinary state of exception vis-à-vis the United States. In addition, the United States had been an extensive military presence in Trinidad in the 1940s, the decade during which the INS first ordered James's deportation to Trinidad.[6] James's imaginary desert island, in contrast, amplifies the repressive and carceral politics of the other spaces, and accordingly, his retching manifests both a visceral response to the food and a political stance that exorcizes the powers that be from his body. The three islands comprise an archipelago that circumvents the maritime space of comparison and the exception as much as it tenders new ways of appreciating the fundamental relay of the world.

Similarly, in their discussion of the psychopathology of hunger in concentration camps, Ryn and Klodzinski note that, while uncommon, some inmates developed an acute revulsion toward the food provided in concentration camps, and some were still disgusted by certain camp staples many years after.[7] Additionally, when asked about the psychic traces left by his experiences in the concentration camp, Marian Zielinsky relayed that he reacted "emotionally to hunger that has been imposed on humans by prevailing/ ruling circumstances [herrschende Umstände]."[8] For Zielinsky, as for James, starvation that is wielded as a political weapon to produce and maintain caesuras differs radically from simple lack of nourishment, which is why both react so strongly to the former. That is, James and Zielinsky know that the assemblages of the flesh they are subject to and subjects of in their particular situations render them not-quite-human. What James brings to the forefront, then, and which remains drowned in Agamben's account of the Muselmann, are the political facets of enfleshment, regardless of the extremity. In addition, James was able to use his enfleshment to produce *Mariners*, as a text and legal testimony, and thus transform his imprisonment into a productive critique of U.S. empire and the nutritional politics of immigration policy. In doing so, James narrates and dwells in the flesh rather than abjuring this domain.

Harriet Jacobs's "loophole of retreat" offers another instructive example in this context, because it presents a protracted process of enfleshment that also functions as a space of freedom.[9] Jacobs inhabits the small, sloped garret space above her grandmother's shed to escape enslavement (although she is still very close to her master) and the sexual advances of her master while still remaining in close proximity to her family, especially her children. Hunger, in this instance, connotes not primarily foodstuff, as it does for James and the Muselmänner, but Jacobs's longing for a territory of bounded manumission. Jacobs cannot stand upright in this space; rats and mice run over her bed; and initially, since the enclosure has no windows, she is unable to distinguish day from night. Soon thereafter Jacobs manages to drill a hole in the wall, "about an inch long and an inch broad," which lifts her spirits because she can now catch a glimpse of and hear her children, but the heat in her lair is still intense, "for nothing but thin shingles protected me from the scorching summer's sun" (*Incidents*, 175). During the relatively mild southern winters, Jacobs "was obliged to lie in bed all day to keep comfortable" and her "shoulders and feet were frostbitten" (175). Although she endured the initial winter, the second cold season brought new challenges: "My limbs were benumbed by inaction, and the cold filled them with cramp. I had a very painful sensation of coldness in my head; even my face and tongue stiffened, and I lost the power of speech" (185). After losing consciousness for sixteen hours and being thought dead by her family, Jacobs came back to life, yet her plight continued as she dwelled for seven years in her garret (described alternatingly as a prison and a retreat), which was nine feet long and seven feet wide while the highest point was just shy of three feet. Jacobs finally broke free from the enclosure long after her lover, Mr. Sands, purchased their children's freedom.

Though Jacobs managed to escape to the North by virtue of having hidden for so long in the loophole of retreat, the enfleshed incapacity produced by her cell haunted her body as disability even in the aftermath of reaching the promised land, thus ensuring that the hieroglyphics of the flesh remained affixed to her physical being-in-the-world in more ways than one. Jacobs's story is instructive for many reasons, not the least of which is the way it casts a stark spotlight on the intimate contiguity of slavery and emancipation, particularly with regard to the severe bodily confinement that served to both curtail and capacitate kinesis, imagination, and liberation. Seeing that Jacobs's confinement resulted from the architectural violence of domesticity and was tethered to having access to her children, her account also draws attention to the (un)gendered provenances of enfleshment. For, in contrast to Douglass, Jacobs—within the generic constraints of the slave narrative and sentimental fiction as well as the nineteenth-century social mores they encode—can neither depict herself as unfettered from familial bonds nor stage her coming to freedom through the conduit of a physical struggle. Though the threat of physical and sexual violence looms large in both Jacobs's and Douglass's cases, Jacobs's scene of enfleshment qua ungendering represents a seven-year marathon in which the ether of physical and psychic brutality is detonated slowly but steadily; the consequences, however, remain just as grievous.[10] Jacobs's injurious sojourn in the garret and James's experience on Ellis Island represent but two of many examples from black cultural archives that typify different manifestations of enfleshment and can therefore be productively placed in conversation with the testimonies of former Muselmänner.

Primo Levi has written perhaps the best-known description of the Muselmann by a camp survivor, which has provided the basis for many subsequent investigations of this figure:

> Their life is short, but their number is endless; they, the Muselmänner, the drowned, form the backbone of the camp, an anonymous mass, continually renewed and always identical, of non-men who march and labour in silence, the divine spark dead within them, already too empty to really suffer. One hesitates to call them living: one hesitates to call their death death, in the face of which they have no fear, as they are too tired to understand. They crowd my memory with their faceless presences, and if I could enclose all the evil of our time in one image, I would choose this image which is familiar to me: an emaciated man, with head dropped and shoulders curved, on whose face and in whose eyes not a trace of a thought is to be seen.[11]

As emblems for the death camps and all that is evil, the Muselmänner haunt Levi, because they represent the embodiments of a radical rupture within modern politics.[12] What is crucial here is that the Muselmänner represent a faceless mass, the drowned, who could no longer be spared, thus highlighting through sheer numerical evidence the severity of evil caused by Nazism. Conversely, for Agamben, even though his theorization of the Muselmann is heavily indebted to Levi, the Muselmänner are individualized figures who symbolize the profound breach in politics and ethics precipitated by Nazism; the Muselmann is "the perfect cipher for the camp" (Remnants, 48).

In both instances, the Muselmänner become ciphers for factors that exceed their own condition: evil, testimony, ethics, the human, and so on, which obscures the flesh of these subjects in an attempt to give back to them a metaphysical body. How might we go about imagining not a disembodied ethics in which the Muselmann serves as template for the inhuman in the human, but the very process of becoming-Muselmann as a form of politics? What formations of habeas viscus do the experiences of Muselmänner make decipherable in a relational opacity?

Not surprisingly, testimony, or rather the lack thereof, occupies a prime location in Agamben's radically novel ethical geography that centers on the Muselmann.[13] Agamben states: "The human being is thus always beyond or before the human, the central threshold through which pass currents of the human and inhuman, subjectification and desubjectification, the living being's becoming speaking and the logos' becoming living. These currents are coextensive, but not coincident; their non-coincidence, the subtle ridge that divides them, is the place of testimony" (Remnants, 135). The Muselmänner are rendered exemplary in this milieu as limit cases for humanity, and they remain, at least in Agamben's thinking, incomparable to others because they have journeyed too far beyond the precincts of the human. Despite Agamben's insistence on testimony's fundamental unfeasibility, which can only stage its own impossibility, the testimonies of the Muselmann figure as the apex of this particular aporia, since Remnants of Auschwitz closes with a collection of quotes from former Muselmänner (all taken from Ryn and Klodzinski's study). Although Agamben engages with authors such as Primo Levi, Jean Améry, and Bruno Bettelheim, all of whom have written about this figure, the words of former Muselmänner themselves are left bare.[14] The testimonies of the Muselmänner appended to the text without commentary by Agamben, a thinker who has written movingly about commentary as an important venue for philosophical reflection, project a rather different image than the completely abject, almost life- and desireless apparitions summoned in the remainder of Remnants.[15]

The testimonies of former Muselmänner, even though they are harrowing in their portrayal of bodily and mental degradation, forcefully dispute the notion according to which "beyond the Muselmann lies only the gas chamber" (Remnants, 85). As Ryn and Klodzinski explain, "the Muselmann was not an exceptional phenomenon but, on the contrary, a quotidian phenomenon."[16] According to the statements featured in their study, prisoners in the camps moved in and out of being-Muselmann, and, depending on the time of year and political situation, 50–80 percent of inmates could be classified as belonging to this category. Moreover, many survivors describe not an inert status but a protracted process, including different stages of physical and psychic decline, of becoming-Muselmann (Muselmannwerdung).[17] Also, other prisoners did not completely shun Muselmänner. Although Agamben writes, "the Muselmann is an absolutely new phenomenon, unbearable to human eyes" (Remnants, 51), some inmates recall feeling pity for the Muselmänner, while others report that "functional inmates" helped Muselmänner if they were friends or part of their family.[18] Even the statements from Ryn and Klodzinski appended to Remnants bear witness to the immense desire for survival and food; one survivor remembers not knowing he was a Muselmann until after the fact; another begins with "I am Muselmann," even though the interview was conducted in 1981–82.

While the Muselmänner may have appeared withdrawn, passive, and lifeless to the other inmates, nourishment moved at the center of their being, because "the Muselmänner retained selective receptivity for all food related stimuli: olfactory, gustatory, and auditory stimuli."[19] All first-person accounts and many of the secondary ones in Ryn and Klodzinski describe, among other things, schemes to secure victuals (118–21), extended conversations fantasizing about the food at home and the devising of fantastic recipes among Muselmänner (94), searching the garbage for discarded scraps of potato peel or animal bones (94), elaborate dreams about food (95, 121), and, at the more extreme end of the spectrum, collective revolts to overpower the inmates responsible for distributing soup (94), and necrophagy (118, 131).

Wladyslaw Fejkiel, who worked as a physician in the infirmary while detained in Auschwitz, remembers that the Muselmänner's nightly mouth-watering dreams were so powerful that they provided conversational sustenance for them throughout their waking hours. The all-embracing affective intensity of the Muselmänner's nocturnal visions allowed the dreams to be transmitted to the functional inmates, and not even Fejkiel, though not a Muselmann himself, was immune to their power:

I once had a dream when I was in the block 28 hospital due to dysentery [Hungerruhr]. I was bathing in a barrel of cream with a pack of cats located in my mother's basement. I trembled at the thought of my mother being able to walk in at any given moment. What was the worst, however, was that I was able to swim, and even submerge myself in the cream but I was not able to drink it. When I awoke, I saw the face of a friend, Muselmann Janusz Krzywicki, who was an officer in Warsaw, which reminded me that I was in the camp.[20]

Fejkiel associates his poetic dream, which interlaces humanity with animality in a remarkable fashion, with the Muselmänner's gastronomic imagination. The visions of being immersed in an unattainable gustatory substance belong, according to Fejkiel, not to him but to the Muselmänner; he is merely a vessel in their transmission. Meanwhile, on waking, the Muselmann Janusz Krzywicki's presence alerts Fejkiel to the fact that he is being detained in the camp. Consequently, the Muselmann inhabits and takes possession of Fejkiel's waking and nonwaking life, but he does so not as an ethereal cipher for human evil or the death camps in general but as a desiring presence in the flesh. This, in turn, creates a relational assemblage of enfleshment that encompasses both the Muselmänner and the functional inmates. Because the Muselmänner no longer possess humanity, dignity, control, willpower, and are barely holding on to what remains of their mere life, the imaginary relation to all that is edible and drinkable becomes the defining feature of their being. That is, while their bodies might no longer exist in the world of Man, the Muselmänner's relational flesh speaks, conjures, intones, and concocts sumptuous universes that are silenced when the Muselmann is confined to the status of an exceptionally disembodied example. For what comes after the Muselmann for those who lived to bear witness to this (in)humanity is survival, as a potentiality or an actuality; and that, at least for some, is nothing but a politics.

Wolfgang Sofsky begins to conceptualize becoming-Muselmann in a different mode than Agamben and others, precisely because he does not insist on using agency and dignity to qualify this status.[21] Such an endeavor, if it is to take seriously the tradition of the oppressed, needs to begin by abandoning volitional agency as the sine qua non of oppositionality; I quote from Sofsky at length to underscore the political challenge posed by the Muselmänner:

The Muselmänner repeatedly violated this self-discipline. They stood in the way everywhere; because they were weakened, they were unable to work as well as the others, and the Kapos punished them brutally for this. They developed edema and boils; they were filthy, stinking, oblivious of what was happening to and with them. They were totally superfluous for the camp's everyday routine. . . . Since they repeatedly violated the rules of order and cleanliness, they were singled out as scapegoats. . . . In the barracks, they dirtied the halls, bunks, and blankets. At meal distribution, they tried to push their way to the front, were shoved aside, and had to look on as the others ate. They relieved themselves in soup bowls; they begged and stole. They did not care about punishments. Thus, many prisoner functionaries declared war on them. . . . If they were shouted at, they were momentarily startled, and did nothing. Punched in the face, they did not react. They were kicked but they felt no pain. They were whipped and beaten, yet in vain. *Their apathy was provocative; it stirred the rage of their tormentors.* The excess of violence was vented specifically against the Muselmänner. Orders accomplished nothing. *Even violence fell flat; it was ineffective. The passivity of the Muselmann was an insult to power.*[22]

Since we cannot surmise whether the Muselmann was an affront because he or she actively fought the powers that be or because of her or his passivity, what might it mean to apply the problematics of resistance and agency to this context? What relational modes of being in the flesh (habeas viscus) come to light when even violence becomes inoperative, as was the case here? What modalities of life are stifled by the rhetoric of exceptionality, which would see only the violence the Muselmänner undergo? In sum, Agamben shies away from commenting on the first-person accounts of former Muselmänner that close *Remnants of Auschwitz* not merely out of piety and respect—at least this is not the only reason—but because he cannot conceive of the Muselmänner as actual, complicated, breathing, living, ravenous, and desiring beings. Or as one former Muselmann, Ignacy Sikora, relates, "I resisted thinking about the possibility that I might die and believed with the doggedness of a madman that we would survive. The hunger and cold were probably the only things that kept me in constant motion."[23] Put simply, in Agamben's system becoming-Muselmann never appears as a politics; rather it remains locked within the constraints of a static example. Had Agamben not simply incorporated but also digested the thoughts and dreams of the Muselmänner, perhaps then genocidal violence would cease to appear as such an absolute force of law from above that negates all other dimensions of the existence and subjectivity of the oppressed. The dialogue about the Muselmann initiated by Agamben does not offer alternatives to our current epistemic cum political order, because it cannot even begin to fathom what it may mean to think about the Muselmänner not as symbols— by sheer virtue of their existence in the death camps—for abstract categories such as evil or dignity but as subjects that lived and dreamed other ways of being human.

But perhaps I should leave the last word on this matter to C. L. R. James, who, as we have seen, was no stranger to the repressive politics of (d)i(n)gestion:

> Then began a four weeks nightmare. . . . I know something of the history of our times. I have read what men have gone through for years in Nazi camps. I know what millions have endured and still endure in the prisons and labor camps behind the Iron Curtain. I have read of the years of torture they have endured and still endure in the Russian concentration camps and prisons. Not a word here implies that Ellis Island is either a Nazi concentration camp or a Russian slave labor camp or anything like them. To the people, unfortunately only too few, who have *digested* what all this means for modern civilization, it may appear that to write about four weeks is an inflation of a minor personal grievance. But far more is involved. (*Mariners*, 136–37; emphasis added)

James, speaking from the vantage point of being enfleshed ("on the island . . . an alien is not a human being"; *Mariners*, 140) also insists on putting his experiences, especially those involving nourishment, side by side with the atrocities of Nazi concentration camps and Stalinist gulags without rendering them directly comparable. The refusal to compare under the rigorous maintenance of a shared horizon and "the processes of bringing-into-relation" impart useful lessons in understanding the vexed workings of modern politics, since they eschew the traces of calculability (political, economic, numeric, ethical, etc.) that appear in scores of comparative analyses of political subjugation and are, as we have seen, integral to the smooth operator that is Man's juridical assemblage.[24]

By refusing the modus operandi of calculability, James leaves the law in the dust and summons the incalculable: justice. "Law is not justice. Law is an element of calculation, and it is just that there be law, but justice is incalculable, it demands that one calculate with the incalculable."[25] James is humble enough to repudiate comparing his situation, whether directly or in a more hushed manner, to that of concentration camp inmates, but also politically astute enough to realize that not-bringing-them-into-relation would only further the divide-and-conquer tactic of modern sovereignty. Despite the fact that James has no access to habeas corpus, his testimony in book form produces a habeas viscus, an extrajuridical law of motion that marshals the relationality of the flesh beyond the laws of comparison. In the end, while the extremity of becoming-Muselmann should by no means be denied, we do well to recall that racism, whether in the colony, the concentration camp, the plantation, the prison, in Guantanamo Bay, or on Ellis Island exhibits no dire need for a legal state of exception, although it has a hard time refusing it when offered as a fringe benefit, or in James's words, "I believe I have given sufficient evidence here to show the grave injustices which are being perpetrated in the name of the law, and that is inconceivable to me" (Mariners, 165). As opposed to a cognitive map of bare life and biopolitics, this dialogue between the Muselmänner, Jacobs, and James prompts an upended affective assemblage of the pharmako-etherial compound: the hieroglyphics of the flesh in which marking, encampment, branding, whipping, imprisonment, denial of nourishment, life, and death concoct a continuum. To properly digest "what all this means for modern civilization," then, is to acknowledge how the ether of the flesh surrounds us as a potentiality in every and all things, not just in states or spaces of exception. Partaking of the flesh, albeit the habeas viscus kind rather than the pure abjection varietal, tenders flavors and textures found in lives of imprisoned freedom, desires for survival, and viscous dreams of life that awaken future anterior humanities, which exceed Man's inesculent culinary laws.

Habeas viscus not only travels alongside the world of Man
but lays bare the fleshy tissue of other humanities.

8 FREEDOM: SOON

In this closing chapter I would like to continue taking up Hortense Spillers's challenge and ask what it might mean to claim the monstrosity of the
flesh as a site for freedom beyond the world of Man in order to heed Baby
Suggs's words in Toni Morrison's *Beloved* about loving the flesh: "In this here
place, we flesh; flesh that weeps, laughs; flesh that dances on bare feet in
grass. Love it. Love it hard. Yonder they do not love your flesh. They despise
it."[1] In order to improperly inhabit and understand the politics and poetics
of habeas viscus, we must return to some of the voices from the previous
two chapters. Revisit them we should, however, not to authenticate them as
acoustic mirrors of the oppressed or to grant them juridical humanity but in
order to listen more closely to prophetic traces of the hieroglyphics of the
flesh in these echoes of the future anterior tense. Many critics assume that
political violence is somehow outside the grasp of linguistic structures. In
her now classic account of the body in pain, Scarry argues that pain in general and torture in particular causes a regression to the "pre-language of cries
and groans," which becomes indicative of the annihilation of the tortured's
world.[2] In making this argument, Scarry assumes that world and language
preexist and are unmade by the act of torture, which imagines political violence as exterior to the normal order rather than as an instrument in the creation of the world and language of Man. Agamben's point about language

and witnessing vis-à-vis Auschwitz, although not quite in the same register, skirts fairly close to making a similar argument: "It is thus necessary that the impossibility of bearing witness, the 'lacuna,' that constitutes human language, collapses, giving way to a different impossibility of bearing witness—that which does not have language" (Remnants, 39). Perhaps it might be more useful to construe "cries and groans," "heart-rending shrieks," "the mechanical murmurs without content" as language that does not rely on linguistic structures, at least not primarily, to convey meaning, sense, or expression.[3] For language, especially in the space-ways of the flesh, comes in many varieties, and functions not only—or even primarily—to create words in the service of conforming to linguistic structures transparent in the world of Man.[4] This approach also cannot imagine that for many of those held captive by Man it is always already "after the end of the world. . . . Don't you know that yet?" long before the actual acts of torture have begun.

Roman Grzyb, a former concentration camp prisoner, for instance, gives the following account of the Muselmann's idiolect: "The Muselmann used his very own jargon by constantly repeating what came to his completely confused mind. The sentences were often incomplete and were illogical, stopping abruptly at random points."[5] As can be gleaned from the testimonies of Muselmänner, slaves, or Ellis Island detainees, what is at stake is not so much the lack of language per se, since we have known for a while now that the subaltern cannot speak, but the kinds of dialects available to the subjected and how these are seen and heard by those who bear witness to their plight. Nevertheless, the suffering voices exemplified by James and the Muselmänner should not be understood as fountains of authenticity but rather as instantiations of a radically different political imaginary that steers clear of reducing the subjectivity of the oppressed to bare life. In R. Radhakrishnan's thinking, this political domain produces "critical knowledge, which in turn empowers the voice of suffering to make its own cognitive-epistemological intervention by envisioning its own utopia, rather than accepting an assigned position within the ameliotary schemes proposed by the dominant discourse."[6] Thus, suffering appears as utopian erudition—or is expressed through hieroglyphics of the flesh to echo Spillers and Zora Neale Hurston—and not as an end unto itself or as a precritical sphere of truth, as the liberal humanist Weltanschauung would have it; rather, "liberalism is tolerant of abundant speech as long as it does not have to take into account voices it does not understand."[7] Where dominant discourse seeks to develop upgrades of the current notions of humanity as Man, improvements are not the aim or product of the imaginaries borne of racializing assemblages and political violence; instead they summon forms of human emancipation that can be imagined but not (yet) described.

While this form of communication does not necessarily conform to the standard definition of linguistic utterance, to hear Aunt Hester's howls or the Muselmann's repetition merely as pre- or nonlanguage absolves the world of Man from any and all responsibility for bearing witness to the flesh. Hardly anterior to language and therefore the human, these rumblings vocalize the humming relay of the world that makes linguistic structures possible, directly corresponding to how the not-quite- and nonhuman give rise to the universe of Man. That is to say, the flesh engulfs not only Man's visually marked others via instruments of torture and the intergenerational transmission of hieroglyphics but emanates rays of potential enfleshment throughout the far-flung corners of Being in the world of Man.

According to Aristotle, even though "higher life (bios) is emphatically the end proposed, yet life itself (zoe) is also an object for which [citizens] unite and maintain the corporate political association; for it is probable that some degree of the higher life is necessarily implied in merely living. . . . Certain it is that the majority of men endure much suffering without ceasing to cling to life—a proof that a certain happiness or *natural sweetness* resides in it."[8] When the hieroglyphics of the flesh are construed not merely as banishments but as transit visas to universes betwixt and between the jurisdictions of Man, they prompt the following question: how is it possible to politicize the "natural sweetness" of the flesh without the limits imposed by the concepts of bare life and biopolitics?

In one of the testimonies that close Agamben's *Remnants of Auschwitz*, former Muselmann Wlodzimierz Borkowski makes a startling statement. According to Agamben's text, when retroactively describing his undergoing becoming-Muselmann, Borkowski asserts, "I felt a strange sweetness." The German translation of Wlodzimierz Borkowski's testimony, originally given in Polish, upon which Agamben bases his translation, reads thus:

Ein Vorgefühl dieses Zustands hatte ich schon erfahren. In der Gefängniszelle lernte ich das Gefühl der Lebensflucht kennen: Alle irdischen Dinge schienen ganz unwichtig. Die körperlichen Funktionen ließen nach. Sogar der Hunger plagte mich weniger. Ich hatte so ein merkwürdig *süßes und angenehmes* Gefühl, nur daß ich keine Kraft mehr hatte, von der Pritsche aufzustehen, und wenn ich es doch tat, dann mußte ich mich auf dem Weg zum Kübel an den Wänden stützen.[9]

And here is the translation from Agamben's text:

> I'd already had a presentiment of this state. In the cell, I felt life leaving me. Earthly things no longer mattered; bodily functions faded away. Even hunger tormented me less. *I felt a strange sweetness.* I just didn't have the strength to get off my cot, and if I did, I had to lean on the walls to make it to the bucket. (*Remnants*, 167)

Everything in this passage has been translated directly from Borkowski's statement but "und angenehmes." The pleasant dimension has been excised in Agamben's own translation of these words found in the original Italian publication of *Remnants*, and it does not appear in Heller-Roazen's English translation.[10] Lest readers chalk the omission up to discrepancies in translation between German and Italian, it should be remarked that Agamben presumably translated this passage himself, since the Italian edition of *Remnants* is based on the German text and no other translators are mentioned. In addition, Agamben, as the editor of the Italian edition of Walter Benjamin's complete works from 1979 through 1994 and a former student of Martin Heidegger, would be at least nominally familiar with German language writings. Agamben indubitably mishears the Muselmann's language—however, whether he does so consciously or not is beyond the scope of my interpretive powers—which is symptomatic of the general Christlike configuration of the Muselmann in Agamben's text. While the misapprehension once more calls attention to Agamben's philological will to power, I am more interested in how this revealing translationary deviation points to the inadequacy of bare life as a global concept that explains the creation of hierarchical differentiation among human groups and to those dimensions of the Muselmänner that are erased by Agamben: the untidy and opaque enfleshment of Muselmänner such as Borkowski. How might Agamben's theorization of bare life have shifted had he paid heed to the beatitude Borkowski associates with his enfleshment?

Furthermore, Borkowski's statement resonates with the special place of sugar and sweetness in the history of human evolution, since Homo sapiens is one of the few species that can taste sugar and has developed to physiologically associate sweetness with life, survival, freedom, and all that is good. However, "our sweet receptors evolved in environments with so little sugar that they may not have a shutoff point," since the majority of humans had no access to sugar before the eighteenth century.[11] Thus, the missing shutoff point becomes a problem only in a world where sugar is readily available for consumption, such as ours. In recent history the abundance of sugar was made possible via the conduit of racial slavery: slavery undergirds humanity's current sucrose surplus crisis. As Sidney Mintz and others have shown, sugar played a central role in the economy of plantation slavery, especially in the Caribbean. Mintz argues that during the Industrial Revolution the newly freed British working classes were at liberty to develop an increasing appetite for sweetness given that sugar was no longer a luxury but, due to slavery and colonialism, had become a common commodity. It also accentuated and accelerated the shift of the primary function of sucrose from a spice or medicine to a sweetener of other, more bitter colonial goods such as tea, coffee, and chocolate, as well as a caloric bolster for the working poor—it was cheap and filling.[12] Hence, the exponential explosion in access to sugar since the eighteenth century, which is out of step with the evolutionary development of human sweet receptors reared in an environment of scarcity, would not have been possible without transatlantic slavery.

In his classic account of the Haitian Revolution, C. L. R. James tells the following story to illustrate how fervent Haitians were about their liberty: "When Chevalier, a black chief, hesitated at the sight of the scaffold, his wife shamed him. 'You do not know how sweet it is to die for liberty!' And refusing to allow herself to be hanged by the executioner, she took the rope and hanged herself."[13] In a similar vein, in her 1831 slave narrative Mary Prince speaks of "the sweets of freedom" and proclaims "to be free is very sweet," which might illuminate Borkowski's description of being a Muselmann insofar as it not only positions this status as one of complete abjection and degradation, but accents the happening of being freed from the restraints of dignity; it also allows for a noncomparative conversation between these different forms of subjection in the flesh.[14] By insisting on the sweetened flavor of liberty, Prince and the unnamed woman render freedom tasteable and digestible, and therefore pleasurable and life saving. The (almost) unlimited capacity for opiate-inducing syrupy tastes and textures, then, frees the potentiality of subjugated subjects such as Prince and Borkowski, since they, deprived of both sugar and liberty, know of the hunger that moves in survival as freedom. To banish these articulations of freedom and/or pleasure into exile in the precinct of inhumanity or prelanguage, as Agamben and others do, not only denies the possibility of life in extreme circumstances but also leaves intact the ruling definition of the human as Man. In other words, as Aunt Hester, Wlodzimierz Borkowski, Harriet Jacobs, C. L. R. James, Shola, and Agamemnon intimate in their differently tuned sociolects, as a way of conceptualizing politics, habeas viscus diverges from the discourses and institutions that yoke the flesh to political violence in the modus of deviance. Instead, it translates the hieroglyphics of the flesh into an originating leap in the imagining of future anterior freedoms and new genres of humanity.

For Agamben, potentiality and freedom are intimately related: "The root of freedom is to be found in the abyss of potentiality. To be free is not to simply have the power to do this or that thing, nor is it simply the power to refuse to do this or that thing. To be free is . . . *to be capable of one's own impotentiality, to be in relation to one's own privation.*"[15] Although the Heideggerian undertones of this passage should not go unnoticed, Agamben's discussion of potentiality arises from an engagement with Aristotle, for whom *paschein* (suffering or undergoing) appears as the example that grounds the movement between potentiality and actuality (*Potentialities*, 184).[16] If subjection in extreme situations of political violence provides freedom's antithesis, especially in Aristotle's context[17]—and "I'd prefer not to" is simply not an option—how do privation, impotentiality, non-Being, lack, and darkness (Agamben uses all these terms to describe the "abyss of potentiality") encounter the flesh and rest in the unfree? Freedom stands at the juncture of the flesh's privation and potentiality: the flesh carries the potential for manumission, although not the actual freedom to undergo and suffer (*paschein*) Man's liberty. Put simply, the world of Man denies the flesh its opulent and hieroglyphic freedom by relegating it to a terrain of utter abjection outside the iron grip of humanity, thereby disavowing how the ether of the flesh represents both a perpetual potentiality and actuality in Man's kingdom, only enveloping some subjects more than others.

Agamben continues, "There is truly potentiality only where the potentiality to not-be does not lag behind actuality but passes fully into it. . . . What is truly potential is thus what has exhausted all its impotentiality in bringing it wholly into the act as such" (*Potentialities*, 183). Impotentiality, once actualized, kindles the originary potentiality that rests in the oppressed, which is nothing other than habeas viscus. Alternatively, the subjugated subject's im/potentiality lies in the mélange of deprivation (the damaging lack of material benefits considered to be basic necessities in a society) and depravation (to make someone immoral or wicked), or, rather, in the deviations that muddle these categories, for instance via Spillers's brilliant conjoining of *porno* and *trope*.[18] The oppressed subject is deprived of freedom, while also being depraved by "a potential for pornotroping." This, in turn, justifies the racialized subject's privation. In the aftermath of colonialism, genocide, and racial slavery, freedom, decolonization, and sovereignty perform the role of impotentiality/non-Being that has passed into actuality only nominally; the hieroglyphics of the flesh, however, remain a potent potential that lingers affixed to the racialized body as not-quite-human, even subsequent to nominal emancipations, disenabling the actualization of a different sort of freedom, and therefore liberty's true potentiality.[19] That is, freedom and humanity conjured from the vantage point of the flesh and not based on its abrogation.

Agamben's theorization of bare life leaves no room for alternate forms of life that elude the law's violent embrace. What seems to have vanished from this description is the *life* in the *bare life* compound; hence the homo sacer remains a thing, whose happening slumbers in bare life without journeying through the rivulets of liberations elsewhere. The potential of bare life as a concept falls victim to a legal dogmatism that equates humanity and personhood with a status bequeathed or revoked by juridical sovereignty in much the same way as human rights discourse and habeas corpus do. Because alternatives do not exist in Agamben's generalized sphere of exception that constitutes bare life, the law denotes the only constituent power in the definition and adjudication of what it means to be human or dehumanized in the contemporary world. If alternate forms of life, what Wynter dubs genres of the human beyond the world of Man, can flourish only after the complete obliteration of the law, then it would follow that our existence, whether it is bare or not, stands and falls with the extant laws in the current codification of Man. This can blind us to the sorrow songs, smooth glitches, miniscule movements, shards of hope, scraps of food, and interrupted dreams of freedom that already swarm the ether of Man's legal apparatus, which does not mean that these formations annul the brutal validity of bare life, biopolitics, necropolitics, social death, or racializing assemblages but that Man's juridical machine can never exhaust the plentitude of our world. The future orientation of political messianism has made the existing realities of oppressed groups more bearable and has inspired some of modernity's greatest thinkers (Karl Marx, W. E. B. Du Bois, and Walter Benjamin, to name only a few), functioning as a politicopoetic imaginary of the flesh—an instantiation of the reveries that lay groundwork for assemblages of liberation in the future anterior tense—with recourse to a worldly and/or a metaphysical restorative force that transpires in the name of affecting redemptive transformations in the hic et nunc.[20] This dimension evaporates in bare life and biopolitics discourse; in its stead Agamben offers us a defanged legal messianism far removed from the traditions of the oppressed while Foucault fails to consider alternative imaginaries. When June Tyson repeatedly intones, "It's after the end of the world. . . . Don't you know that yet?" at the beginning of the Sun Ra Arkestra's 1974 film *Space Is the Place*, she directs our attention to the very real likelihood that another world might not only be possible but that this universe may already be here in the NOW.[21] The only question that remains: do we have the tools required to apprehend other worlds such as the one prophesied by June Tyson and Sun Ra, or will we remain infinitely detained by the magical powers of Man's juridical assemblage as a result of having consumed too much of his treacly Kool-Aid?

The idea of the flesh, as theorized by Spillers, while by no means drinking from the bountiful fountain of messianism, constitutes a liminal zone comprising legal and extralegal subjection, violence, and torture as well as lines of flight from the world of Man in the form of practices, existences, thoughts, desires, dreams, and sounds contemporaneously persisting in the law's spectral shadows. The enfleshed modalities of humanity, however, are not uncritical reiterations of the humanist episteme or insistences on the exceptional particularity of racialized humanity, and, as a consequence, they do not represent mere legal or moral bids for inclusion into or critiques of the shortcomings of western liberal humanism. For habeas viscus does not obey the logic of legal possession and remains even after the body's demise; it refuses to pass on but is, nonetheless, passed down as the remainder of the hieroglyphics of the flesh. In the absence of and in contradistinction to habeas corpus, how might the flesh incarnate alternate forms of liberty and humanity that dwell among us in the NOW, which, "as a model of messianic time, comprises the entire history of humanity in an enormous abbreviation, coincides exactly with the place the history of humanity occupies in the universe"?[22] If it's after the end of the world and we just don't know that yet, surviving in the space of the flesh might just be tantamount to inhabiting a future anterior elsewhere in which "contemporary events throw a penetrating light into the past and thereby illuminate the future."[23]

Agamben repeatedly quotes Walter Benjamin's famous proclamation from "On the Concept of History": "The tradition of the oppressed teaches us that 'the state of exception' (Ausnahmezustand) in which we live is not the exception but the rule. We must attain a conception of history that is commensurate with this insight. Then we will clearly see that it is our task to bring about a real state of exception, and this will improve our position in the struggle against fascism"; yet he rarely comments on Benjamin's references to the tradition of the oppressed or the fight against fascism ("On the Concept of History," 392).[24] Far more interested in the law as the locus for the universalization of the state of exception than he is in the pedagogy of the oppressed, Agamben's omission amplifies his almost exclusive focus on bare life from the horizon of jurisprudence and hegemony, thus leaving intact the homo sacer qua homo sacer by repeating the very procedure by which modern racializing assemblages invent and maintain this category. In his numerous discussions of Benjamin, Agamben also does not consider the question of historical materialism: "The historical materialist approaches a historical object only where it confronts him as a monad. In this structure he recognizes the sign of a messianic arrest of happening [Stillstellung], or (to put it differently) a revolutionary chance in the fight for the oppressed past" ("On the Concept of History," 396). For Benjamin, the dialectical struggle of historical materialism seeks not to universalize the particular oppressed past to but to generate the revolutionary restitution of temporality in which the messianic arrest of happening functions as an assemblage of freedom.

In his most extended consideration of the concept of messianic redemption as it appears in the Benjaminian oeuvre, Agamben dismisses exegeses of "On the Concept of History" that insist on replacing the history of the ruling classes with historical narratives about the tradition of the oppressed, because this presumes "that the tradition of the oppressed classes is, in its goals and in its structures, altogether analogous to the tradition of the ruling classes (whose heir it would be); the oppressed class, according to this theory, would differ from the ruling classes only with respect to its content" (Potentialities, 153). The radical nonfungibility of the ruling and oppressed classes vis-à-vis history vanishes after this point so that Agamben can appeal to an abstract sphere of historical cessation qua messianic salvation. In Agamben's narration, Benjamin's aim is not to emancipate the past and "re-

store its true dignity, to transmit it anew as an inheritance for future generations." Instead, what is at stake "is an interruption of tradition in which the
past is fulfilled and thereby brought to its end once and for all. For humanity
as for the individual human, to redeem the past is to put an end to it, to cast
upon it a gaze that fulfills it" (*Potentialities*, 153). The opposition between a
reconstructive and destructive relationship to the past that Agamben postulates, while in the spirit of Benjamin, misses its mark because it does not
consider the question of historical materialism so fundamental to the way
Benjamin imagines the oppressed's world historical role in bringing about
a real state of exception. Excavating the subjugated past constitutes a revolutionary endeavor since the tradition of the oppressed cannot differ from
ruling-class history purely in its epiphenomenal content.[25] Not only does
the oppressed past call into question the hubris of empty homogenous time
but it also, and more significantly, requires a distinctive ontologico-formal
assemblage in order to appear in the clearing of history. Which is to say that
the oppressed qua flesh must be summoned as an assemblage of revolutionary freedom so as not to fall prey to the limits of traditional dialectical materialism. Consequently, as opposed to the constraints of the traditional dialectical form in which "every negation has its value solely as background for
the delineation of the lively, the positive," Benjamin's versioning of the dialectic emphasizes that "a new partition be applied to this initially excluded,
negative component so that, by a displacement of the angle of vision (but
not of the criteria!), a positive element emerges anew in it too—something
different from that previously signified. And so on, ad infinitum, until the
entire past is brought into the present in *a historical apocatastasis*."[26] Benjamin
is after the transubstantiation of the originally discounted, negative factor
(the oppressed/revolutionary classes or the flesh), for it is in this prehen-
sive shift that the echoing omen of revolutionary redemption can be found.
As Benjamin writes, the oppressed class (the flesh/Man's others) appears
in this dialectical drama as "the avenger that completes the task of liberation in the name of generations of the downtrodden" ("On the Concept
of History," 394). In accordance with his usage of other religious and cosmological concepts, Benjamin secularizes but does not dispense completely
with the metaphysical and otherworldly resonances of "the restitution of
all things of which God has spoken" (Acts 3:21), although he does further
specify the temporal cum liberationist dimensions of apocatastasis, which
addresses "the resolve to gather again, in revolutionary action and in revo-

lutionary thinking, precisely the elements of the 'too early' and the 'too late' of the first beginning and the final decay."[27] Much too tardy for salvation while anticipating the epoch of revolution, the ether of the flesh is situated at the crossing of the first creation of what was and the ultimate arrest of what is. As such the flesh provides the ground, the loophole of retreat, the liminal space, and the archipelago for those revolutions that will have occurred but remain largely imperceptible within Man's political and critical idioms: "It's after the end of the world. . . . Don't you know that yet?"

Because black cultures have frequently not had access to Man's language, world, future, or humanity, black studies has developed a set of assemblages through which to perceive and understand a world in which subjection is but one path to humanity, neither its exception nor its idealized sole feature. Yet black studies, if it is to remain critical and oppositional, cannot fall prey to juridical humanity and its concomitant pitfalls, since this only affects change in the domain of the map but not the territory. In order to do so, the hieroglyphics of the flesh should not be conceptualized as just exceptional or radically particular, since this habitually leads to the comparative tabulation of different systems of oppression that then serve as the basis for defining personhood as possession. As Frantz Fanon states: "All forms of exploitation are identical, since they apply to the same 'object': man."[28] Accordingly, humans are exploited as part of the Homo sapiens species for the benefit of other humans, which at the same time yields a surplus version of the human: Man. Man represents the western configuration of the human as synonymous with the heteromasculine, white, propertied, and liberal subject that renders all those who do not conform to these characteristics as exploitable nonhumans, literal legal no-bodies. If we are to affect significant systemic changes, then we must locate at least some of the struggles for justice in the region of humanity as a relational ontological totality (an object of knowledge) that cannot be reduced to either the universal or particular. According to Wynter, this process requires us to recognize the "emancipation from the psychic dictates of our present . . . genre of being human and therefore from 'the unbearable wrongness of being,' of desetre, which it imposes upon . . . all non-white peoples, as an imperative function of its enactment as such a mode of being[;] this emancipation had been effected at the level of the map rather than at the level of the territory."[29] The level of the map encompasses the nominal inclusion of nonwhite subjects in the false universality of western humanity in the wake of radical movements of the 1960s, while the territory Wynter invokes in this context, and in all of her work, is the figure of Man as a racializing assemblage.

Wielding this very particular and historically malleable classification is not an uncritical reiteration of the humanist episteme or an insistence on the exceptional particularity of black humanity. Rather, Afro-diasporic cultures provide singular, mutable, and contingent figurations of the human, and thus do not represent mere bids for inclusion in or critiques of the shortcomings of western liberal humanism. The problematic of humanity, however, needs to be highlighted as one of the prime objects of knowledge of black studies, since not doing so will sustain the structures, discourses, and institutions that detain black life and thought within the strictures of particularity so as to facilitate the violent conflation of Man and the human. Otherwise, the general theory of how humanity has been lived, conceptualized, shrieked, hungered into being, and imagined by those subjects violently barred from this domain and touched by the hieroglyphics of the flesh will sink back into the deafening ocean of prelinguistic particularity. This, in turn, will also render apparent that black studies, especially as it is imagined by thinkers such as Spillers and Wynter, is engaged in engendering forms of the human vital to understanding not only black cultures but past, present, and future humanities. As a demonic island, black studies lifts the fog that shrouds the laws of comparison, particularity, and exception to reveal an aquatic outlook "far away from the continent of man."[30]

The poetics and politics that I have been discussing under the heading of habeas viscus or the flesh are concerned not with inclusion in reigning precincts of the status quo but, in Cedric Robinson's apt phrasing, "the continuing development of a collective consciousness informed by the historical struggles for liberation and motivated by the shared sense of obligation to preserve [and I would add also to reimagine] the collective being, the ontological totality."[31] Though the laws of Man place the flesh outside the ferocious and ravenous perimeters of the legal body, habeas viscus defies domestication both on the basis of particularized personhood as a result of suffering, as in human rights discourse, and on the grounds of the universalized version of western Man. Rather, habeas viscus points to the terrain of humanity as a relational assemblage exterior to the jurisdiction of law given that the law can bequeath or rescind ownership of the body so that it becomes the property of proper persons but does not possess the authority to nullify the politics and poetics of the flesh found in the traditions of the oppressed. As a way of conceptualizing politics, then, habeas viscus diverges from the discourses and institutions that yoke the flesh to political violence in the modus of deviance. Instead, it translates the hieroglyphics of the flesh into a potentiality in any and all things, an originating leap in the imagining of future anterior freedoms and new genres of humanity.

To envisage habeas viscus as a forceful assemblage of humanity entails leaving behind the world of Man and some of its attendant humanist pieties. As opposed to depositing the flesh outside politics, the normal, the human, and so on, we need a better understanding of its varied workings in order to disrobe the cloak of Man, which gives the human a long-overdue extreme makeover; or, in the words of Sylvia Wynter, "the struggle of our new millennium will be one between the ongoing imperative of securing the well-being of our present ethnoclass (i.e. western bourgeois) conception of the human, Man, which overrepresents itself as if it were the human itself, and that of securing the well-being, and therefore the full cognitive and behavioral autonomy of the human species itself/ourselves."[32] Claiming and dwelling in the monstrosity of the flesh present some of the weapons in the guerrilla warfare to "secure the full cognitive and behavioral autonomy of the human species," since these liberate from captivity assemblages of life, thought, and politics from the tradition of the oppressed and, as a result, disfigure the centrality of Man as the sign for the human. As an assemblage of humanity, habeas viscus animates the elsewheres of Man and emancipates the true potentiality that rests in those subjects who live behind the veil of the permanent state of exception: freedom; assemblages of freedom that sway to the temporality of new syncopated beginnings for the human beyond the world and continent of Man.

German R&B group Glashaus's track "Bald (und wir sind frei) [Soon (and We Are Free)]" performs this overdetermined idea of freedom as disarticulated from Man both graphically and sonically. Paying tribute to both the nineteenth-century spiritual "We'll Soon Be Free," written on the eve of the American Civil War, and Donny Hathaway's 1973 recording, "Someday We'll All Be Free," Glashaus's title

"Bald (und wir sind frei)"

enacts the disrupted yet intertwined notions of freedom, temporality, and sociality that I am gesturing to here.[33] In contrast to its predecessors, which are resolutely located in the future via the use of *soon/someday* and the future tense, Glashaus's version renders freedom in the present tense, albeit qualified by the imminent future of "bald [soon]" and by the typographical parenthetical enclosure of "(und wir sind frei) [and we are free]." The flow of the parentheses intimates both distance and nearness, ragging the homogeneous, empty future of "soon" with a potential present of a "responsible freedom" (Spillers) and/as sociality. The *and* and the parentheses are the conduits for bringing-into-relation freedom's nowtime and its constitutive potential futurity without resolving their tension. The lyrics of "Bald (und wir sind frei)" once again exemplify this complementary strain in that the words in the verses are resolutely future oriented, ending with the invocation of "bald" just before the chorus, which, held in the potential abyss of the present, repeats, "und wir sind frei." Likewise, in the verses, Glashaus's singer Cassandra Steen, accompanied only by a grand piano, just about whispers, whereas she opens up to a more mellifluous style of singing in the chorus; as a result, the verses (bald/future) sound constricted and restrictive but only when heard in relation to the expansive spatiality of the chorus (present). What initially looks like a bracketed afterthought on the page punctures the putatively central point in the sonic realm. It is not a vacant, uniform, or universal future that sets in motion liberty but rather the future as it is seen, felt, and heard from the enfleshed parenthetical present of the oppressed, since this group's NOW is always already bracketed (held captive and set aside indefinitely) in, if not antithetical to, the world of Man. The domain of habeas viscus represents one significant mechanism by which the world of Man constrains subjects to the parenthetical, while at the same time disavowing this tendency via recourse to the abnormal and/ or inhuman. Heard, seen, tasted, felt, and lived in the ethereal shadows of Man's world, however, a habeas viscus unearths the freedom that exists within the hieroglyphics of the flesh. For the oppressed the future will have been now, since Man tucks away this group's present in brackets. Consequently, the future anterior transmutes the simple (parenthetical) present of the dysselected into the nowtime of humanity during which the fleshy hieroglyphics of the oppressed will have actualized the honeyed prophecy of another kind of freedom (which can be imagined but not [yet] described) in the revolutionary apocatastasis of human genres.

To have been touched by the flesh, then, is the path to the abolition of Man: this is part of the lesson of our world.

NOTES

INTRODUCTION

1 Besides the work of Wynter and Spillers, my thinking about racialization is indebted to Frantz Fanon and W. E. B. Du Bois. See Frantz Fanon, *The Wretched of the Earth*, trans. Richard Philcox (1963; reprint, New York: Grove, 2004), 150; Frantz Fanon, *Black Skin, White Masks*, trans. Richard Philcox (1952; reprint, New York: Grove, 2008), 89–120; and W. E. B. Du Bois, *The Souls of Black Folk* [1903], ed. Donald B. Gibson (New York: Penguin Classics, 1996), 3–12.

2 Dylan Rodríguez, *Forced Passages: Imprisoned Radical Intellectuals and the U.S. Prison Regime* (Minneapolis: University of Minnesota Press, 2006), 11.

3 Following Sylvia Wynter, I use Man to designate the modern, secular, and western version of the human that differentiates full humans from not-quite-humans and nonhumans on the basis of biology and economics.

4 As of April 2012, Google Scholar lists 19,800 entries for *biopolitics*, 11,400 for *homo sacer*, and 8,790 for *bare life* but only 917 for *necropolitics*, 1,060 for *Sylvia Wynter*, and 2,050 for *Hortense Spillers*.

5 Ann DuCille, "The Occult of True Black Womanhood: Critical Demeanor and Black Feminist Studies," *Signs* 19.3 (1994): 603.

6 Dwight McBride notices a similar tendency in the resonances between Foucault's conception of historical discontinuities and the writings of Toni Morrison and Maxine Hong Kingston, writing, "Often much of what western theory imagines as the 'new' can only be understood as such when the object of critique is delimited

so as not to include the cultural production of, or the experiences of, marginalized subjects." Dwight A. McBride, "The Ghosts of Memory: Representing the Past in *Beloved* and *The Woman Warrior*," in *Re-placing America: Conversations and Contestations: Selected Essays*, ed. Ruth Hsu, Cynthia G. Franklin, and Suzanne Kosanke (Honolulu: University of Hawai'i Press, 2000), 164.

7 Junot Díaz, "Díaz and Paula M.L. Moya: The Search for Decolonial Love, Part I," *Boston Review*, June 26, 2012.

8 Even though Agamben's description of bare life does not advocate it as a field unscathed by political identities per se, it nevertheless lends itself to this line of thinking, because this description imagines an alternative to bare life only in a sphere of indivisible ontological plenitude in the aftermath of the most extreme forms of political violence, for instance, in Agamben's point about the Muselmann as an "absolute biological substance" or in the consideration of a form of life in which it is no longer possible to sequester bare life from life as such. Giorgio Agamben, *Means without End: Notes on Politics*, trans. Cesare Cesarino and Vincenzo Binetti (Minneapolis: University of Minnesota Press, 2000), 3–12.

9 Edward W. Said, "Traveling Theory," in *The World, the Text, and the Critic* (Cambridge, MA: Harvard University Press, 1983), 241.

10 Within post-Enlightenment European thought, Denise da Silva distinguishes between the transparent white master subject of Man and his various affectable non-European others. Global raciality, then, "produces both (a) the affectable (subaltern) subjects that can be excluded from juridical universality without unleashing an ethical crisis and (b) the self-determined things who should enjoy the entitlements afforded and protected by the principle of universality said to govern modern social configurations." Denise Ferreira da Silva, *Toward a Global Idea of Race* (Minneapolis: University of Minnesota Press, 2007), 35.

11 See Alfred Tarski, *Introduction to Logic and to the Methodology of Deductive Sciences*, 4th ed., ed. Jan Tarski (New York: Oxford University Press, 1936), 110.

12 On the coloniality of being and knowledge in modernity, see Maria Lugones, "Heterosexualism and the Colonial/Modern Gender System," *Hypatia* 22.1 (2007): 186–219; Dipesh Chakrabarty, *Provincializing Europe: Postcolonial Thought and Historical Difference* (Princeton, NJ: Princeton University Press, 2000); Kuan-Hsing Chen, *Asia as Method: Toward Deimperialization* (Durham, NC: Duke University Press, 2010); Anibal Quijano, "Coloniality and Modernity/Rationality," *Cultural Studies* 21.2–3 (2007): 168–78; Anibal Quijano, "Coloniality of Power, Knowledge, and Latin America," *Nepantla: Views from South* 1.3 (2000): 533–80; Linda Tuhiwai Smith, *Decolonizing Methodologies: Research and Indigenous Peoples* (London: Zed, 1999); Sylvia Wynter, "Unsettling the Coloniality of Being/Power/Truth/Freedom: Towards the Human, After Man, Its Overrepresentation—an Argument," CR: *The New Centennial Review* 3.3 (2003): 257–337.

13 Michel Foucault, *The Order of Things: Archaeology of the Human Sciences*, trans. Alan Sheridan (New York: Vintage, 1970), 387.

14 Besides the thinkers discussed here, see Aihwa Ong, "Experiments with Freedom: Milieus of the Human," *American Literary History* 18 (2006): 229–44; and Aihwa Ong, *Neoliberalism as Exception: Mutations in Citizenship and Sovereignty* (Durham, NC: Duke University Press, 2006); Ronald Judy, "Provisional Note on Formations of Planetary Violence," *boundary 2* 33.3 (2006): 141–50; Walter Mignolo, "Citizenship, Knowledge, and the Limits of Humanity," *American Literary History* 18.2 (2006): 312–31; Pheng Cheah, *Inhuman Conditions: On Cosmopolitanism and Human Rights* (Cambridge, MA: Harvard University Press, 2006); Anupama Rao, "Violence and Humanity: Or, Vulnerability as Political Subjectivity," *Social Research: An International Quarterly* 78.2 (2011): 607–32; Paul Gilroy, *Postcolonial Melancholia* (New York: Columbia University Press, 2005); Neferti M. Tadiar, "In the Face of Whiteness as Value: Fall-Outs of Metropolitan Humanness," *Qui Parle* 13.2 (2003): 143–82; and Neferti M. Tadiar, "Metropolitan Life and Uncivil Death," *PMLA* 122.1 (2007): 316–20; Katherine McKittrick, *Demonic Grounds: Black Women and the Cartographies of Struggle* (Minneapolis: University of Minnesota Press, 2006); R. Radhakrishnan, *History, the Human, and the World Between* (Durham, NC: Duke University Press, 2008); Samera Esmeir, "On Making Dehumanization Possible," *PMLA* 121.5 (2006): 1544–51.

15 For a résumé of antihumanism's genesis in post–World War II French intellectual history thought, see Stefanos Geroulano, *An Atheism That Is Not Humanist Emerges in French Thought* (Palo Alto, CA: Stanford University Press, 2010).

16 Important early interventions include Jacques Derrida, "The Ends of Man" [1969], in *Margins of Philosophy*, trans. Alan Bass, 109–36 (Chicago: University of Chicago Press, 1982); and Jacques Derrida, "White Mythology: Metaphor in the Text of Philosophy" [1974], in *Margins of Philosophy*, trans. Alan Bass, 207–71 (Chicago: University of Chicago Press, 1982); Foucault, *The Order of Things*; Gilles Deleuze and Félix Guattari's invocation of Oedipus as an "interior colony" in *Anti-Oedipus: Capitalism and Schizophrenia*, trans. Robert Hurley, Mark Seem, and Helen Lane (Minneapolis: University of Minnesota Press, 1983). For the place of the Algerian war and decolonization in the genesis of post-structuralism, see Robert Young, *White Mythologies: Writing History and the West* (New York: Routledge, 2004); Pal Ahluwalia, *Out of Africa: Post-structuralism's Colonial Roots* (New York: Routledge, 2010).

17 See Wlad Godzich, *The Culture of Literacy* (Cambridge, MA: Harvard University Press, 1994); and Hortense J. Spillers, "The Crisis of the Negro Intellectual: A Post-date," in *Black, White, and in Color: Essays on American Literature and Culture*, 428–70 (Chicago: University of Chicago Press, 2003). See also Nahum D. Chandler, "Originary Displacement," *boundary 2* 27.3 (2000): 249–86. I have addressed some of these questions in the discussion of "identity" and "the subject" as critical

categories; see Alexander G. Weheliye, *Phonographies: Grooves in Sonic Afro-Modernity* (Durham, NC: Duke University Press, 2005), 46–72.

18 See, for instance, N. Katherine Hayles, *How We Became Posthuman: Virtual Bodies in Cybernetics, Literature, and Informatics* (Chicago: University of Chicago Press, 1999). For an elaboration of the nexus between posthumanism and black culture, see Alexander G. Weheliye, "Feenin: Posthuman Voices in Contemporary Black Popular Music," *Social Text* 20.2 (2002): 21–47.

19 This is a reference to Marjorie Spiegel's *The Dreaded Comparison: Human and Animal Slavery* (Hong Kong: Mirror Books, 1996).

20 Hortense J. Spillers, "Introduction—Peter's Pans: Eating in the Diaspora," in *Black, White, and in Color: Essays on American Literature and Culture*, 1–64 (Chicago: University of Chicago Press, 2003), 20.

21 Cary Wolfe, *Animal Rites: American Culture, the Discourse of Species, and Posthumanist Theory* (Chicago: University of Chicago Press, 2003), 7.

22 Saidiya V. Hartman, *Scenes of Subjection: Terror, Slavery, and Self-Making in Nineteenth-Century America* (New York: Oxford University Press, 1997), 123.

23 Aimé Césaire, *Discourse on Colonialism*, trans. Joan Pinkham (1955; reprint, New York: Monthly Review Press, 1972), 73.

24 Hartman, *Scenes of Subjection*, 5–10.

25 Édouard Glissant, *Poetics of Relation*, trans. Betsy Wing (Ann Arbor: University of Michigan Press, 1997), 171–72.

26 Richard Iton, "Still Life," *Small Axe* 17.1 40 (2013): 33.

27 Lisa M. Lowe, "The Intimacies of the Four Continents," in *Haunted by Empire: Geographies of Global Intimacy in North American History*, ed. Ann Laura Stoler (Durham, NC: Duke University Press, 2006), 205. See also Grace Kyungwon Hong and Roderick A. Ferguson, *Strange Affinities: The Gender and Sexual Politics of Comparative Racialization* (Durham, NC: Duke University Press, 2011), especially Hong and Ferguson's introduction, which proposes an alternative mode of comparison—one based not on similarity but difference—derived from women-of-color feminism and queer-of-color critique. In addition to Glissant's "poetics of relation," I have found Stuart Hall's notion of "articulation" and Deleuze and Guattari's "assemblages" most generative in devising noncomparative modes of historical, economic, political, and racial associations across seemingly disparate contexts.

28 Andrea Smith, "Heteropatriarchy and the Three Pillars of White Supremacy," in *Color of Violence: The Incite! Anthology*, ed. Incite! Women of Color against Violence, 66–73 (Boston: South End, 2006).

29 See Wendy Brown, *States of Injury: Power and Freedom in Late Modernity* (Princeton, NJ: Princeton University Press, 1995), 52–76.

30 See Asma Abbas, *Liberalism and Human Suffering: Materialist Reflections on Politics, Ethics, and Aesthetics* (New York: Palgrave Macmillan, 2010), 229.

31 The manifestos mentioned in the text and others can be found at Beautone, http:// beautone.tumblr.com/search/manifesto.

32 Tim Haslett, "Hortense Spillers Interviewed by Tim Haslett for the Black Cultural Studies Web Site Collective in Ithaca, NY," February 4, 1998, accessed June 5, 2012, http://www.blackculturalstudies.org/spillers/spillers_intvw.html.

33 See Kathleen Fitzpatrick, Planned Obsolescence: Publishing, Technology, and the Future of the Academy (New York: NYU Press, 2011).

34 Aimé Césaire, "Culture and Colonization," trans. Brent Hayes Edwards (1956), Social Text 28.2 103 (2010): 133.

1 BLACKNESS

1 C. L. R. James, "Black Studies and the Contemporary Student" [1969], in The C.L.R. James Reader, ed. Anna Grimshaw (Cambridge, MA: Blackwell, 1992), 397.

2 Spillers, "The Crisis of the Negro Intellectual," 464. Hereafter parenthetically cited in the body of the text. See also Hortense J. Spillers, "The Crisis of the Black Intellectual," in A Companion to African-American Philosophy, ed. Tommy Lee Lott and John P. Pittman, 87–106 (Malden, MA: Blackwell, 2003).

3 See Louis Althusser and Étienne Balibar, Reading Capital, trans. Ben Brewster (London: Verso, 1970), especially 34–52.

4 While I use blackness and black people to illustrate this particular point, for Spillers, the community takes center stage as that which functions as a real object in black studies when, in fact, it should be construed as an object of knowledge ("The Crisis of the Negro Intellectual," 457–58).

5 Althusser and Balibar, Reading Capital, 107.

6 Viewing race as an arrangement of relations that produces commonsensical racial identities corresponds to Teresa De Lauretis's characterization of the subject of feminism, which "is a theoretical construct (a way of conceptualizing, of understanding, of accounting for certain processes, not women)." Teresa De Lauretis, Technologies of Gender: Essays on Theory, Film, and Fiction (Bloomington: Indiana University Press, 1987), 10.

7 Whenever I deploy the locutions black subject, blackness, or racialized subject, I do so with regard to their attendant gendered and sexualized opacities and to the ways in which they rest and transmute in history and geography.

8 I am using the designation Negro not simply to remain loyal to Du Bois's terminology but to emphasize the conceptual dimension of this category in Du Bois's thought, one analogous to the place of the "working class" in Marx or "power" in Foucault, and to keep in view the historical contingency of racial designators. For different formulations of Du Bois's methodology concerning the systematic study of the Negro, see W. E. B. Du Bois, "The Study of the Negro Problems," Annals

of the American Academy of Political and Social Science 11.1 (1898): 1–23; "The Laboratory in Sociology at Atlanta University," *Annals of the American Academy of Political and Social Science* 21.3 (1903): 502–5; and "Die Negerfrage in Den Vereinigten Staaten (The Negro Question in the United States)" [1906], trans. J. G. Fracchia, CR: The *New Centennial Review* 6.3 (2007): 241–90.

For the most sustained critical account of the place of the Negro as a central category in Du Bois's early system of thought, see Nahum Chandler, "Of Exorbitance: The Problem of the Negro as a Problem for Thought," *Criticism* 50.3 (2009): 345–410.

9 Ronald Judy, "Untimely Intellectuals and the University," *boundary 2* 27.1 (2000): 131–32.

10 In their respective considerations of black studies, both Spillers and Wynter warn against the blunting of the field's radical edge by the forces of commercialization (Spillers) and its pacification through the embrace of liberalist tenets under the guise of critiquing the essentialism of previous formations of black studies (Wynter). See Spillers, "The Crisis of the Negro Intellectual," 465; and Sylvia Wynter, "On How We Mistook the Map for the Territory and Re-imprisoned Ourselves in Our Unbearable Wrongness of Being, of Désêtre: Black Studies toward the Human Project," in *Not Only the Master's Tools: African-American Studies in Theory and Practice*, ed. Lewis Ricardo Gordon and Jane Anna Gordon (Boulder, CO: Paradigm, 2006), 110–15.

11 The quotations about inventive critical practices are taken respectively from Brian Massumi, *Parables for the Virtual: Movement, Affect, Sensation* (Durham, NC: Duke University Press, 2002), 12–13; and Edward Said, "The Text, the World, the Critic," *Bulletin of the Midwest Modern Language Association* 8.2 (1975): 22.

12 See David Scott and Sylvia Wynter, "The Re-enchantment of Humanism: An Interview with Sylvia Wynter," *Small Axe* 8 (September 2000): 207.

13 Sylvia Wynter, "Beyond Miranda's Meanings: Un/Silencing the 'Demonic Ground' of Caliban's 'Woman,'" in *Out of the Kumbla: Caribbean Women and Literature*, ed. Carole Boyce Davies and Elaine Savory, 355–70 (Trenton, NJ: Africa World Press, 1990). In her elaboration of Wynter, Katherine McKittrick draws attention to the twofold signification of the demonic as being at home in the supernatural (spirits, the devil, etc.) and natural sciences, where it designates "a working system that cannot have a determined, or knowable outcome" (McKittrick, *Demonic Grounds*, xxiv). Walter Benjamin also summons the demonic, especially as it traverses the figure of UnMan (Unmensch) as a technology toward achieving "real humanism." See Walter Benjamin, "Karl Kraus" [1931], in *Walter Benjamin: Selected Writings*, vol. 2, part 2: 1931–1934, ed. Howard Eiland and Michael W. Jennings, trans. Edmund Jephcott, 433–56 (Cambridge, MA: Harvard University Press, 2005).

14 Judith Butler, *Undoing Gender* (New York: Routledge, 2004), 13. In contrast to But-

ler, Ross Posnock (although his is basically the same idiom in a different register) conceives of Afro-diasporic intellectuals as anti-identitarian cosmopolitans: "Neither Du Bois nor Fanon regarded nationalism or Negritude as an endpoint or a fixed identity; instead they were moments, critical stages to reach a telos of the universal." Ross Posnock, *Color and Culture: Black Writers and the Making of the Modern Intellectual* (Cambridge, MA: Harvard University Press, 2000), 91–92. Scholars such as Posnock have an immense need to uplift minority thinkers, which both smacks of condescension and echoes colonial "civilizing" missions. Minority intellectuals are either put in their particularized cum identitarian place, as occurs in Butler, or granted access to the master's house via the teleportation capacities of universal cosmopolitanism.

15 On black women's liminal vantage point in Wynter's work, see McKittrick, *Demonic Grounds*, 133–36.

16 Greg Thomas, "PROUD FLESH Inter/Views: Sylvia Wynter," *ProudFlesh: New Afrikan Journal of Culture, Politics, and Consciousness* 4 (2006). See also Scott and Wynter, "The Re-enchantment of Humanism," 183–87; Sylvia Wynter, "Human Being as Noun? Or *Being Human as Praxis*—Towards the Autopoetic Turn/Overturn: A Manifesto," August 25, 2007, otl2.wikispaces.com/file/view/The+Autopoetic+Turn.pdf; Sylvia Wynter, "Beyond Liberal and Marxist Leninist Feminisms: Towards an Autonomous Frame of Reference" (San Francisco: Institute for Research on Women and Gender, 1982); and Wynter, "Beyond Miranda's Meanings."

17 Gayatri Chakravorty Spivak, "Can the Subaltern Speak?," in *Marxism and the Interpretation of Culture*, ed. Cary Nelson and Lawrence Grossberg (Champaign: University of Illinois Press, 1988), 275. Of course, Spivak, in what has now become a locus classicus of postcolonial critical theorizing, is referencing the limitations of Michel Foucault's and Gilles Deleuze's work vis-à-vis subaltern subjectivity. See also Gayatri Chakravorty Spivak, *A Critique of Postcolonial Reason: Toward a History of the Vanishing Present* (Cambridge, MA: Harvard University Press, 1999), 248–66.

18 This does not deviate from Butler's treatment of nonwhite thinkers in her other works. For instance, in *Antigone's Claim* Butler invokes race in relation to the questions of kinship at the core of her argument. Citing Angela Davis, Orlando Patterson, and Carol Stack, Butler contends that racial slavery eradicated any traditional notions of kinship for black subjects. Yet at the close of the text Butler posits kinship as the precondition of the human, showing how Antigone asks us to imagine "a new field of the human, . . . when gender is displaced, and kinship founders on its own founding laws." Here race drops out of the picture, subsumed by a universal variant of gender, and Butler's earlier arguments about race, kinship, and slavery remain a mere footnote. However, New World slavery did not merely abolish normative kinship structures but positioned black subjects as nonhuman, and, as Butler acknowledges, one is the precondition of the other. This seems in-

dicative of not only Butler's otherwise admirable work but the majority of Anglo-American post-structuralist–inflected cultural studies, where questions of race are a sideshow at best. Judith Butler, *Antigone's Claim: Kinship between Life and Death* (New York: Columbia University Press, 2000), 72–82.

19 Thomas, "PROUD FLESH Inter/Views."

20 See May Opitz, Katharina Oguntoye, and Dagmar Schultz, eds., *Showing Our Colors: Afro-German Women Speak Out* (1986; reprint, Amherst: University of Massachusetts Press, 1992); Cherríe Moraga and Gloria Anzaldúa, eds., *This Bridge Called My Back: Writings by Radical Women of Color*, 2nd ed. (New York: Kitchen Table: Women of Color Press, 1983); Barbara Smith, ed., *Home Girls: A Black Feminist Anthology* (New York: Kitchen Table: Women of Color Press, 1983); Carole Boyce Davies and Elaine Savory, eds., *Out of the Kumbla: Caribbean Women and Literature* (Trenton, NJ: Africa World, 1990).

21 Wynter, "Beyond Liberal and Marxist Leninist Feminisms," 14.

22 Wynter, "Beyond Liberal and Marxist Leninist Feminisms," 16.

23 Hortense J. Spillers, "'Mama's Baby, Papa's Maybe': An American Grammar Book," in *Black, White, and in Color: Essays on American Literature and Culture* (Chicago: University of Chicago Press, 2003), 229.

24 Combahee River Collective, "A Black Feminist Statement," in *This Bridge Called My Back: Writings by Radical Women of Color*, 2nd ed., ed. Cherríe Moraga and Gloria Anzaldúa (New York: Kitchen Table: Women of Color Press, 1983), 215.

25 Audra Simpson, "On Ethnographic Refusal: Indigeneity, 'Voice' and Colonial Citizenship," *Junctures: The Journal for Thematic Dialogue* 9 (2007): 67–80.

26 Spillers, "Introduction—Peter's Pans," 21.

27 Sylvia Wynter, "Beyond the Word of Man: Glissant and the New Discourse of the Antilles," *World Literature Today* 63.4 (1989): 637–48; and Sylvia Wynter, "On Disenchanting Discourse: 'Minority' Literary Criticism and Beyond," *Cultural Critique* 7 (1987): 207–44.

28 Wynter, "Beyond the Word of Man, 645.

29 Wynter also lists the native, woman, worker, mad, and unfit as further ontological others; however, she insists that the designation "nigger" holds a particularly volatile position in the "Man as Man" configuration. Wynter, "Beyond the Word of Man," 642.

30 Scott and Wynter, "The Re-enchantment of Humanism," 183.

31 For the terms *theodicy* and *biodicy*, see Scott and Wynter, "The Re-enchantment of Humanism," 142. Wynter, "Unsettling the Coloniality of Being/Power/Truth/Freedom," 318.

32 In the following discussion of Wynter's culturobiological notion of the human, I draw primarily on Wynter's essay about Fanon's sociogeny: Sylvia Wynter, "Towards the Sociogenic Principle: Fanon, Identity, the Puzzle of Conscious Experi-

ence, and What It Is Like to Be 'Black,'" in *National Identities and Sociopolitical Changes in Latin America*, ed. Mercedes F. Durán-Cogan and Antonio Gómez-Moriana, 30–66 (New York: Routledge, 2001); and on Wynter's comments in Scott and Wynter, "The Re-enchantment of Humanism."

33 German Darwinist Ernst Haeckel, who was also one of the founders of the modern eugenics movement, popularized the phrase "ontogeny recapitulates phylogeny" and its ideological superstructure "recapitulation theory" (also known as the "biogenetic constitution") in the late nineteenth century. While Sigmund Freud referenced this theoretical construct throughout his work, its conceptual impact is most evident in the central contention of his 1913 work *Totem and Taboo: Some Points of Agreement between the Mental Lives of Savages and Neurotics*. For a compact overview of recapitulation theory's history, see Stephen Jay Gould, *Ontogeny and Phylogeny* (Cambridge, MA: Harvard University Press, 1977).

34 Fanon, *Black Skin, White Masks*, xv.

35 Fanon, *Black Skin, White Masks*, 90. See also Wynter, "Towards the Sociogenic Principle," 50–54; hereafter parenthetically cited in the body of the text.

36 Wynter, "Towards the Sociogenic Principle."

37 Even though fully reconstructing Wynter's intricate and challenging claims about the interplay of biology and culture in the construction of humanity lies beyond the scope of this book, I would like to note that Wynter's contentions concerning human cognition and the neurochemical reward system are in dialogue with, among others, the following "scientific" texts: Gregory Bateson, *Steps to an Ecology of Mind* (Chicago: University of Chicago Press, 1972); James F. Danielli, "Altruism and the Internal Reward System or the Opium of the People," *Journal of Social and Biological Systems* 3.2 (1980): 87–94; Avram Goldstein, *Addiction: From Biology to Drug Policy* (New York: Oxford University Press, 2001).

38 Antonio de Nicolas quoted in Sylvia Wynter, "'Genital Mutilation' or 'Symbolic Birth'? Female Circumcision, Lost Origins, and the Aculturalism of Feminist/Western Thought," *Case Western Reserve Law Review* 47 (1997): 512.

39 For sociobiological treatments of racial thinking, see Edouard Machery and Luc Faucher, "Why Do We Think Racially? A Critical Journey in Culture and Evolution," in *Handbook of Categorization in Cognitive Science*, ed. Henri Cohen and Claire Lefebvre, 1009–33 (London: Elsevier, 2005); Lawrence Hirschfeld, *Race in the Making: Cognition, Culture, and the Child's Construction of Human Kinds* (Cambridge, MA: MIT Press, 1998); and David Livingstone Smith, *Less Than Human: Why We Demean, Enslave, and Exterminate Others* (New York: St. Martin's, 2011).

40 Wynter offers another formulation of this dynamic: "What causes these specific neural firings to be activated in a specific modality is not a property of the brain itself (of ontogeny). Instead, it is a property of the verbal codes in whose positive/negative (good/evil, symbolic life/death) systems of meaning we institute

ourselves as specific genres of being human. . . . Since the causal source of the
nature of our response does not lie in the neurophysiological mechanisms of the
brain, which implement that response . . . it is its meaning systems that determine
how the mechanisms of the brain will implement our experience of being human,
in the terms of each culture's specific conception." Scott and Wynter, "The Re-
enchantment of Humanism," 189.

41 Fanon, *Black Skin, White Masks*, 93.

42 Wynter, "Towards the Sociogenic Principle," 31.

43 Scott and Wynter, "The Re-enchantment of Humanism," 180. Wynter describes
the difference between the selected/eugenic and dysselected/dysgenic as follows:
"All members of the population group of European descent, classified as the white
race, allegedly proven by the very nature of their dominant position in the global
order over all other groups, now classified as non-white 'native' races, that they
had been, as a 'race,' optimally selected by evolution to embody ostensibly the
biological *norm* of being human. With, therefore, this institutionalized dialectic
between the two groups, each discursively and institutionally represented, one as
the norm, the other as the anti-norm, now made indispensable to the enactment
of the new *eugenic/dysgenic* sociogenic code, as the code in whose terms the Western
bourgeoisie, unable hitherto to legitimate its role as a ruling class on the basis
of the noble blood and birth model of the landed aristocracy, was now to legitimate itself as a *naturally selected* ruling class, because the bearers and transmitters
of an alleged eugenic line of descent." Wynter, "On How We Mistook the Map for
the Territory," 127.

44 Wynter, "Unsettling the Coloniality of Being/Power/Truth/Freedom," 260–61.

45 See Dorothy Roberts, *Fatal Invention: How Science, Politics, and Big Business Re-create
Race in the Twenty-First Century* (New York: New Press, 2011); and Keith Wailoo,
Alondra Nelson, and Catherine Lee, eds., *Genetics and the Unsettled Past: The Collision
of DNA, Race, and History* (New Brunswick, NJ: Rutgers University Press, 2012).

46 See Wynter, "On How We Mistook the Map for the Territory."

47 The phrase "planetary imagination" stems from Gayatri Chakravorty Spivak, *Death
of a Discipline* (New York: Columbia University Press, 2003), 96. See also Paul Gilroy,
Against Race: Imagining Political Culture beyond the Color Line (Cambridge, MA: Harvard
University Press, 2000). The presence of (African) American cultural artifacts in the
global domain is not tantamount to political, cultural, or economic hegemony per
se. In addition, this discussion is partially a response to an emergent consensus—
among both U.S. and European scholars of the African diaspora—at several con-
ferences about an African American hegemony vis-à-vis other black populations.
Frequently, the long histories of black studies in the United States—and the lack
thereof outside the United States—and the global circulation of African American
cultural artifacts are summoned to stand in as the grounds for said hegemony.

Even though I'm not disputing these two points, I would strongly caution against the invocation of hegemony for the reasons I mention above, as well as the underfunded status of many U.S. black studies programs and the mass impoverishment, criminalization, and incarceration of so many people of African descent in the United States.

48 Katherine McKittrick, "I Entered the Lists . . . Diaspora Catalogues: The List, The Unbearable Territory, and Tormented Chronologies—Three Narratives and a Weltanschauung," XCP: Cross Cultural Poetics 17 (2007): 20.

49 Etienne Balibar, "The Nation Form: History and Ideology," in Race, Nation, Class: Ambiguous Identities, ed. Etienne Balibar and Immanuel Maurice Wallerstein (New York: Verso, 1991), 96.

50 Fanon, Black Skin, White Masks, 204.

51 My argument does not concern the existence and value of diasporic groups per se but the ways in which they have been conceptualized in critical discourse. For an elaboration of this point, see Alexander G. Weheliye, "My Volk to Come: Peoplehood in Recent Diaspora Discourse and Afro-German Popular Music," in Black Europe and the African Diaspora, ed. Trica Danielle Keaton, Stephen Small, and Darlene Clark Hine (Champaign: University of Illinois Press, 2009).

52 Althusser and Balibar, Reading Capital, 108.

2 BARE LIFE

1 Giorgio Agamben, Homo Sacer: Sovereign Power and Bare Life, trans. Daniel Heller-Roazen (Palo Alto, CA: Stanford University Press, 1998). Hereafter parenthetically cited in the body of the text.

2 For a succinct sketch of Agamben's ideas about bare life and modern politics, see Jacques Rancière, Dissensus: On Politics and Aesthetics, trans. Steve Corcoran (New York: Continuum, 2010), 64–67. For an introduction to the discourse of biopolitics in Foucault, Agamben, and beyond, see Thomas Lemke, Biopolitics: An Advanced Introduction (New York: NYU Press, 2011).

3 Daniel Heller-Roazen translates Agamben's la nuda vita as bare life, while Vincenzo Binetti and Cesare Casarino use naked life. In his essay "Critique of Violence," from which Agamben takes this phrase, Walter Benjamin termed this compound bloßes Leben, which has been rendered as mere life by Edmund Jephcott in the English language edition of Benjamin's selected works. Paradoxically, the German translation of Agamben uses nacktes Leben despite its origin in the Benjaminian notion of bloßes Leben. In a personal communication, Heller-Roazen noted that he chose bare life to signify both the mere and nude dimensions of the homo sacer. I will use mere, bare, and naked life to mark both the palimpsestic structure of this phrase in its various translationary afterlives and, at times, to highlight particular aspects, such

as nakedness, of the homo sacer figure. See Agamben, *Homo Sacer: Sovereign Power*; Giorgio Agamben, *Homo Sacer: Die souveräne Macht und das nackte Leben*, trans. Hubert Thüring (Frankfurt am Main: Suhrkamp, 2002); Agamben, *Means without End*; Walter Benjamin, "Critique of Violence" [1921], in *Walter Benjamin: Selected Writings*, vol. 1: 1913–1926, ed. Marcus Paul Bullock and Michael William Jennings, trans. Edmund Jephcott, 236–52 (Cambridge, MA: Harvard University Press, 2004).

4 Waziyatawin A. Wilson, "Decolonizing the 1862 Death Marches," *American Indian Quarterly* 28.1–2 (2004): 185–215; Vicki Rozema, *Voices from the Trail of Tears* (Winston-Salem, NC: John F. Blair, 2003); Jennifer Denetdale, *The Long Walk: The Forced Navajo Exile* (Philadelphia: Chelsea House, 2007); James L. Dickerson, *Inside America's Concentration Camps: Two Centuries of Internment and Torture* (Chicago: Chicago Review Press, 2010).

5 Since the former slaves were not yet legally emancipated when these camps were initially constructed, the Union designated them as property, as contraband of war. For an extensive discussion of these contraband camps, see Leon F. Litwack, *Been in the Storm So Long: The Aftermath of Slavery* (New York: Knopf, 1979).

6 Klaus Mühlhahn, "The Concentration Camp in Global Historical Perspective," *History Compass* 8.6 (2010): 543–61; Iain R. Smith and Andreas Stucki, "The Colonial Development of Concentration Camps (1868–1902)," *Journal of Imperial and Commonwealth History* 39.3 (2011): 417–37; Dylan Rodríguez, *Suspended Apocalypse: White Supremacy, Genocide, and the Filipino Condition* (Minneapolis: University of Minnesota Press, 2009).

7 Mahmood Mamdani, *When Victims Become Killers: Colonialism, Nativism, and the Genocide in Rwanda* (Princeton, NJ: Princeton University Press, 2002), 10.

8 Gilroy, *Against Race*, 142–43; Volker Langbehn and Mohammad Salama, eds., *German Colonialism: Race, the Holocaust, and Postwar Germany* (New York: Columbia University Press, 2011).

9 We might also observe in passing the striking resemblances between the legal cum ideological apparatuses of Jim Crow in the United States, German Nuremberg laws, and South African apartheid laws. See Jürgen Zimmerer, *Von Windhuk nach Auschwitz: Beiträge zum Verhältnis von Kolonialismus und Holocaust* (Munster: LIT Verlag, 2007); Bill Ezzell, "Laws of Racial Identification and Racial Purity in Nazi Germany and the United States: Did Jim Crow Write the Laws That Spawned the Holocaust," *Southern University Law Review* 30.1 (2002): 1–13; Thomas Borstelmann, *Apartheid's Reluctant Uncle: The United States and Southern Africa in the Early Cold War* (New York: Oxford University Press, 1993).

10 Agamben, *Homo Sacer*, 166.

11 Pascal Grosse, *Kolonialismus, Eugenik und bürgerliche Gesellschaft* (Frankfurt am Main: Campus Verlag, 2000); and Pascal Grosse, "From Colonialism to National Socialism to Postcolonialism: Hannah Arendt's *Origins of Totalitarianism*," *Postcolonial*

Studies 9.1 (2006): 35–52. See also Stefan Kühl, *The Nazi Connection: Eugenics, American Racism, and German National Socialism* (New York: Oxford University Press, 1994). While Hannah Arendt does not probe the direct historical connections between colonial and National Socialist encampments, her argument lays the groundwork for conceptualizing racialization qua modern terror in relational terms, as does Aimé Césaire. See Hannah Arendt, *The Origins of Totalitarianism* (1951; reprint, New York: Houghton Mifflin Harcourt, 1994); and Césaire, *Discourse on Colonialism*.

12 As opposed to Britain, France, or Spain, Germany entered the colonial marketplace through the Berlin Conference (1884–85), during which the European powers partitioned the African continent, ushering in the scramble for Africa. Germany lost its African colonies (Namibia, Tanzania, Cameroon, Togo) in the aftermath of World War I. On the history of German colonialism, especially as it traverses questions of racialization, see Eric Ames, Marcia Klotz, and Lora Wildenthal, eds., *Germany's Colonial Pasts* (Lincoln: University of Nebraska Press, 2005); Sara Friedrichsmeyer, Sara Lennox, and Susanne Zantop, eds., *The Imperialist Imagination: German Colonialism and Its Legacy* (Ann Arbor: University of Michigan Press, 1998); Shelley Baranowski, *Nazi Empire: German Colonialism and Imperialism from Bismarck to Hitler* (New York: Cambridge University Press, 2010).

13 See, for instance, Neferti Tadiar, *Things Fall Away: Philippine Historical Experience and the Makings of Globalization* (Durham, NC: Duke University Press, 2009); Scott Morgensen, "The Biopolitics of Settler Colonialism: Right Here, Right Now," *Settler Colonial Studies* 1.1 (2011): 52–76; Lisa M. Lowe, "Reckoning Nation and Empire: Asian American Critique," in *A Concise Companion to American Studies*, ed. John Carlos Rowe, 229–44 (Malden, MA: Wiley-Blackwell, 2010); Colin Dayan, *The Law Is a White Dog: How Legal Rituals Make and Unmake Persons* (Princeton, NJ: Princeton University Press, 2011); Ong, *Neoliberalism as Exception*; Avery F. Gordon, "Abu Ghraib: Imprisonment and the War on Terror," *Race and Class* 48.1 (2006): 42–59; and Avery F. Gordon, "The United States Military Prison: The Normalcy of Exceptional Brutality," in *The Violence of Incarceration*, ed. Phil Scraton and Jude McCulloch, 164–86 (New York: Routledge, 2008); Mark Rifkin, "Indigenizing Agamben: Rethinking Sovereignty in Light of the 'Peculiar' Status of Native Peoples," *Cultural Critique* 73 (2009): 88–124; John Márquez, "Nations Re-bound: Race and Biopolitics at EU and US Borders," in *Europe in Black and White: Immigration, Race, and Identity in the "Old Continent,"* ed. Manuela Ribeiro Sanches, Joao Ferreira Duarte, and Fernando Clara, 38–49 (Bristol, UK: Intellect, 2011); Jodi Kim, *Ends of Empire: Asian American Critique and the Cold War* (Minneapolis: University of Minnesota Press, 2010); Dean Spade, *Normal Life: Administrative Violence, Critical Trans Politics, and the Limits of Law* (Boston: South End, 2011); Sylvester Johnson, *The Myth of Ham in Nineteenth-Century American Christianity: Race, Heathens, and the People of God* (New York: Palgrave Macmillan, 2004); João H. Costa Vargas, *Never Meant to Survive: Genocide and Utopias in*

Black Diaspora Communities (Lanham, MD: Rowman and Littlefield, 2008); Antonio Viego, *Dead Subjects: Toward a Politics of Loss in Latino Studies* (Durham, NC: Duke University Press, 2007); Patricia Clough and Craig Willse, eds., *Beyond Biopolitics: Essays on the Governance of Life and Death* (Durham, NC: Duke University Press, 2011); Eric Stanley, "Near Life, Queer Death Overkill and Ontological Capture," *Social Text* 29.2 107 (2011): 1–19; Rodríguez, *Suspended Apocalypse*; Nicholas De Genova, "Theoretical Overview," in *The Deportation Regime: Sovereignty, Space, and the Freedom of Movement*, ed. Nathalie Peutz and Nicholas De Genova, 33–65 (Durham, NC: Duke University Press, 2010); Ewa Ponowska Ziarek, *Feminist Aesthetics and the Politics of Modernism* (New York: Columbia University Press, 2012); Kalpana Seshadri, *Humanimal: Race, Law, Language* (Minneapolis: University of Minnesota Press, 2011); Jasbir Puar, *Terrorist Assemblages: Homonationalism in Queer Times* (Durham, NC: Duke University Press, 2007); Andrea Smith, *Conquest: Sexual Violence and American Indian Genocide* (Boston: South End, 2005).

14 Gilroy, *Against Race*, 60; see also 81–95.

15 William Goodell's 1853 *Slave Code* states the following about the laws and statutes governing the killing of slaves in the United States: "At present, the willful [sic], malicious, and deliberate murder of a slave, by whomsoever perpetrated, is declared to be punishable with death, in every State. The exclusion of all testimony of colored persons, bond or free, is a feature sufficient, of itself, to render these laws nugatory. The 'owner' or 'overseer' may command the slave to attend him to any secret spot, and there murder him with impunity. Or he may do it openly, (it has often been done,) in the sight of many colored persons, with equal impunity." W. Goodell, *The American Slave Code in Theory and Practice: Its Distinctive Features Shown by Its Statutes, Judicial Decisions, and Illustrative Facts* (New York: American and Foreign Anti-Slavery Society, 1853), 178.

16 For Patterson, slavery is synonymous with social death, and he distinguishes between intrusive and extrusive forms thereof. In the intrusive variant of social death "the slave was ritually incorporated as the permanent enemy on the inside"; conversely, in the extrusive model "the dominant image of the slave was that of an insider who had fallen, one who had ceased to belong and had been expelled from normal participation in the community." Agamben's notion of homo sacer would seem to occupy the zone of indistinction between these two forms of social death. Orlando Patterson, *Slavery and Social Death: A Comparative Study* (Cambridge, MA: Harvard University Press, 1982), 39.

17 Glissant, *Poetics of Relation*, 75.

18 On the question of genocide in the African diaspora, see Civil Rights Congress, *We Charge Genocide: The Historic Petition to the United Nations for Relief from a Crime of the United States Government against the Negro People* (New York: Civil Rights Congress, 1951); and Vargas, *Never Meant to Survive*.

19 Hortense J. Spillers et al., "'Whatcha Gonna Do?': Revisiting 'Mama's Baby, Papa's Maybe: An American Grammar Book'; A Conversation with Hortense Spillers, Saidiya Hartman, Farah Jasmine Griffin, Shelly Eversley, and Jennifer L. Morgan," *Women's Studies Quarterly* 35.1/2 (2007): 300.

20 Whereas I concentrate on the concept of the flesh, Spillers has theorized slavery's impact on black subjectivity primarily through a psychoanalytically inflected investigation of symbolic structures, demonstrating the different ways in which the familial constellations of the plantation continue to shape the ontological condition of black subjects in the west.

21 Spillers, "'Mama's Baby, Papa's Maybe,'" 206. Hereafter parenthetically cited in the body of the text.

22 For elaborations of Spillers's distinction between body and flesh, see Abdul Jan-Mohamed, *The Death-Bound-Subject: Richard Wright's Archaeology of Death* (Durham, NC: Duke University Press, 2005); Darieck Scott, *Extravagant Abjection: Blackness, Power, and Sexuality in the African American Literary Imagination* (New York: NYU Press, 2010); Sharon Holland, *Raising the Dead: Readings of Death and (Black) Subjectivity* (Durham, NC: Duke University Press, 2000); Robert Reid-Pharr, *Black Gay Man: Essays* (New York: NYU Press, 2001); Hartman, *Scenes of Subjection*; and Nicole Fleetwood, *Troubling Vision: Performance, Visuality, and Blackness* (Chicago: University of Chicago Press, 2011).

23 Wynter, "Beyond Miranda's Meanings," 358. See also Wynter, "On How We Mistook the Map for the Territory," 115; Wynter, "'Genital Mutilation' or 'Symbolic Birth'?," 509, and Scott and Wynter, "The Re-enchantment of Humanism," 200.

24 This is a reference to the Detroit electro group Drexciya, who in their Afrofuturist recasting of the Middle Passage imagined that this genocidal trauma produced a new species. These Drexciyans are nautically transmuted progenies of "pregnant America-bound African slaves thrown overboard by the thousands during labour for being sick and disruptive cargo." Drexciya, *The Quest* (CD, Detroit: Submerge, 1997).

25 All definitions are from the *Oxford Dictionary of English*, 3rd ed. (New York: Oxford University Press, 2010).

26 I should clarify that my argument here is not about casting Wynter's thinking in an antifeminist light or that her work has no relevance for studies of gender but rather an occasion to expand the Wynterian project—in dialogue with Spiller's ideas—so that it addresses the gendered dimensions of racializing assemblages. For analyses indebted to Wynter that center gender and sexuality, see Greg Thomas, *The Sexual Demon of Colonial Power: Pan-African Embodiment and Erotic Schemes of Empire* (Bloomington: Indiana University Press, 2007); and McKittrick, *Demonic Grounds*.

27 Darlene Clark Hine, "Rape and the Inner Lives of Black Women in the Middle West," *Signs* 14.4 (1989): 912–20; Angela Y. Davis, *Blues Legacies and Black Feminism:*

Gertrude "Ma" Rainey, Bessie Smith, and Billie Holiday (New York: Pantheon, 1998);
Claudia Tate, Domestic Allegories of Political Desire: The Black Heroine's Text at the Turn
of the Century (New York: Oxford University Press, 1992); Julia C. Oparah, "Feminism and the (Trans)gender Entrapment of Gender Nonconforming Prisoners,"
UCLA Women's Law Journal 18.2 (2012): 239–73; Hazel V. Carby, Reconstructing Womanhood: The Emergence of the Afro-American Woman Novelist (New York: Oxford University Press, 1987); Patricia Hill Collins, Black Feminist Thought: Knowledge, Consciousness, and the Politics of Empowerment, 2nd ed. (New York: Routledge, 2000); Cathy J.
Cohen, "Punks, Bulldaggers, and Welfare Queens: The Radical Potential of Queer
Politics?," GLQ: A Journal of Lesbian and Gay Studies 3.4 (1997): 437–65; Evelynn Hammonds, "Black (W)holes and the Geometry of Black Female Sexuality," Differences:
A Journal of Feminist Cultural Studies 6.2/3 (1994): 126–45.

28 Cohen, "Punks, Bulldaggers, and Welfare Queens," 455.

29 Spillers, "Introduction—Peter's Pans," 21, emphasis original. See also Spillers et
al., "'Whatcha Gonna Do?'"

30 While I largely agree with Denise da Silva's recent consideration of global raciality and strongly endorse the spirit that animates da Silva's categorical rethinking
of race qua subjectivity, there are two points of divergence that distinguish our
respective projects: first, I would insist on the relational process-ness of the way
race creates and grazes modern humanity, and second, da Silva dismisses too easily perspectives from black and ethnic studies as being invested only in the pin-
pointing of "social logics of exclusion." As my argument shows, while minority
discourse seemingly traffics in rhetorics of marginalization and inclusion, as an
intellectual project, which is at least partially defined by racializing assemblages,
this field cannot but address itself to the logics of the global human subject. See
da Silva, Toward a Global Idea of Race.

31 Luce Irigaray, This Sex Which Is Not One, trans. Catherine Porter (Ithaca, NY: Cornell
University Press, 1985), especially 170–91.

32 Hortense J. Spillers, "Interstices: A Small Drama of Words," in Black, White, and in
Color: Essays on American Literature and Culture (Chicago: University of Chicago Press,
2003), 155.

33 Hortense J. Spillers, Black, White, and in Color: Essays on American Literature and Culture
(Chicago: University of Chicago Press, 2003), 395.

34 Maurice Merleau-Ponty, The Visible and the Invisible; Followed by Working Notes, ed.
Claude Lefort, trans. Alphonso Lingis (Evanston, IL: Northwestern University
Press, 1968), 139.

35 Elizabeth A. Grosz, "Merleau-Ponty and Irigaray in the Flesh," Thesis Eleven 36.1
(1993): 54; see also Elizabeth A. Grosz, Time Travels: Feminism, Nature, Power
(Durham, NC: Duke University Press, 2005), especially 124–29.

36 Nas, "Ether," on *Stillmatic* (New York: Columbia Records, 2001). This is also a reference to the Aristotelian idea that "aether" represents the fifth element located in the higher stratums of the heavens rather than the earthly world the other four elements inhabit.

37 Jacques Derrida, "Differance" [1973], in *Margins of Philosophy*, trans. Alan Bass (Chicago: University of Chicago Press, 1982), 16.

3 ASSEMBLAGES

1 See Gilles Deleuze and Felix Guattari, *A Thousand Plateaus: Capitalism and Schizophrenia*, trans. Brian Massumi (Minneapolis: University of Minnesota Press, 1987), 87–88. Hereafter parenthetically cited in the body of the text as *Plateaus*. See also Puar, *Terrorist Assemblages*, 211–16. Puar has done much to create a conversation between Deleuze and Guattari's idea of assemblages and questions of identity, especially sexuality and race, taking place in queer and race studies. Her treatment of assemblages, however, construes these as wholly in flux and counter to the fixed racialized, sexualized, and nationalized identities found in theories of intersectionality, neglecting that assemblages are marked as much by territorialization as they are by deterritorialization.

2 Manuel DeLanda, *A New Philosophy of Society: Assemblage Theory and Social Complexity* (New York: Continuum, 2006), 28.

3 Massumi, *Parables for the Virtual*; Kara Keeling, *The Witch's Flight: The Cinematic, the Black Femme, and the Image of Common Sense* (Durham, NC: Duke University Press, 2007); Rosi Braidotti, *Metamorphoses: Towards a Materialist Theory of Becoming* (Boston: Polity, 2002); Elizabeth A. Grosz, *Becoming Undone: Darwinian Reflections on Life, Politics, and Art* (Durham, NC: Duke University Press, 2011); DeLanda, *A New Philosophy of Society*; Puar, *Terrorist Assemblages*.

4 Simone Bignall and Paul Patton, eds., *Deleuze and the Postcolonial* (Edinburgh: Edinburgh University Press, 2010). The dispute between Miller and Holland about how to properly interpret Deleuze can be found in the following essays: Eugene W. Holland, "Representation and Misrepresentation in Postcolonial Literature and Theory," *Research in African Literatures* 34.1 (2003): 159–73; Christopher L. Miller, "'We Shouldn't Judge Deleuze and Guattari': A Response to Eugene Holland," *Research in African Literatures* 34.3 (2003): 129–41; and Christopher L. Miller, "The Post-identitarian Predicament in the Footnotes of a Thousand Plateaus: Nomadology, Anthropology, and Authority," *Diacritics* 23.3 (1993): 6–35. Rosi Braidotti discusses the relationship between feminism and orthodox Deleuzianism in *Nomadic Subjects: Embodiment and Sexual Difference in Contemporary Feminist Theory*, 2nd ed. (New York: Columbia University Press, 2011), 276–82.

5 Barbara Christian, "The Race for Theory," *Cultural Critique* 6 (1987): 51–63; Stuart Hall, "Who Needs 'Identity'?," in *Questions of Cultural Identity*, ed. Paul Du Gay and Stuart Hall, 1–17 (London: Sage, 1996); Spivak, "Can the Subaltern Speak?"

6 Spivak, "Can the Subaltern Speak?," 273. Hortense Spillers makes a correlative point about the psychoanalytic protocols of Jacques Lacan: "Lacanian psychoanalytic theory is simply heavenly, insofar as it has no eyes for the grammar and politics of power." Spillers, *Black, White, and in Color*, 386.

7 Stuart Hall, "On Postmodernism and Articulation: An Interview with Stuart Hall," in *Stuart Hall: Critical Dialogues in Cultural Studies*, ed. David Morley and Kuan-Hsing Chen (New York: Routledge, 1986), 146. Hall is referring to Ernesto Laclau and Chantal Mouffe's 1985 text *Hegemony and Socialist Strategy: Towards a Radical Democratic Politics*, 2nd ed. (London: Verso, 2001).

8 Stuart Hall, "Race, Articulation, and Societies Structured in Dominance," in *Sociological Theories: Race and Colonialism*, 303–45 (Paris: UNESCO, 1980).

9 Stuart Hall, "Signification, Representation, Ideology: Althusser and the Post-structuralist Debates," *Critical Studies in Media Communication* 2.2 (1985): 93. See also Althusser and Balibar, *Reading Capital*; and Brent Hayes Edwards, *The Practice of Diaspora: Literature, Translation, and the Rise of Black Internationalism* (Cambridge, MA: Harvard University Press, 2003). The idea of articulation (*soziale Gliederung*) can be traced back to Marx's writings on political economy, where he writes about the need "to grasp the specific social articulation of modern production [die moderne Produktion in ihrer bestimmten sozialen Gliederung aufzufassen]." Karl Marx, "Grundrisse der Kritik der politischen Ökonomie," in *Ökonomische Manuskripte 1857/58. Karl Marx, Friedrich Engels Gesamtausgabe* (MEGA), vol. 2/1.1 (Berlin: Dietz, 1988), 33. It was Althusser and Balibar's *Reading Capital* that first provided a theoretical elaboration of the term or concept "articulation," which they define thus: "The structure of the whole is articulated as the structure of an organic hierarchized whole. The co-existence of limbs and their relations in the whole is governed by the order of a dominant structure which introduces a specific order into the articulation (Gliederung) of the limbs and their relations." Althusser and Balibar, *Reading Capital*, 99. *Gliederung* has often been translated as *structure* in earlier English versions of Marx's texts, but Althusser and Balibar use both the German term and the French *articulation* throughout the original French text of *Lire le Capital*; Ben Brewster's English translation of this text also uses *articulation* and *Gliederung*.

10 Hall, "Race, Articulation, and Societies Structured in Dominance," 330.

11 For a discussion of the way Deleuze and Guattari mobilize and conscript the figure of the American Indian in *A Thousand Plateaus*, see Jodi A. Byrd, *The Transit of Empire: Indigenous Critiques of Colonialism* (Minneapolis: University of Minnesota Press, 2011), 11–18.

12 This corresponds to the ways multiracial discourse simultaneously disavows (in the name of transcending primitive notions thereof) and reinstates (by embracing racial intermixture as a utopian ideal) a limited notion of race. See Jared Sexton, *Amalgamation Schemes: Antiblackness and the Critique of Multiracialism* (Minneapolis: University of Minnesota Press, 2008).

13 Spivak, "Can the Subaltern Speak?," 279.

14 Dayan, *The Law Is a White Dog*, 50, emphasis added.

15 Roberts, *Fatal Invention*, 4.

16 Wynter, "'Genital Mutilation' or 'Symbolic Birth'?," 513.

17 Zora Neale Hurston, "Characteristics of Negro Expression" [1934], in *Folklore, Memoirs, and Other Writings*, ed. Cheryl A. Wall (New York: Library of America, 1995), 831. This confers an altogether different signification on the biblical adage "and the Word was made flesh, and dwelt among us" (John 1:14).

18 Merleau-Ponty, *The Visible and the Invisible*, 132.

4 RACISM

1 See Zdzislaw Ryn and Stanslav Klodzinski, "An der Grenze zwischen Leben und Tod. Eine Studie über die Erscheinung des 'Muselmann' im Konzentrationslager," in *Die Auschwitz-Hefte: Texte der polnischen Zeitschrift "Przeglad Lekarski" über historische, psychische und medizinische Aspekte des Lebens und Sterbens in Auschwitz*, 1: 89–154 (Hamburg: Rogner und Bernhard Verlag, 1994), which is the most extensive study of the Muselmann, consisting of a collection of interviews with concentration camp survivors about the Muselmann, including some by former Muselmänner. All translations from this text are mine. Agamben draws on this study in his central argument about the Muselmann in *Remnants of Auschwitz*, especially in the text's appendix, which consists of first-person testimonies by former Muselmänner taken from Ryn and Klodzinski's study. For other earlier, largely historiographical and biographical accounts of this figure, see Wolfgang Sofsky, *The Order of Terror: The Concentration Camp* (Princeton, NJ: Princeton University Press, 1997); Eugen Kogon, *Der SS-Staat: Das System der deutschen Konzentrationslager* (Zurich: Europa Verlag, 1946); Emil Langbein, *People in Auschwitz*, trans. Harry Zohn (1972; reprint, Chapel Hill: University of North Carolina Press, 2004), 89–105; Benedikt Kautsky, *Teufel und Verdammte: Erfahrungen und Erkenntnisse aus sieben Jahren in deutschen Konzentrationslagern* (Zurich: Büchergilde Gutenberg, 1946), 167–69; Viktor Frankl, *Trotzdem Ja zum Leben sagen: Ein Psychologe erlebt das Konzentrationslager* (Munich: Deutscher Taschenbuch Verlag, 1982). Agamben's *Remnants of Auschwitz* has single-handedly introduced the term *Muselmann* to Anglo-American critical discourse, leading to the rather uninterrogated ubiquity of this term in current discussions of modern political violence. Agamben's phil-

osophical claims about Auschwitz and the camp as the nomos of modernity have been scrutinized much more closely in European scholarship.

2 Sofsky, *The Order of Terror*, 201. Sofsky further notes that most Muselmänner were Russian and Polish Jews, who were already deemed to belong to the lowest social strata in the camp and, thus, excepted from the camp supply chain (203).

3 One observer compares the intensity with which Muselmänner sought provender to the ferocity of the attack dogs used in the camps, another to starving canines. A former Muselmann notes that he wandered about the camp akin to an abandoned dog, while one even goes so far as to state that the Muselmänner had lost not only the semblances of humanity but all mammalian ones as well. Ryn and Klodzinski, "An der Grenze zwischen Leben und Tod," 102, 119, 134–35, 102.

4 According to the *Oxford English Dictionary*, *Mussalman* was used in the English language until the middle of the twentieth century, while *mussulmano* (Italian) and *musulman* (French) are still widely utilized today.

5 Giorgio Agamben, *Remnants of Auschwitz*, 45. Hereafter parenthetically cited in the body of the text. Ryn and Klodzinski, "An der Grenze zwischen Leben und Tod," 98–101.

6 Focusing on the theological aporia in Agamben's consideration of Auschwitz, Gil Anidjar is one of the few critics who does not simply gloss over the significance of the name *Muselmann*. I would extend Anidjar's point about religion into the political, seeing that the designation *Muselmann* encodes not merely a religious identity but also a racialized one. In contrast to Agamben and his critics in the English-speaking world, Anidjar translates *Muselmann* to *Muslim*, which is an important first step in calling attention to the often-elided politics of naming in this situation. I have chosen not do so here in order to mark the difference between *Muselmann*—as a catachrestic marker for the particular historical manifestation of *Muselmann* within the death camps—and the more common German *Muselmane*. Gil Anidjar, *The Jew, the Arab: A History of the Enemy* (Stanford, CA: Stanford University Press, 2003), 138–49.

7 Even if the term *Muselmann* itself was not pejorative at this historical juncture, we need only consult some of the alternate expressions used to designate this state: *Kamel* (camel), *Knochengerippe* (ragabones), *Tölpel* (slob/yokel), *Bettler* (beggar), *Gimpel* (dunce), *Kretinerl* (cretin), and *Krüppel* (cripple), for instance, to see that it was far from admiring. Ryn and Klodzinski, "An der Grenze zwischen Leben und Tod," 99. Since 2009, the term has been legally recognized as derogatory in Germany.

8 Ruth Wilson Gilmore, "Race and Globalization," in *Geographies of Global Change: Remapping the World*, ed. Ronald John Johnston, Peter James Taylor, and Michael Watts, 261–74 (Malden, MA: Wiley-Blackwell, 2002), 261.

9 Michel Foucault, *Society Must Be Defended: Lectures at the Collège de France, 1975–76*, trans. David Macey (New York: St. Martin's, 2003), 255, 258. Hereafter parenthet-

ically cited in the body of the text. See also Michel Foucault, *The Birth of Biopolitics: Lectures at the Collège de France, 1978–1979*, trans. Graham Burchell (New York: Picador, 2010); and Michel Foucault, *The History of Sexuality*, vol. 1: *An Introduction*, trans. Robert Hurley (New York: Vintage, 1978), especially 133–59.

10 Foucault, *The Order of Things*.

11 See Michel Foucault, *Abnormal: Lectures at the Collège de France, 1974–1975*, ed. Valerio Marchetti and Antonella Salomoni, trans. Graham Burchell (New York: Picador, 2003), 316–17; Foucault, *The Birth of Biopolitics*, 228; Michel Foucault, *Security, Territory, Population: Lectures at the Collège de France, 1977–78*, ed. Michel Senellart, trans. Graham Burchell (New York: Palgrave Macmillan, 2007).

12 Foucault states, "This will allow power to treat that population as a mixture of races, or to be more accurate, to treat the species, to subdivide the species it controls, into the subspecies known, precisely, as races. That is the first function of racism: to fragment, to create caesuras within the biological continuum" (*Society*, 255).

13 Michel Foucault, "Questions on Geography," in *Power/Knowledge: Selected Interviews and Other Writings, 1972–1977*, ed. Colin Gordon (New York: Random House, 1980), 67–68. Emphases added.

14 Mbembe holds that it is somewhat immaterial whether the ideological and administrative roots of Nazism are located in plantations and colonies or whether, as Foucault argues, they grew within Europe; what remains significant for understanding our current global political order is that "in modern philosophical thought and European political practice and imaginary, the colony represents the site where sovereignty consists fundamentally in the exercise of a power outside the law." Achille Mbembe, "Necropolitics," *Public Culture* 15 (2003): 23.

15 On the biopolitical laboratories of colonialism, see Phillippa Levine, "Anthropology, Colonialism, and Eugenics," in *The Oxford Handbook of the History of Eugenics*, ed. Alison Bashford and Phillippa Levine, 43–61 (New York: Oxford University Press, 2010); Grosse, *Kolonialismus, Eugenik und bürgerliche Gesellschaft*; Helen Tilley, *Africa as a Living Laboratory: Empire, Development, and the Problem of Scientific Knowledge, 1870–1950* (Chicago: University of Chicago Press, 2011); and for the long history of (illicit) medical experimentation on nonwhite subjects in the United States, see, for instance, Smith, *Conquest*; Susan Lederer, *Subjected to Science: Human Experimentation in America before the Second World War* (Baltimore, MD: Johns Hopkins University Press, 1997); James Howard Jones, *Bad Blood: The Tuskegee Syphilis Experiment* (New York: Simon and Schuster, 1993); Harriet Washington, *Medical Apartheid: The Dark History of Medical Experimentation on Black Americans from Colonial Times to the Present* (New York: Random House, 2008). For a history of African American health activism that arose partially as resistance to these experiments, see Alondra Nelson, *Body and Soul: The Black Panther Party and the Fight against Medical Discrimination* (Min-

neapolis: University of Minnesota Press, 2011), especially 23–48. Moreover, as David Mitchell and Sharon Snyder show, psychiatric institutions also served as laboratories for the biopolitics of Nazism, which also included the killing of disabled subjects as well as the enforced sterilization of this group and Afro-Germans. See "The Eugenic Atlantic: Race, Disability, and the Making of an International Eugenic Science, 1800–1945," *Disability and Society* 18.7 (2003): 843–64. We also do well to consider the many nonmedical modes of biologized population control that proliferated in these sites such as the selected breeding of the enslaved and colonized or the biopolitical dimensions of indigenous genocide in the Americas.

16 I would distinguish the socialist racism Foucault invokes here from the racializing assemblages that I have been discussing only on the grounds that the former does not necessitate the optic cum biological grounding of difference among human groups that is the defining property of ethnic racism. Foucault makes a similar point in the lectures from the previous year, when he postulates the difference between the "traditional, historical" form of ethnic racism and the racism "against the abnormal" unleashed by psychiatry, an "internal racism that permits the screening of every individual within a given society." I am not so much taking issue with the fact that Foucault emphasizes the historical shifts in racializing assemblages as I am pointing out that he does not define or explain *ethnic racism*, which results in the naturalization of racial difference. Foucault, *Abnormal*, 316–17.

17 Foucault writes of the "boomerang effect" "colonial practice can have on the juridico-political structures of the West. . . . While colonization, with its techniques and its political and juridical weapons, obviously transported European models to other continents, it also had a considerable boomerang effect on the mechanisms of power in the West, and on the apparatuses, institutions, and techniques of power. A whole series of colonial models was brought back to the West, and the result was that the West could practice something resembling colonization, or an internal colonialism, on itself" (*Society*, 103). Foucault takes this idea from Hannah Arendt without citing its source: see Arendt, *The Origins of Totalitarianism*, 155, 206, and 223. Also, in much the same way as Foucault's uncredited utilization of Angela Davis's and George Jackson's ideas that I discuss shortly, in *Society Must Be Defended* Foucault reviews many of the same sources that Arendt deployed in the "Race-Thinking before Racism" chapter of *The Origins of Totalitarianism* without mentioning Arendt in his lectures.

18 The quoted phrases are taken from Ann Stoler's summary of Foucault's lectures on racism. Ann Stoler, *Race and the Education of Desire: Foucault's History of Sexuality and the Colonial Order of Things* (Durham, NC: Duke University Press, 1995), 66, 60.

19 For an analogous critique of Foucault's erasure of racialized, gendered, and colo-

nial violence in his argument about the changing nature of modern punishment and incarceration in Discipline and Punish, see Joy James, Resisting State Violence: Radicalism, Gender, and Race in U.S. Culture (Minneapolis: University of Minnesota Press, 1996), 24–43.

20 Brady Thomas Heiner, "Foucault and the Black Panthers," City: Analysis of Urban Trends, Culture, Theory, Policy, Action 11.3 (2007): 315. See the partial translation of Foucault's writing about the murder of George Jackson: Michel Foucault, Catharine von Bülow, and Daniel Defert, "The Masked Assassination" [1971], in Warfare in the American Homeland: Policing and Prison in a Penal Democracy, ed. Joy James, trans. Sirene Farb, 140–58 (Durham, NC: Duke University Press, 2007); and Foucault's comments about race and imprisonment in "Michel Foucault on Attica: An Interview," Social Justice 18.3 (45) (1991): 29. Heiner also notes that while Foucault's ideas about biopolitics are first developed through a discussion of state racism in the unpublished 1975–76 lectures, the published incarnation of this concept in The History of Sexuality, vol. 1, substitutes sex and sexuality for the references to racism ("Foucault and the Black Panthers," 336). Similarly, Jasbir Puar mentions that where queer theory has concentrated on Foucault's discussion of the repressive hypothesis in this text, critical ethnic studies scholars have taken up the idea of biopolitics instead (Terrorist Assemblages, 34). Pal Ahluwalia and Robert Young have both analyzed the significance of Foucault's sojourn in Tunisia 1966–68, where he wrote The Archeology of Knowledge. Ahluwalia, Out of Africa, 145–49; Robert Young, Postcolonialism: An Historical Introduction (Malden, MA: Wiley-Blackwell, 2001), 395–98. In contrast to Foucault, Gilles Deleuze was far more direct in acknowledging his indebtedness to the ideas of the BPP and George Jackson. See Michelle Koerner, "Line of Escape: Gilles Deleuze's Encounter with George Jackson," Genre 44.2 (2011): 157–80.

21 For a history of how the French Left came to abandon anticolonialism in the aftermath of 1968 and why it has largely been hostile to postcolonial studies, multiculturalism, and identity politics since then, see Kristin Ross, May '68 and Its Afterlives (Chicago: University of Chicago Press, 2002), especially 158–69; and Robert Stam and Ella Shohat, Race in Translation: Culture Wars around the Postcolonial Atlantic (New York: NYU Press, 2012). See also Robin Kelley, Freedom Dreams: The Black Radical Imagination (Boston: Beacon, 2002); and Jean Paul Sartre, Colonialism and Neocolonialism (New York: Routledge, 2001).

22 Achille Mbembe, "Provincializing France?," Public Culture 23.1 (2011): 119. Hollande used Kanye West and Jay-Z's song "Niggas in Paris" as the soundtrack for a promotional spot in his 2012 presidential campaign. The spot features primarily nonwhite French citizens and, naturally, in its utilization of a recording by two African Americans rather than Afro-, Arab-, or Asian-French performers, locates

the problematic of race in France's *autre lieu*. For an extended consideration of how German whiteness is maintained by locating race, racism, and people of color in the nation's elsewhere, see Weheliye, *Phonographies*, 145–97.

23 *Territoires d'outre-mer*: French overseas territories.

24 In *State of Exception* Agamben deems the internment of Japanese Americans in 1942 to be the "most spectacular violation of civil rights" in the history of the United States, especially since it was based "solely [on] racial motivation." Giorgio Agamben, *State of Exception*, trans. Kevin Attell (Chicago: University of Chicago Press, 2005), 22. As Sora Han points out, Agamben's emphasis on the racial animus of this internment "conspicuously marks the absence of the history of race in the paradigm of the camp," seeing that the internment of Japanese Americans represents neither the most remarkable breach of the civil rights contract in U.S. history nor the only one based on race. Sora Han, "Strict Scrutiny: The Tragedy of Constitutional Law," in *Beyond Biopolitics: Essays on the Governance of Life and Death*, ed. Patricia Ticineto Clough and Craig Willse (Durham, NC: Duke University Press, 2011), 112.

25 David Scott, "Preface: Soul Captives Are Free," *Small Axe* 11.2 23 (2007): viii.

26 See Mike Davis, "Fortress Los Angeles: The Militarization of Urban Space," in *Variations on a Theme Park: The New American City and the End of Public Space*, ed. Michael Sorkin, 154–80 (New York: Macmillan, 1992); Ruth Wilson Gilmore, *Golden Gulag: Prisons, Surplus, Crisis, and Opposition in Globalizing California* (Berkeley: University of California Press, 2007).

27 The term *ginger*, when used to describe people with red hair and fair skin, refers back to nineteenth-century English prejudices against the Scottish and Irish populations among whom these traits were thought to be more prevalent and whom the English deemed racially inferior; it is still used as a derogatory epithet in the United Kingdom today.

28 Gilles Deleuze, *Pure Immanence: Essays on a Life*, trans. Anne Boyman (New York: Zone, 2005), 28.

29 In 1991, a version of "Born Free" was recorded by British comedian Vic Reeves, who appeared earlier on a segment of a television show titled *Knock Down Ginger*, which was named after a children's game commonly referred to in the United States as Ding Dong Ditch.

30 Ronald A. T. Judy, "Democracy or Ideology," *boundary 2* 33.3 (2006): 57.

31 For a delineation of the racialization of Muslims that references the discourse of Foucault and Agamben, see Junaid Rana, *Terrifying Muslims: Race and Labor in the South Asian Diaspora* (Durham, NC: Duke University Press, 2011), especially 26–94. See also Puar, *Terrorist Assemblages*.

32 Gilmore, *Golden Gulag*, 243–44.

33 Here is the passage from Homo Sacer in its original form: "The novelty of modern biopolitics lies in the fact that the biological given is as such immediately political, and the political is as such immediately the biological given" (148).

5 LAW

1 Nuruddin Farah, Sardines: A Novel (Variations on the Theme of an African Dictatorship) (1981; reprint, Saint Paul, MN: Graywolf, 1992), 195–96.

2 W. E. B. Du Bois, The Correspondence of W. E. B. Du Bois, vol. 3: Selections 1944–1963, ed. Herbert Aptheker (Amherst: University of Massachusetts Press, 1997), 23. For treatments of Du Bois's engagement with human rights on behalf of African Americans and colonized peoples across the globe, see Samuel Moyn, The Last Utopia: Human Rights in History (Cambridge, MA: Harvard University Press, 2010), 100–110; Nikhil Pal Singh, Black Is a Country: Race and the Unfinished Struggle for Democracy (Cambridge, MA: Harvard University Press, 2004), 155–59.

3 Wendy Brown, States of Injury: Power and Freedom in Late Modernity (Princeton, NJ: Princeton University Press, 1995), 74–75.

4 For different delineations of the kinds of sexual violence not recognized by the liberal state and treatments of how these acts must conform to certain narrative structures in order to be recognized by the police, national governments, or supranational entities, see Smith, Conquest; Will Storr, "The Rape of Men," Guardian, July 17, 2011, http://www.guardian.co.uk/society/2011/jul/17/the-rape-of-men; Beth Richie, Arrested Justice: Black Women, Violence, and America's Prison Nation (New York: NYU Press, 2012); Randall Williams, The Divided World: Human Rights and Its Violence (Minneapolis: University of Minnesota Press, 2010).

5 Esmeir, "On Making Dehumanization Possible," 1544. In his consideration of the limits that are part and parcel of Indigenous claims for legal recognition in Canada, Glen Coulthard demonstrates how "the state institutional and discursive fields within and against which Indigenous demands for recognition are made and adjudicated can subtly shape the subjectivities and worldviews of the Indigenous claimants involved." In addition to molding the conditions of possibility for indigenous subjectivity, legal forms of recognition are based on categories (personhood, property, injury, etc.) that "are profoundly hierarchical and power-laden, and as such have the ability to asymmetrically mold and govern how indigenous subjects think and act." Glen S. Coulthard, "Subjects of Empire: Indigenous Peoples and the 'Politics of Recognition' in Canada," Contemporary Political Theory 6.4 (2007): 452.

6 This is the wording of the relevant passage in the U.S. Constitution: "The privilege of the Writ of Habeas Corpus shall not be suspended, unless when in Cases

of Rebellion or Invasion the public Safety may require it." On the history of habeas corpus, see Cary Federman, *The Body and the State: Habeas Corpus and American Jurisprudence* (Albany: State University of New York Press, 2007); and Paul Delaney Halliday, *Habeas Corpus: From England to Empire* (Cambridge, MA: Harvard University Press, 2010). For a consideration of habeas corpus and legal states of exception within the context of British colonialism, see Nasser Hussain, *The Jurisprudence of Emergency: Colonialism and the Rule of Law* (Ann Arbor: University of Michigan Press, 2003).

7 For a historical overview of Native Americans' relationship with U.S. law, see Vine Deloria and Clifford Lytle, *American Indians, American Justice* (Austin: University of Texas Press, 1983).

8 *Scott v. Sandford (TANEY, C.J., Opinion of the Court)*, 60 U.S. 393 (U.S. Supreme Court 1857).

9 *Scott v. Sandford.* Priscilla Wald also reads the comparison of Native and African Americans in terms of the subject-producing powers of the U.S. Supreme Court. However, Wald emphasizes the court's propensities for making and unmaking not juridical humans but American citizens. Although the human and the citizen are intimately related, especially in the wake of the *Rights of Man*, it is important for my argument to highlight that the latter is often the compulsory precondition for the former. Priscilla Wald, *Constituting Americans: Cultural Anxiety and Narrative Form* (Durham, NC: Duke University Press, 1995), 16–63. For other considerations of this case and the comparison between black and indigenous subjects, see Vine Deloria, "Minorities and the Social Contract," *Georgia Law Review* 20.4 (1986): 917–34.

10 See Cheryl I. Harris, "Whiteness as Property," *Harvard Law Review* 106.8 (1993): 1707–70. For the complex racialization of Arab Americans, including in U.S. legal history, see Amaney Jamal and Nadine Naber, eds., *Race and Arab Americans before and after 9/11: From Invisible Citizens to Visible Subjects* (Syracuse, NY: Syracuse University Press, 2008); Lisa S. Majaj, "Arab-Americans and the Meanings of Race," in *Postcolonial Theory and the United States: Race, Ethnicity, and Literature*, ed. Amritjit Singh and Peter Schmidt, 320–37 (Jackson: University Press of Mississippi, 2000). For a critical chronicle of Native American racialization via the U.S. legal apparatus, see Robert A. Williams, *Like a Loaded Weapon: The Rehnquist Court, Indian Rights, and the Legal History of Racism in America* (Minneapolis: University of Minnesota Press, 2005); and Scott Richard Lyons, *X-Marks: Native Signatures of Assent*, Indigenous Americas (Minneapolis: University of Minnesota Press, 2010). For a genealogy of legal whiteness in U.S. law, see Ian Haney-López, *White by Law: The Legal Construction of Race* (New York: NYU Press, 1996).

11 J. Kēhaulani Kauanui, *Hawaiian Blood: Colonialism and the Politics of Sovereignty and Indigeneity* (Durham, NC: Duke University Press, 2008), 10.

12 See, for instance, Andrea Smith, "Boarding School Abuses, Human Rights, and Reparations," *Social Justice* 31.4 98 (2004): 89–102; and David Wallace Adams, *Education for Extinction: American Indians and the Boarding School Experience, 1875–1928* (Lawrence: University Press of Kansas, 1995).

13 Williams, *The Divided World*, xiv.

14 On Henrietta Lacks, see Rebecca Skloot, *The Immortal Life of Henrietta Lacks* (New York: Random House, 2010); Karla F. C. Holloway, *Private Bodies, Public Texts: Race, Gender, and a Cultural Bioethics* (Durham, NC: Duke University Press, 2011), 2–6; Gilroy, *Against Race*, 19–24; da Silva, *Toward a Global Idea of Race*, 8–10; Michael Gold, *A Conspiracy of Cells: One Woman's Immortal Legacy and the Medical Scandal It Caused* (Albany: State University of New York Press, 1986).

15 On the racialization of genetics, see Roberts, *Fatal Invention*; Troy Duster, "Buried Alive: The Concept of Race in Science," in *Genetic Nature/Culture: Anthropology and Science beyond the Two-Culture Divide*, ed. Alan H. Goodman, Deborah Heath, and M. Susan Lindee, 258–77 (Berkeley: University of California Press, 2003); Nikolas Rose, *The Politics of Life Itself: Biomedicine, Power, and Subjectivity in the Twenty-First Century* (Princeton, NJ: Princeton University Press, 2008); Kimberly TallBear, "DNA, Blood, and Racializing the Tribe," *Wicazo Sa Review* 18.1 (2003): 81–107.

16 Hannah Landecker, "Between Beneficence and Chattel: The Human Biological in Law and Science," *Science in Context* 12.1 (1999): 205. It should be noted that what is at stake in both Henrietta Lacks's and John Moore's cases are cell lines taken from human bodies, since the U.S. Supreme Court had ruled in favor of patenting of human-made organisms in the *Diamond v. Chakrabarty* case (1980). In her comparison of Mo (patented) and HeLa (not patented), Landecker shows how after 1980 human cell lines "became property that could be restricted to a particular individual, institution, or company rather than the scientific community in general. That restriction took the form not of an affirmative right to the cell line but the right to exclude others from using it to commercial ends" (215).

17 Landecker, "Between Beneficence and Chattel," 204.

18 *Moore v. Regents of University of California* (1990) 51 C3d 120 (Supreme Court of California 1990), Armand Arabian.

19 *Moore v. Regents.*

20 *Moore v. Regents*, Edward Panelli. According to Robert C. King, *A Dictionary of Genetics*, 7th ed. (Oxford: Oxford University Press, 2006), lymphokines are "a heterogeneous group of glycoproteins released from T lymphocytes after contact with a cognate antigen. Lymphokines affect other cells of the host rather than reacting directly with antigens."

21 See Purnima Bose, "General Electric, Corporate Personhood and the Emergence of the Professional Manager," in *Cultural Critique and the Global Corporation*, ed. Laura E. Lyons and Purnima Bose, 28–63 (Bloomington: Indiana University Press, 2010).

As Charles Mills reminds us, "'person' is not co-extensive with 'human' because to be human is neither necessary nor sufficient for personhood. Non-human entities exist that count as persons while human entities exist that do not count as persons. Not all humans have been granted the moral status to which their presumptive personhood should have entitled them." Charles W. Mills, "The Political Economy of Personhood," On the Human: A Project of the National Humanities Center, April 4, 2011, http://onthehuman.org/2011/04/political-economy-of-personhood/. See also Mills's argument about how what he terms "the racial contract" creates a version of the human synonymous with white supremacy: Charles W. Mills, The Racial Contract (Ithaca, NY: Cornell University Press, 1997).

22 Spade, Normal Life, 128.

23 In a fashion consonant to the incorporation of white, middle-class women into the world of Man, the post–civil rights (partial) integration of the black middle class "into the consumer horizon of expectation of the generic class (the white middle class)" is accompanied by the relegation of the black poor into "increasingly criminalized underclasses . . . interned in 'the hood' (i.e., the jobless inner-city ghettoes and their prison-system extension)." Sylvia Wynter, "On How We Mistook the Map for the Territory," 158. It is also accompanied by the almost absolute precariousness of the black middle class; see Mary E. Pattillo, Black Picket Fences: Privilege and Peril among the Black Middle Class (Chicago: University of Chicago Press, 1999).

24 Julia C. Oparah, "Maroon Abolitionists: Black Gender-Oppressed Activists in the Anti-prison Movement in the US and Canada," in Captive Genders: Trans Embodiment and the Prison Industrial Complex, ed. Nat Smith and Eric A. Stanley (Oakland, CA: AK Press, 2011), 294. See also Oparah, "Feminism and the (Trans)gender Entrapment of Gender Nonconforming Prisoners."

25 Spade, Normal Life, 33. Spade provides several examples of what such a politics might look like IRL, especially in the final chapter of this text.

26 Agamben, State of Exception, 88. Hereafter parenthetically cited in the body of the text.

27 I discuss Benjamin's notion of nowtime (Jetztzeit) later.

28 Antonio Negri, "The Ripe Fruit of Redemption," trans. Arianna Bove, Generation-online.org, July 26, 2003, http://www.generation-online.org/t/negriagamben.htm.

29 In addition to the homo sacer project, which addresses alternate forms-of-life in the yet-to-come obliquely, The Open: Man and Animal and The Coming Community most recognizably exhibit the opposition between the utter legal corruption of the present and a future utopia not beholden to legal sovereignty.

30 See Wynter, "Unsettling the Coloniality," 331; and Fanon, Black Skin, White Masks, 204.

31 Benjamin, "Critique of Violence," 250.

32 Benjamin's essay is an extended meditation on Georges Sorel's distinction between the political strike (focused on specific demands) and the proletarian general strike (focused on the anarchic overturning of the current socioeconomic order). The Spartacists were a German communist group during the Weimar Republic, led by Rosa Luxemburg and Karl Liebknecht, who attempted to take over Berlin in 1919 to usher in a broad social and political revolution. The revolt was violently crushed by the paramilitary troops of the Freikorps—with the support of the Weimar government—who murdered Luxemburg and Liebknecht in the aftermath of the uprising.

33 Benjamin, "Critique of Violence," 252.

34 What is more commonly referred to as a state of emergency usually occurs when democratic governments, in response to crises (war or civil disorder, for instance), legally suspend some or all laws of the nation or municipality in question, transferring most of the power to either the government or the military. States of emergency have often been utilized to withdraw basic civil rights from citizens and as a tool of state violence, for example, the suspension of habeas corpus in 1942, which allowed for the legal internment of Japanese Americans, or the measures instituted by the USA Patriot Act in 2001.

35 See Giorgio Agamben, *The Open: Man and Animal*, trans. Kevin Attel (Palo Alto, CA: Stanford University Press, 2004); and Giorgio Agamben, *The Time That Remains: A Commentary on the Letter to the Romans*, trans. Patricia Dailey (Palo Alto, CA: Stanford University Press, 2005).

36 Agamben, *State of Exception*, 52–53. On Schmitt's anti-Semitism during the Third Reich and beyond, see Raphael Gross, *Carl Schmitt und die Juden: Eine deutsche Rechtslehre* (Frankfurt am Main: Suhrkamp, 2005). The recent leftist reanimation of Schmitt's work by thinkers such as Agamben, Antonio Negri, Chantal Mouffe, and Jacques Derrida tends to downplay and neglect these aspects of his life and thought. Other critics have offered much more grounded considerations of the "scandalous Benjamin-Schmitt dossier," for example, Jacob Taubes, *Ad Carl Schmitt: Reflexive Harmony*, trans. Keith Tribe (New York: Columbia University Press, 2011); and Samuel Weber, "Taking Exception to Decision: Walter Benjamin and Carl Schmitt," *Diacritics* 22.3/4 (1992): 5–18; Horst Bredekamp, "From Walter Benjamin to Carl Schmitt, via Thomas Hobbes," trans. Melissa T. Hause and Justin Bond, *Critical Inquiry* 25.2 (1999): 247–66.

37 Walter Benjamin, *The Origin of German Tragic Drama* [1928], trans. John Osborne (London: Verso, 1998), 81. Rolf Tiedemann, *Niemandsland: Studien mit und über Theodor W. Adorno* (Munich: Edition Text + Kritik, 2007), 88–90. I thank Michael Schwarz from the Walter Benjamin Archiv in Berlin for bringing Tiedemann's response to my attention. Likewise, in *The Time That Remains*, Agamben establishes

the influence of St. Paul's Letter to the Romans on Benjamin's philosophy on the basis of a few philological speculations: the typographical spacing out of the word "s c h w a c h e [weak]" in "weak messianic power" found in one of the extant manuscript versions of "On the Concept of History," the quotation marks Benjamin places around "Jetztzeit," and a remark by Benjamin's friend Gershom Scholem "implying an identification with Paul on the part of Benjamin." Agamben, *The Time That Remains*, 145. See also Jacques Derrida's observation about Agamben's philological obsession with "firsts" in Jacques Derrida, *The Beast and the Sovereign*, vol. 1, ed. Michel Lisse, Marie-Louise Mallet, and Ginette Michaud, trans. Geoffrey Bennington (Chicago: University of Chicago Press, 2009), 135–39, 431–43.

38 This misconstrues the core insights of Foucault's *Discipline and Punish*, since confinement represents only a minor factor in the microphysics of power found in modern imprisonment, which includes the racialization of the prisoner as not-quite-human, what Foucault describes as the creation of his soul. See Michel Foucault, *Discipline and Punish: The Birth of the Prison*, trans. Alan Sheridan (New York: Vintage, 1977), especially 16–31.

39 See Angela Davis, *Abolition Democracy: Beyond Empire, Prisons, and Torture* (New York: Seven Stories Press, 2005); Dayan, *The Law Is a White Dog*; Gilmore, *Golden Gulag*; Gordon, "The United States Military Prison"; Dylan Rodríguez, *Forced Passages: Imprisoned Radical Intellectuals and the U.S. Prison Regime* (Minneapolis: University of Minnesota Press, 2006).

40 Dayan, *The Law Is a White Dog*, 181. In a related piece, Joan Dayan notes, "The legal turn to meaning vacates the human. In the repeated attempts to decipher the meaning of Eighth Amendment language, interpretation makes possible the denial of inmate claims while negating the humanity of the confined body." Joan Dayan, "Legal Slaves," *Nepantla: Views from South* 2 (2001): 22.

41 Davis, *Abolition Democracy*, 124.

42 See Agamben, *State of Exception*, 2.

43 Carl Schmitt, *Political Theology: Four Chapters on the Concept of Sovereignty*, trans. George Schwab (Chicago: University of Chicago Press, 1985), 5.

44 Judy, "Provisional Note on Formations of Planetary Violence," 143. And Patrick Wolfe, writing about the complex status of Native Americans vis-à-vis U.S. law, has suggested the term *exceptionism*, which he contrasts with both U.S. exceptionalism and Schmitt's theorization of the state of exception, to denote "the structural exclusion of particular groups from the operation of human rights, as opposed to the temporary suspension of human rights across society as a whole." Patrick Wolfe, "Corpus Nullius: The Exception of Indians and Other Aliens in US Constitutional Discourse," *Postcolonial Studies* 10.2 (2007): 145.

An earlier and shorter incarnation of this chapter appeared as "Pornotropes," *Journal of Visual Culture* 7.1 (April 2008).

1 Martin Heidegger, *What Is a Thing*, trans. W. B. Barton and Vera Deutsch (South Bend, IN: Gateway Editions, 1967), 48 (translation modified). Page duBois maps a terrain in which the extraction of truth from the pained slave body via torture in ancient Greece both initiates and haunts the very idea of truth as Alethiea/unconcealment (Entbergung) in western philosophy from Plato to Heidegger. See Page duBois, *Torture and Truth* (New York: Routledge, 1991), especially 127–40.

2 Hartman, *Scenes of Subjection*, 51.

3 Heidegger, *What Is a Thing?*, 48, translation modified.

4 Although *gefesselt* signifies captivity and bondage—the most literal translation would be tied up or handcuffed—in the Heideggerian context, echoes of *riveted* and *enraptured* also rest in this word, which locates, for our purposes, the happening of the slave *Ding* in the province of bondage and rapture, and which we will encounter later under the rubric of pornotroping.

5 Daphne Brooks, *Bodies in Dissent: Spectacular Performances of Race and Freedom, 1850–1910* (Durham, NC: Duke University Press, 2006), 6.

6 Hayden White, *Tropics of Discourse: Essays in Cultural Criticism* (Baltimore, MD: Johns Hopkins University Press, 1978), 2.

7 Pornotroping also significantly recasts Deleuze's concept of the pornological. In *Coldness and Cruelty*, Gilles Deleuze places the pornological above merely descriptive pornography in its confrontation with the perimeter of "non-language" in which "violence does not speak" and "eroticism remains unspoken." He goes on to write, "The imperative and descriptive function must transcend itself toward a higher function." Gilles Deleuze, *Coldness and Cruelty*, in Gilles Deleuze and Leopold Sacher-Masoch, *Masochism* (New York: Zone, 1989), 22–23. Pornotroping tenders a vernacular in which political violence chatters insistently with its fellow traveler eroticism.

8 Hartman, *Scenes of Subjection*, 27.

9 Mary Prince was also no stranger to pornotroping, since nakedness and the pleasure of the sovereign frequently go hand in hand with flogging in her narrative; see, for instance, *The History of Mary Prince* [1831], ed. Sarah Salih (New York: Penguin, 2000), 14. Further, Prince's testimony links the sensation of taste qua erotics ("their pleasure") to the whipping of slaves with the repeated invocation of "licking": "They were raw with licks. Lick—lick—. . . . I was licked" (15). The tongue and the whip form a rhythm (licks, lick, lick) that situates pornotroping beyond the visual and auditory, all the while not leaving these two domains in the dust.

10 Sharpe, *Monstrous Intimacies: Making Post-slavery Subjects* (Durham, NC: Duke University Press, 2010), 4.

11 The erotics of subjection in the domains that are my concern here have been addressed most dynamically in relation to black gay male sexuality, and I am very much indebted to the important line of inquiry initiated by Samuel Delany, Gary Fischer, Robert Reid-Pharr, and Darieck Scott. Samuel R. Delany, *Shorter Views: Queer Thoughts and the Politics of the Paraliterary* (Middletown, CT: Wesleyan University Press, 1999); Gary Fisher, *Gary in Your Pocket: Stories and Notebooks of Gary Fisher*, ed. Eve Kosofsky Sedgwick (Durham, NC: Duke University Press, 1996); Reid-Pharr, *Black Gay Man*; Scott, *Extravagant Abjection*. More generally, Anthony Paul Farley suggests that "the culture of the colorline, that is American culture, is an S&M culture in denial." Anthony Paul Farley, "The Black Body as Fetish Object," *Oregon Law Review* 76 (1997): 465. My point, however, wishes to bracket—with the full knowledge that this may well be impossible—questions of agency and subjective pleasure, albeit without foreclosing them, in order to understand how the asubjective dimensions of pornotroping contribute to the construction of habeas viscus, or the hieroglyphics of the flesh.

12 Hartman, *Scenes of Subjection*, 3.

13 See Fred Moten, *In the Break: The Aesthetics of the Black Radical Tradition* (Minneapolis: University of Minnesota Press, 2003), 1–24.

14 Moten, *In the Break*, 4, 22. Although Moten argues that "for Hartman the very specter of enjoyment is reason enough to repress the encounter," and his opening chapter rests on the interanimation of Aunt Hester's screams and Douglass's portrayal of the sorrow songs, Hartman does not shy away from the viscous density of pleasure in this context, and she discusses the nexus of shrieks and sorrow songs throughout *Scenes of Subjection*. For instance, she writes, "the profane association of song and suffering raises a host of issues that exceed the fascination or disapprobation incited by the apparently unsettling juxtaposition of the festive and the obscene. Foremost among these issues is the thorny status of pleasure, given such instrumental uses, the instability of agency when conspicuous displays of willfulness only serve to undermine the subject, and the perviousness of pain and pleasure at various sites of amusement, inclusive of slaves striking it smart on the auction block, the popular stage, and the breakdown performed in the quarters" (Hartman, *Scenes*, 33).

15 Frederick Douglass, *Narrative of the Life of Frederick Douglass, an American Slave* (Boston: Anti-Slavery Office, 1845), 8–9. Hereafter cited parenthetically in the body of the text.

16 See also Sharpe, *Monstrous Intimacies*, especially 5–13.

17 Glissant, *Poetics of Relation*, 73.

18 See Ronald Judy, *(Dis)forming the American Canon: African-Arabic Slave Narratives and the Vernacular* (Minneapolis: University of Minnesota Press, 1993), especially chapter 2,

for a sustained treatment of the canonization of slave narratives as literary artifacts in black studies.

19 Deborah McDowell, "In the First Place: Making Frederick Douglass and the Afro-American Narrative Tradition," in *Critical Essays on Frederick Douglass*, ed. William L. Andrews (Boston: GK Hall, 1991), 210.

20 On Jacob's loophole of retreat, see McKittrick, *Demonic Grounds*; and Valerie Smith, "'Loopholes of Retreat': Architecture and Ideology in Harriet Jacobs's *Incidents in the Life of a Slave Girl*," in *Reading Black, Reading Feminist*, ed. Henry Louis Gates, 212–26 (New York: Meridian, 1990). I also discuss this passage in chapter 7 of *Habeas Viscus*.

21 For critics besides Hartman and Moten discussing Aunt Hester, see, for instance, Sharpe, *Monstrous Intimacies*; Lindon Barrett, "African-American Slave Narratives: Literacy, the Body, Authority," *American Literary History* 7.3 (1995): 415–42; Maurice O. Wallace, *Constructing the Black Masculine: Identity and Ideality in African American Men's Literature and Culture, 1775–1995* (Durham, NC: Duke University Press, 2002); Robert Reid-Pharr, *Conjugal Union: The Body, the House, and the Black American* (New York: Oxford University Press, 1999); Tate, *Domestic Allegories of Political Desire*.

22 The refashioning of these scenes in Douglass's subsequent autobiography *My Bondage, My Freedom* (1855) underscores my points by making the pornotropic aspects even more explicit than the 1845 *Narrative*.

23 Maurice Wallace describes the link between the two scenes thus: "Unmistakably, the portrayal of Covey, enraged by the slave's insubordination ripping the slave-boy's clothes from his body . . . is a graphic recapitulation of Anthony's savage assault on Hester." Wallace, *Constructing the Black Masculine*, 92.

24 Aliyyah Abdur-Rahman, *Against the Closet: Identity, Political Longing, and Black Figuration* (Durham, NC: Duke University Press, 2012), 42. Abdur-Rahman, though astutely exploring the queer dimensions of slave narratives, does not mention Douglass's struggle with Covey but focuses instead on the representation of Aunt Hester and how this bespeaks Douglass's anxiety about having being sired through rape. See also Thomas Foster, "The Sexual Abuse of Black Men under American Slavery," *Journal of the History of Sexuality* 20.3 (2011): 445–64; and Charles Nero, "Toward a Black Gay Aesthetic: Signifying in Contemporary Black Gay Literature," in *Brother to Brother: New Writings by Black Gay Men*, ed. Essex Hemphill (Boston: Alyson, 1991).

25 The phrase "ahistorical Stoff of sexuality" is taken from Eve Kosofsky Sedgwick, *Between Men: English Literature and Male Homosocial Desire* (New York: Columbia University Press, 1985), 6.

26 Fanon, *Black Skin, White Masks*, 123.

27 Here I am thinking of the reports of murder and sexual assault in the New Orleans

Superdome in the aftermath of Katrina. We should also recall the many ways in which lynching and sexualization were imbricated.

28 Gayl Jones, *Corregidora* (Boston: Beacon, 1986), 135.

29 For a general consideration of the centrality of racialization and sexuality to colonial domination, see Robert Young, *Colonial Desire: Hybridity in Theory, Culture, and Race* (New York: Routledge, 1995).

30 For Sylvia Wynter, Judeo-Christianity's fallen flesh/redeemed spirit dyad inaugurates the production of western Man's nonhuman others, which in later periods get transubstantiated to the domains of biology and economics: "The master code of symbolic life ('the name of what is good') and death ('the name of what is evil') would now become that of reason/sensuality, rationality/irrationality in the reoccupied place of the matrixcode of Redeemed Spirit/Fallen Flesh." Wynter, "Unsettling the Coloniality," 287.

31 On the link between martyrology and the tortured black body, especially in the nineteenth-century abolitionist context, see Marcus Wood, *Blind Memory: Visual Representations of Slavery in England and America* (New York: Routledge, 2000), 215–91. Karen Halttunen has shown that the rise of Anglo-American humanitarianism at the end of the eighteenth century and the beginning of the nineteenth trafficked significantly in the "pornography of pain" and that pain became an integral part of pornography in this period. See Karen Halttunen, "Humanitarianism and the Pornography of Pain in Anglo-American Culture," *American Historical Review* 100.2 (1995): 303–34.

32 Keeling, *The Witch's Flight*, 59.

33 This scene is re-created almost in its entirety, with the exception of the presence of the boy, in Quentin Tarrantino's 2012 film *Django Unchained*. The film's second half owes much to *Mandingo*.

34 In Ryn and Klodzinski, concentration camp survivors report that extreme passivity was one of the defining features of being Muselmann and that other inmates felt fear, disgust, and anger due to this passivity. Ryn and Klodzinski, "An der Grenze zwischen Leben und Tod," 116–17. See also the passage from Sofsky cited in chapter 7 that explains how the Muselmann's passivity posed a threat to the normal order of the camp.

35 See Wilhelm Reich, *The Mass Psychology of Fascism* [1933], trans. Theodore Wolfe (New York: Orgone Institute Press, 1946); Herbert Marcuse, *Eros and Civilization* (Boston: Beacon, 1955); Klaus Theweleit, *Male Fantasies: Women, Floods, Bodies, History*, trans. Stephen Conway, Erica Carter, and Chris Turner (Minneapolis: University of Minnesota Press, 1987); Susan Sontag, "Fascinating Fascism," in *Under the Sign of Saturn*, 73–105 (New York: Doubleday, 1980).

36 Giorgio Agamben, *Profanations*, trans. Jeff Fort (New York: Zone, 2007), 91.

37 Walter Benjamin, "Franz Kafka: On the Tenth Anniversary of His Death" [1934],

in *Walter Benjamin: Selected Writings*, vol. 2, part 2: 1931–1934, ed. Howard Eiland and Michael W. Jennings, trans. Harry Zohn (Cambridge, MA: Harvard University Press, 2005), 802.

38 See, for instance, Jeffrey Toobin, "Killing Habeas Corpus: Arlen Specter's About-Face," *New Yorker*, December 4, 2006, 46–52. Many books chronicle the systematic use of torture by the U.S. military since 9/11, especially in relation to the Abu Ghraib scandal; see, for instance, Mark Danner, *Torture and Truth: America, Abu Ghraib, and the War on Terror* (New York: New York Review Books, 2004); and Karen J. Greenberg and Joshua L. Dratel, *The Torture Papers: The Road to Abu Ghraib* (Cambridge: Cambridge University Press, 2005).

7 DEPRIVATION

1 W. E. B. Du Bois, *John Brown* (Philadelphia: George W. Jacobs, 1909), 344.

2 See Anna Grimshaw and Keith Hart, "American Civilization: An Introduction," in *American Civilization*, 1–25 (Malden, MA: Blackwell, 1993).

3 Donald Pease has written extensively about how James's text is framed by and in dialogue with the McCarran-Walter Act. See Donald Pease, "C.L.R. James, *Moby-Dick* and the Emergence of Transnational American Studies," in *The Futures of American Studies*, ed. Donald Pease and Robyn Wiegman, 135–63 (Durham, NC: Duke University Press, 2002).

4 Donald Pease, "Introduction," in C. L. R. James, *Mariners, Renegades, and Castaways: The Story of Herman Melville and the World We Live In* (Hanover, NH: University Press of New England, 2001), xxv.

5 C. L. R. James, *Mariners, Renegades, and Castaways: The Story of Herman Melville and the World We Live In* (1953; reprint, Hanover, NH: University Press of New England, 2001), 135. Hereafter parenthetically cited in the body of the text.

6 See Harvey R. Neptune, *Caliban and the Yankees: Trinidad and the United States Occupation* (Chapel Hill: University of North Carolina Press, 2007).

7 Zdzislaw Ryn and Stanslav Klodzinski, "Zur Psychopathologie von Hunger und Hungererleben im Konzentrationslager," in *Die Auschwitz-Hefte: Texte der polnischen Zeitschrift "Przeglad Lekarski" über historische, psychische und medizinische Aspekte des Lebens und Sterbens in Auschwitz*, vol. 2 (Hamburg: Rogner und Bernhard Verlag, 1994), 122–24.

8 Ryn and Klodzinski, "Zur Psychopathologie von Hunger," 131.

9 Harriet Ann Jacobs, *Incidents in the Life of a Slave Girl*, ed. Lydia Maria Child (Boston: Published for the Author, 1861), 173–88. Hereafter parenthetically cited in the body of the text.

10 While I do not discuss it exhaustively here, it bears mentioning that the text Jacobs submits to the court of public opinion (*Incidents*) also differs radically in form, con-

tent, and function from the one James tenders as part of his defense (*Mariners*). In fact, one way to read the final chapter of *Mariners*, "A Natural but Necessary Conclusion," is as a testimony to James's ungendering, since he is forced to summon autobiography in order to depict his physical deterioration and can therefore not fall back on the masculine authorial detachment of the earlier chapters concerned with Melville's *Moby-Dick*. Jacobs, however, must write autobiographically and reference her physical embodiment throughout *Incidents*.

11 Primo Levi, *Survival in Auschwitz: The Nazi Assault on Humanity*, trans. Stuart Woolf (1958; reprint, New York: Simon and Schuster, 1996), 90.

12 Omer Bartov argues that Jean Améry and Primo Levi, who were assimilated western European Jews, diverge from Holocaust survivors such as Eli Wiesel and Ka-Tzetnik, who grew up in Eastern European religiously defined environments. Where Levi and Améry construe the Holocaust as a radical rupture in the Enlightenment ideals of western modernity, Ka-Tzetnik and Wiesel imagine the Shoah in theological terms, accenting questions of chosenness and the nature of evil. As a result, Bartov notes the latter two were not nearly as pessimistic as Améry and Levi. In this way, Agamben's reliance on the work of Améry, and especially Levi, can be seen as both an extension of this school and also as his evasion of more overdetermined modes of thinking about Nazi concentration camps and their implication for modern politics. See Omer Bartov, *Mirrors of Destruction: War, Genocide, and Modern Identity* (New York: Oxford University Press, 2000), 196–97; Ka-Tzetnik 135633, *House of Dolls* (London: Senate, 1977); Jean Améry, *At the Mind's Limits: Contemplations by a Survivor on Auschwitz and Its Realities*, trans. Sidney Rosenfeld and Stella Rosenfeld (Bloomington: Indiana University Press, 1998); Elie Wiesel, *The Night Trilogy: Night, Dawn, Day* (New York: Farrar, Straus and Giroux, 2008).

13 Here, Agamben does not depart significantly from the majority of recent academic writings about the Holocaust, which are dominated by testimony, along with trauma, as the central category of analysis. See, for instance, Shoshona Felman and Dori Laub, *Testimony: Crises of Witnessing in Literature, Psychoanalysis, and History* (New York: Routledge, 1992); and Dominick LaCapra, *History and Memory after Auschwitz* (Ithaca, NY: Cornell University Press, 1998).

14 See Améry, *At the Mind's Limits*; Bruno Bettelheim, *Informed Heart: Autonomy in a Mass Age* (1960; reprint, London: Penguin, 1986); Levi, *Survival in Auschwitz*.

15 See Agamben, *The Time That Remains*.

16 Ryn and Klodzinski, "Zur Psychopathologie von Hunger," 104.

17 Although Agamben mentions this term, translated by Heller-Roazen as *Muselmannization*, in the penultimate paragraph of *Remnants*, it inflects neither his description nor his analysis of the Muselmann (*Remnants*, 145).

18 See Ryn and Klodzinski, "Zur Psychopathologie von Hunger," 111 and 127.

19 Jozef Kret quoted in Ryn and Klodzinski, "Zur Psychopathologie von Hunger," 119.

20 Wladyslaw Fejkiel quoted in Zdzislaw Ryn and Stanslav Klodzinski, "An der Grenze zwischen Leben und Tod: Eine Studie über die Erscheinung des 'Muselmann' im Konzentrationslager," in *Die Auschwitz-Hefte: Texte der polnischen Zeitschrift "Przeglad Lekarski" über historische, psychische und medizinische Aspekte des Lebens und Sterbens in Auschwitz*, 1: 89–154 (Hamburg: Rogner und Bernhard Verlag, 1994), 95.

21 Consider, for instance, this passage from *Remnants of Auschwitz* wherein Agamben notes how the traditional moral categories do not apply to the Muselmann: "If one establishes a limit beyond which one ceases to be human, and all or most of humankind passes beyond it, this proves not the inhumanity of human beings but, instead, the insufficiency and abstraction of the limit" (*Remnants*, 63). Yes, the limit must be reconfigured so as to encompass the fleshliness of the Muselmän-ner, while we must also query the grounds upon which we declare the Musel-mann's inhumanity. Agamben then tells the following story in order to illustrate his point: "Imagine that the ss let a preacher enter the camp and that he tried with every possible means to convince the Muselmänner of the necessity of keeping their dignity and self-respect even at Auschwitz. The preacher's gesture would be odious; his sermon would be an atrocious jest in the face of those who were be-yond not only the possibility of persuasion, but even of all human help" (*Remnants*, 63). Yet the preacher's homily would only be detestable if he or she were operating within the insufficient and abstract borders between the human and the inhuman. More fundamentally, why must a preacher (rather than a functional inmate, a phi-losopher, a historian, or a novelist) occupy the role of the moral criminal in this context? Why would this preacher be concerned about the Muselmann's dignity and self-respect? Agamben then reveals that to deny the Muselmann's humanity would be tantamount to corroborating the "verdict of the ss."

22 Sofsky, *The Order of Terror*, 202–4, emphasis added. Similarly, Konrad Szweda asks, "Perhaps, in his mental crippling, bodily decay, and in his total impassiveness, [the Muselmann] was protesting against crime and injustice?" Szweda quoted in Ryn and Klodzinski, "An der Grenze zwischen Leben und Tod," 150.

23 Ignacy Sikora quoted in Ryn and Klodzinski, "An der Grenze zwischen Leben und Tod," 122.

24 Quote from Glissant, *Poetics of Relation*, 95.

25 Jacques Derrida, "Force of Law: The Mystical Foundation of Authority," in *Acts of Religion*, ed. Gil Anidjar, trans. Mary Quaintance (New York: Routledge, 2002), 244.

8 FREEDOM

1 Toni Morrison, *Beloved* (New York: Signet, 1987), 103. While inspired by Spillers's injunction, I should note that she is referring not to the flesh per se but to Afri-

can American women's potential "insurgent ground as female social subject" that might be established by "actually claiming the monstrosity (of a female with the potential to 'name'), which her culture imposes in blindness[;] 'Sapphire' might rewrite after all a radically different text for a female empowerment." Hortense J. Spillers, "'Mama's Baby, Papa's Maybe': An American Grammar Book" [1987], in *Black, White, and in Color: Essays on American Literature and Culture*, 203–29 (Chicago: University of Chicago Press, 2003), 229.

2 Here is the full passage: "To witness the moment when pain causes a reversion to the pre-language of cries and groans is to Witness the destruction of language; but conversely, to be present when a person moves up out of that pre-language and projects the facts of sentience into speech is almost to have been permitted to be present at the birth of language itself." Elaine Scarry, *The Body in Pain: The Making and Unmaking of the World* (New York: Oxford University Press, 1987), 6. In Scarry's recapitulationist model, the fallen flesh of prelanguage ascends to the redeemed spirit of speech as sentience.

3 Quotes from Zdzislaw Ryn and Stanslav Klodzinski, "An der Grenze zwischen Leben und Tod: Eine Studie über die Erscheinung des 'Muselmann' im Konzentrationslager," in *Die Auschwitz-Hefte: Texte der polnischen Zeitschrift "Przeglad Lekarski" über historische, psychische und medizinische Aspekte des Lebens und Sterbens in Auschwitz*, 1: 89–154 (Hamburg: Rogner und Bernhard Verlag, 1994), 117.

4 On the reduction of language to linguistic structures in the aftermath of structuralism and the problems this poses for the study of black cultures, see Weheliye, *Phonographies*, 30–36.

5 Roman Grzyb quoted in Ryn and Klodzinski, "An der Grenze zwischen Leben und Tod," 116, translation mine.

6 Rajagopalan Radhakrishnan, *Theory in an Uneven World* (Malden, MA: Wiley-Blackwell, 2003), 97.

7 Asma Abbas, "Voice Lessons: Suffering and the Liberal Sensorium," *Theory and Event* 13.2 (2010).

8 Aristotle, *The Politics of Aristotle*, trans. J. E. C. Welldon (London: Macmillan, 1883), 116–17.

9 Ryn and Klodzinski, "An der Grenze zwischen Leben und Tod," 122.

10 See Giorgio Agamben, *Quel che resta di Auschwitz: L'archivio e il testimone: Homo sacer 3* (Turin: Bollati Boringhieri, 1998).

11 See Burkhard Bilger, "The Search for Sweet: Building a Better Sugar Substitute," *New Yorker*, May 22, 2006, 40.

12 See Sidney Wilfred Mintz, *Sweetness and Power: The Place of Sugar in Modern History* (New York: Viking, 1985), especially 74–150.

13 C. L. R. James, *The Black Jacobins: Toussaint L'Ouverture and the San Domingo Revolution* (1938; reprint, New York: Vintage, 1989), 361. James also notes the centrality of the

sugar plantation to the history of the Caribbean, writing that "it has been the most civilizing as well as the most demoralizing influence in West Indian development. When three centuries ago the slaves came to the West Indies, they entered directly into the large-scale agriculture of the sugar plantation, which was a modern system. It further required that the slaves live together in a social relation far closer than any proletariat of the time. The cane when reaped had to be rapidly transported to what was factory production. The product was shipped abroad for sale. Even the cloth the slaves wore and the food they ate was imported. The Negroes, therefore, from the very start lived a life that was in its essence a modern life." James, *The Black Jacobins*, 392.

14 See Prince, *The History of Mary Prince*, 62, 31, and 38. Prince's editor, Thomas Pringle, quotes Prince as saying "the sweets of freedom" in the supplement to the narrative. The sweetness of liberty finds its counterpart in the saltiness of slavery, when Prince is forced to labor in the salt works, where their "feet and legs, from standing in the salt water for so many hours, soon became full with dreadful boils, which eat down in some cases to the very bone, afflicting the sufferers with great torment," 19.

15 Giorgio Agamben, *Potentialities: Collected Essays in Philosophy*, trans. Daniel Heller-Roazen (Palo Alto, CA: Stanford University Press, 1999), 182–83. Hereafter parenthetically cited in the body of the text.

16 See also Agamben, *Homo Sacer*, 46. *Paschein* is also frequently translated as "acted upon" and is distinguished from *poiein* (to act).

17 As Michel Foucault notes, freedom in the ancient Greek context connotes nonslavery, and thus slavery serves as liberty's categorical impotentiality. Michel Foucault, *Ethics: Subjectivity and Truth*, ed. Paul Rabinow, trans. Robert Hurley (New York: New Press, 1997), 286.

18 The definitions of *deprivation* and *depravation* are taken from the *Oxford American Dictionary*.

19 Besides Hartman, who, as we have seen, shows that the recognition of black humanity before and subsequent to emancipation was used to subjugate black subjects in much more insidious and elaborate ways than slavery, my thinking here and in what follows is also in dialogue with Moten's notion of a "freedom drive," Robin Kelley's account of the "freedom dreams" in and of the black radical tradition, Richard Iton's conceptualization of "the black fantastic," and José Muñoz's account of utopia and queer futurity. See Moten, *In the Break*, 7, 70–71; Kelley, *Freedom Dreams*; Richard Iton, *In Search of the Black Fantastic: Politics and Popular Culture in the Post–Civil Rights Era* (New York: Oxford University Press, 2008); and José Esteban Muñoz, *Cruising Utopia: The Then and There of Queer Futurity* (New York: NYU Press, 2009). Also, pertinent in this context is what Best and Hartman describe as "black noise," which is always in excess of the law, since it transports "the kinds of political aspirations that are inaudible and illegible within the prevailing formulas of

political rationality; these yearnings are illegible because they are so wildly utopian and derelict to capitalism." Stephen Best and Saidiya Hartman, "Fugitive Justice," *Representations* 92.1 (2005): 9.

20 *Hic et nunc* means "here and now" in Latin. On messianism in the traditions of the oppressed, see, for instance, Vittorio Lanternari, *The Religions of the Oppressed: A Study of Modern Messianic Cults* (New York: New American Library, 1965); Jean-Pierre Filiu, *Apocalypse in Islam*, trans. M. B. DeBevoise (Berkeley: University of California Press, 2011); Eddie Glaude, *Exodus! Religion, Race, and Nation in Early Nineteenth-Century Black America* (Chicago: University of Chicago Press, 2000); Susannah Gottlieb, *Regions of Sorrow: Anxiety and Messianism in Hannah Arendt and W. H. Auden* (Palo Alto, CA: Stanford University Press, 2003); Michael Löwy, *Redemption and Utopia: Jewish Libertarian Thought in Central Europe: A Study in Elective Affinity*, trans. Hope Heaney (Palo Alto, CA: Stanford University Press, 1992); Wilson Jeremiah Moses, *Black Messiahs and Uncle Toms: Social and Literary Manipulations of a Religious Myth* (State College, PA: Penn State University Press, 1993).

21 John Coney, dir., *Sun Ra and His Intergalactic Arkestra: Space Is the Place* (Plexifilm, 1974). Here is a brief synopsis of *Space Is the Place*: Through the medium of music Sun Ra and his Arkestra travel to another planet. However, in order to populate this planet with black people, Ra and his Arkestra must voyage back to earth and, using their advanced sonic arsenal, save black people from the wicked Man. Eventually, planet Earth combusts after the saviors (Sun Ra and his Arkestra) have returned to their new home planet.

22 Walter Benjamin, "On the Concept of History" [1940], in *Selected Writings*, vol. 4: 1938–1940, trans. Harry Zohn (Cambridge, MA: Harvard University Press, 2003), 396 (translation modified). Hereafter parenthetically cited in the body of the text.

23 C. L. R. James, "Dialectical Materialism and the Fate of Humanity," in *The C.L.R. James Reader*, ed. Anna Grimshaw (Cambridge, MA: Blackwell, 1992), 167. Writing about James's *Mariners, Renegades, and Castaways*, Donald Pease describes the work of the "future anterior" in this text as connecting "a past event with a possible future on which the past event depends for its significance. The split temporality intrinsic to the future anterior describes an already existing state of affairs at the same time that it stages the temporal practice through which that state of affairs will have been produced." Pease, "Doing Justice to CLR James's *Mariners, Renegades, and Castaways*," *boundary 2* 27.2 (2000): 19. See also da Silva, *Toward a Global Idea of Race*, 253–67; and Muñoz, *Cruising Utopia*.

24 For Agamben's citations of Benjamin's phrase without discussing the tradition of the oppressed, see Agamben, *Homo Sacer*, 55; *Means without End* 6; *Potentialities*, 160; *State of Exception*, 6, 57.

25 Walter Benjamin, *The Arcades Project*, ed. Rolf Tiedemann, trans. Howard Eiland and Kevin McLaughlin (Cambridge, MA: Harvard University Press, 1999), 459.

26 Benjamin, *Arcades Project*, 459, emphasis added. Apocatastasis (derived from the Greek) signifies the reconstitution, restitution, or restoration to an original or primordial state, and it has led an illustrious life in the annals of the three Abrahamic religions, as well as the Buddhist idea of Nirvana. Most recently the concept has been affiliated with Christian universalism, where it is associated with universal salvation and reconciliation. Before its theological turn, it referred to the planetary realignment of the cosmos in the aftermath of the apocalyptic conflagration in Stoic thought. Given Benjamin's career-spanning interest in astrology and cosmology, ranging from early publications such as *The Origin of German Tragic Drama* to the *Arcades Project*, which he was working on before he died, Benjamin was likely drawn to the idea of apocatastasis because it blurs the lines between the religious, revolutionary, and cosmological.

27 Benjamin, *Arcades Project*, 698.

28 Fanon, *Black Skin, White Masks*, 69.

29 Wynter, "On How We Mistook the Map for the Territory," 118.

30 Benjamin, "Franz Kafka," 802.

31 Cedric J. Robinson, *Black Marxism: The Making of the Black Radical Tradition* (London: Zed, 1983), 245–46.

32 Wynter, "Unsettling the Coloniality," 260.

33 Hathaway's song has become a modern standard and has been recorded by many other artists including Aretha Franklin, Bobby Womack, Regina Belle, George Benson, Chaka Khan, Sergio Mendes, and Teena Marie. Chic's "At Last I Am Free" (1978) is another pertinent statement in this context given its twinning of temporality and freedom.

BIBLIOGRAPHY

Abbas, Asma. *Liberalism and Human Suffering: Materialist Reflections on Politics, Ethics, and Aesthetics*. New York: Palgrave Macmillan, 2010.

———. "Voice Lessons: Suffering and the Liberal Sensorium." *Theory and Event* 13.2 (2010).

Abdur-Rahman, Aliyyah. *Against the Closet: Identity, Political Longing, and Black Figuration*. Durham, NC: Duke University Press, 2012.

Adams, David Wallace. *Education for Extinction: American Indians and the Boarding School Experience, 1875–1928*. Lawrence: University Press of Kansas, 1995.

Agamben, Giorgio. *Die souveräne Macht und das nackte Leben*. Translated by Hubert Thüring. Frankfurt am Main: Suhrkamp, 2002.

———. *Homo Sacer: Sovereign Power and Bare Life*. Translated by Daniel Heller-Roazen. Palo Alto, CA: Stanford University Press, 1998.

———. *Means without End: Notes on Politics*. Translated by Cesare Cesarino and Vincenzo Binetti. Minneapolis: University of Minnesota Press, 2000.

———. *The Open: Man and Animal*. Translated by Kevin Attel. Palo Alto, CA: Stanford University Press, 2004.

———. *Potentialities: Collected Essays in Philosophy*. Translated by Daniel Heller-Roazen. Palo Alto, CA: Stanford University Press, 1999.

———. *Profanations*. Translated by Jeff Fort. New York: Zone, 2007.

———. *Quel che resta di Auschwitz: L'archivio e il testimone: Homo sacer 3*. Turin: Bollati Boringhieri, 1998.

———. *Remnants of Auschwitz: The Witness and the Archive.* Translated by Daniel Heller-Roazen. New York: Zone, 1999.

———. *State of Exception.* Translated by Kevin Attel. Chicago: University of Chicago Press, 2005.

———. *The Time That Remains: A Commentary on the Letter to the Romans.* Translated by Patricia Dailey. Palo Alto, CA: Stanford University Press, 2005.

Ahluwalia, Pal. *Out of Africa: Post-structuralism's Colonial Roots.* New York: Routledge, 2010.

Althusser, Louis. *For Marx.* Translated by Ben Brewster. New York: Verso, 1969.

Althusser, Louis, and Étienne Balibar. *Reading Capital.* Translated by Ben Brewster. London: Verso, 1970.

Améry, Jean. *At the Mind's Limits: Contemplations by a Survivor on Auschwitz and Its Realities.* Translated by Sidney Rosenfeld and Stella Rosenfeld. Bloomington: Indiana University Press, 1998.

Ames, Eric, Marcia Klotz, and Lora Wildenthal, eds. *Germany's Colonial Pasts.* Lincoln: University of Nebraska Press, 2005.

Anidjar, Gil. *The Jew, the Arab: A History of the Enemy.* Stanford, CA: Stanford University Press, 2003.

Arendt, Hannah. *The Origins of Totalitarianism.* 1951. Reprint, New York: Houghton Mifflin Harcourt, 1994.

Aristotle. *The Politics of Aristotle.* Translated by J. E. C. Welldon. London: Macmillan, 1883.

Balibar, Etienne. "The Nation Form: History and Ideology." In *Race, Nation, Class: Ambiguous Identities,* edited by Etienne Balibar and Immanuel Maurice Wallerstein, 86–106. New York: Verso, 1991.

———. "Violence and Civility: On the Limits of Political Anthropology." *differences: A Journal of Feminist Cultural Studies* 20.2–3 (2009): 9–35.

Balibar, Etienne, and Immanuel Maurice Wallerstein, eds. *Race, Nation, Class: Ambiguous Identities.* New York: Verso, 1991.

Baranowski, Shelley. *Nazi Empire: German Colonialism and Imperialism from Bismarck to Hitler.* New York: Cambridge University Press, 2010.

Barrett, Lindon. "African-American Slave Narratives: Literacy, the Body, Authority." *American Literary History* 7.3 (1995): 415–42.

Bartov, Omer. *Mirrors of Destruction: War, Genocide, and Modern Identity.* New York: Oxford University Press, 2000.

Bateson, Gregory. *Steps to an Ecology of Mind.* Chicago: University of Chicago Press, 1972.

Benjamin, Walter. *The Arcades Project* [1982]. Edited by Rolf Tiedemann, translated by Howard Eiland and Kevin McLaughlin. Cambridge, MA: Harvard University Press, 1999.

———. "Critique of Violence" [1921]. In *Walter Benjamin: Selected Writings*, vol. 1: 1913–1926, edited by Marcus Paul Bullock and Michael William Jennings, translated by Edmund Jephcott, 236–52. Cambridge, MA: Harvard University Press, 2004.

———. "Franz Kafka: On the Tenth Anniversary of His Death" [1934]. In *Walter Benjamin: Selected Writings*, vol. 2, part 2: 1931–1934, edited by Howard Eiland and Michael W. Jennings, translated by Harry Zohn, 795–818. Cambridge, MA: Harvard University Press, 2005.

———. "Karl Kraus" [1931]. In *Walter Benjamin: Selected Writings*, vol. 2, part 2: 1931–1934, edited by Howard Eiland and Michael W. Jennings, translated by Edmund Jephcott, 433–56. Cambridge, MA: Harvard University Press, 2005.

———. "On the Concept of History" [1940]. In *Selected Writings*, vol. 4: 1938–1940, translated by Harry Zohn, 389–401. Cambridge, MA: Harvard University Press, 2003.

———. *The Origin of German Tragic Drama* [1928]. Translated by John Osborne. London: Verso, 1998.

Best, Stephen, and Saidiya Hartman. "Fugitive Justice." *Representations* 92.1 (2005): 1–15.

Bettelheim, Bruno. *Informed Heart: Autonomy in a Mass Age*. 1960. Reprint, London: Penguin, 1986.

Bignall, Simone, and Paul Patton, eds. *Deleuze and the Postcolonial*. Edinburgh: Edinburgh University Press, 2010.

Bilger, Burkhard. "The Search for Sweet: Building a Better Sugar Substitute." *New Yorker*, May 22, 2006, 40.

Borstelmann, Thomas. *Apartheid's Reluctant Uncle: The United States and Southern Africa in the Early Cold War*. New York: Oxford University Press, 1993.

Bose, Purnima. "General Electric, Corporate Personhood and the Emergence of the Professional Manager." In *Cultural Critique and the Global Corporation*, edited by Laura E. Lyons and Purnima Bose, 28–63. Bloomington: Indiana University Press, 2010.

Boyce Davies, Carole, and Elaine Savory, eds. *Out of the Kumbla: Caribbean Women and Literature*. Trenton, NJ: Africa World, 1990.

Braidotti, Rosi. *Metamorphoses: Towards a Materialist Theory of Becoming*. Boston: Polity, 2002.

———. *Nomadic Subjects: Embodiment and Sexual Difference in Contemporary Feminist Theory*, 2nd ed. New York: Columbia University Press, 2011.

Bredekamp, Horst. "From Walter Benjamin to Carl Schmitt, via Thomas Hobbes." Translated by Melissa T. Hause and Justin Bond. *Critical Inquiry* 25.2 (1999): 247–66.

Brooks, Daphne. *Bodies in Dissent: Spectacular Performances of Race and Freedom, 1850–1910*. Durham, NC: Duke University Press, 2006.

Brown, Wendy. *States of Injury: Power and Freedom in Late Modernity.* Princeton, NJ: Princeton University Press, 1995.

Burleigh, D. Michael, and Wolfgang Wippermann. *The Racial State: Germany, 1933–1945.* Cambridge: Cambridge University Press, 1991.

Butler, Judith. *Antigone's Claim: Kinship between Life and Death.* Wellek Library Lectures. New York: Columbia University Press, 2000.

———. *Undoing Gender.* New York: Routledge, 2004.

Byrd, Jodi A. *The Transit of Empire: Indigenous Critiques of Colonialism.* Minneapolis: University of Minnesota Press, 2011.

Carby, Hazel V. *Reconstructing Womanhood: The Emergence of the Afro-American Woman Novelist.* New York: Oxford University Press, 1987.

Carver, Steve, dir. *Drum.* United Artists, 1976.

Cavani, Liliana, dir. *The Night Porter.* AVCO Embassy Pictures, 1974.

Césaire, Aimé. "Culture and Colonization." Translated by Brent Hayes Edwards. 1956. Reprint, *Social Text* 28.2 103 (2010): 127–44.

———. *Discourse on Colonialism.* Translated by Joan Pinkham. 1955. Reprint, New York: Monthly Review Press, 1972.

Chakrabarty, Dipesh. *Provincializing Europe: Postcolonial Thought and Historical Difference.* Princeton, NJ: Princeton University Press, 2000.

Chandler, Nahum D. "Of Exorbitance: The Problem of the Negro as a Problem for Thought." *Criticism* 50.3 (2009): 345–410.

———. "Originary Displacement." *boundary 2* 27.3 (2000): 249–86.

Cheah, Pheng. *Inhuman Conditions: On Cosmopolitanism and Human Rights.* Cambridge, MA: Harvard University Press, 2006.

Chen, Kuan-Hsing. *Asia as Method: Toward Deimperialization.* Durham, NC: Duke University Press, 2010.

Chomsky, Marvin J., and John Erman, dirs. *Roots.* American Broadcasting Company (ABC), January 23, 1977.

Christian, Barbara. "The Race for Theory." *Cultural Critique* 6 (1987): 51–63.

Civil Rights Congress. *We Charge Genocide: The Historic Petition to the United Nations for Relief from a Crime of the United States Government against the Negro People.* New York: Civil Rights Congress, 1951.

Clough, Patricia Ticineto, and Craig Willse, eds. *Beyond Biopolitics: Essays on the Governance of Life and Death.* Durham, NC: Duke University Press, 2011.

Cohen, Cathy J. "Punks, Bulldaggers, and Welfare Queens: The Radical Potential of Queer Politics?" *GLQ: A Journal of Lesbian and Gay Studies* 3.4 (1997): 437–65.

Collins, Patricia Hill. *Black Feminist Thought: Knowledge, Consciousness, and the Politics of Empowerment,* 2nd ed. New York: Routledge, 2000.

Combahee River Collective. "A Black Feminist Statement." In *This Bridge Called My*

Back: Writings by Radical Women of Color, 2nd ed., edited by Cherríe Moraga and Gloria Anzaldúa, 210–18. New York: Kitchen Table: Women of Color Press, 1983.

"Concentration Camp." *Encyclopædia Britannica*, 2011. http://www.britannica.com/EB checked/topic/130884/concentration-camp.

Coney, John, dir. *Sun Ra and His Intergalactic Arkestra: Space Is the Place*. Plexifilm, 1974.

Coulthard, Glen S. "Subjects of Empire: Indigenous Peoples and the 'Politics of Recognition' in Canada." *Contemporary Political Theory* 6.4 (2007): 437–60.

Danielli, James F. "Altruism and the Internal Reward System or the Opium of the People." *Journal of Social and Biological Systems* 3.2 (1980): 87–94.

Danner, Mark. *Torture and Truth: America, Abu Ghraib, and the War on Terror*. New York: New York Review Books, 2004.

da Silva, Denise Ferreira. *Toward a Global Idea of Race*. Minneapolis: University of Minnesota Press, 2007.

Davis, Angela Y. *Abolition Democracy: Beyond Empire, Prisons, and Torture*. New York: Seven Stories Press, 2005.

———. *Blues Legacies and Black Feminism: Gertrude "Ma" Rainey, Bessie Smith, and Billie Holiday*. New York: Pantheon, 1998.

———. "Reflections on the Black Woman's Role in the Community of Slaves." *Black Scholar* 12.6 (1981): 2–15.

Davis, Mike. "Fortress Los Angeles: The Militarization of Urban Space." In *Variations on a Theme Park: The New American City and the End of Public Space*, edited by Michael Sorkin, 154–80. New York: Macmillan, 1992.

Dayan, Colin. *The Law Is a White Dog: How Legal Rituals Make and Unmake Persons*. Princeton, NJ: Princeton University Press, 2011.

Dayan, Joan. "Legal Slaves and Civil Bodies." *Nepantla: Views from South* 2 (2001): 3–39.

DeLanda, Manuel. *A New Philosophy of Society: Assemblage Theory and Social Complexity*. New York: Continuum, 2006.

Delany, Samuel R. *Shorter Views: Queer Thoughts and the Politics of the Paraliterary*. Middletown, CT: Wesleyan University Press, 1999.

De Lauretis, Teresa. *Technologies of Gender: Essays on Theory, Film, and Fiction*. Bloomington: Indiana University Press, 1987.

Deleuze, Gilles. *Coldness and Cruelty*. In Gilles Deleuze and Leopold Sacher-Masoch, *Masochism*. New York: Zone, 1989.

———. *Pure Immanence: Essays on a Life*. Translated by Anne Boyman. New York: Zone, 2005.

Deleuze, Gilles, and Félix Guattari. *Anti-Oedipus: Capitalism and Schizophrenia*. Translated by Robert Hurley, Mark Seem, and Helen Lane. Minneapolis: University of Minnesota Press, 1983.

————. *A Thousand Plateaus: Capitalism and Schizophrenia*. Translated by Brian Massumi. Minneapolis: University of Minnesota Press, 1987.

Deloria, Vine. "Minorities and the Social Contract." *Georgia Law Review* 20.4 (1986): 917–34.

Deloria, Vine, and Clifford Lytle. *American Indians, American Justice*. Austin: University of Texas Press, 1983.

Demme, Jonathan, dir. *Beloved*. Touchstone Pictures, 1998.

Denetdale, Jennifer. *The Long Walk: The Forced Navajo Exile*. Philadelphia: Chelsea House, 2007.

Derrida, Jacques. *The Beast and the Sovereign*, vol. 1. Edited by Michel Lisse, Marie-Louise Mallet, and Ginette Michaud, translated by Geoffrey Bennington. Chicago: University of Chicago Press, 2009.

————. "Differance" [1973]. In *Margins of Philosophy*, translated by Alan Bass, 3–27. Chicago: University of Chicago Press, 1982.

————. "The Ends of Man" [1969]. In *Margins of Philosophy*, translated by Alan Bass, 109–36. Chicago: University of Chicago Press, 1982.

————. "Force of Law: The Mystical Foundation of Authority." In *Acts of Religion*, edited by Gil Anidjar, translated by Mary Quaintance, 228–98. New York: Routledge, 2002.

————. "White Mythology: Metaphor in the Text of Philosophy" [1974]. In *Margins of Philosophy*, translated by Alan Bass, 207–71. Chicago: University of Chicago Press, 1982.

Deslauriers, Guy, dir. *The Middle Passage (Passage du milieu)*. HBO Home Video, 2001.

Díaz, Junot. "Junot Díaz and Paula M. L. Moya: The Search for Decolonial Love, Part I." *Boston Review*, June 26, 2012.

Dickerson, James L. *Inside America's Concentration Camps: Two Centuries of Internment and Torture*. Chicago: Chicago Review Press, 2010.

Douglass, Frederick. *Narrative of the Life of Frederick Douglass, an American Slave*. Boston: Anti-Slavery Office, 1845.

Drexciya. *The Quest*. CD. Detroit: Submerge, 1997.

duBois, Page. *Torture and Truth*. New York: Routledge, 1991.

Du Bois, W. E. B. *The Correspondence of W. E. B. Du Bois*, vol. 1: *Selections 1877–1934*. Edited by Herbert Aptheker. Amherst: University of Massachusetts Press, 1997.

————. *The Correspondence of W. E. B. Du Bois*, vol. 3: *Selections 1944–1963*. Edited by Herbert Aptheker. Amherst: University of Massachusetts Press, 1997.

————. "Die Negerfrage in den Vereinigten Staaten (The Negro Question in the United States)" [1906]. Translated by J. G. Fracchia. CR: *The New Centennial Review* 6.3 (2007): 241–90.

————. *John Brown*. Philadelphia: George W. Jacobs, 1909.

————. "The Laboratory in Sociology at Atlanta University." *Annals of the American Academy of Political and Social Science* 21.3 (1903): 502–5.

————. *The Souls of Black Folk* [1903]. Edited by Donald B. Gibson. New York: Penguin Classics, 1996.

————. "The Study of the Negro Problems." *Annals of the American Academy of Political and Social Science* 11.1 (1898): 1–23.

DuCille, Ann. "The Occult of True Black Womanhood: Critical Demeanor and Black Feminist Studies." *Signs* 19.3 (1994): 591–629.

Duster, Troy. "Buried Alive: The Concept of Race in Science." In *Genetic Nature/Culture: Anthropology and Science beyond the Two-Culture Divide*, edited by Alan H. Goodman, Deborah Heath, and M. Susan Lindee, 258–77. Berkeley: University of California Press, 2003.

Edwards, Brent Hayes. *The Practice of Diaspora: Literature, Translation, and the Rise of Black Internationalism*. Cambridge, MA: Harvard University Press, 2003.

Enns, Diane. "Political Life before Identity." *Theory and Event* 10.1 (2007).

Esmeir, Samera. "On Making Dehumanization Possible." PMLA 121.5 (2006): 1544–51.

Ezzell, Bill. "Laws of Racial Identification and Racial Purity in Nazi Germany and the United States: Did Jim Crow Write the Laws That Spawned the Holocaust." *Southern University Law Review* 30.1 (2002): 1–13.

Fanon, Frantz. *Black Skin, White Masks* [1952]. Translated by Richard Philcox. New York: Grove, 2008.

————. *The Wretched of the Earth* [1963]. Translated by Richard Philcox. New York: Grove, 2004.

Farah, Nuruddin. *Sardines: A Novel (Variations on the Theme of an African Dictatorship)*. 1981. Reprint, Saint Paul, MN: Graywolf, 1992.

Farley, Anthony Paul. "The Black Body as Fetish Object." *Oregon Law Review* 76 (1997): 457–535.

Federman, Cary. *The Body and the State: Habeas Corpus and American Jurisprudence*. Albany: State University of New York Press, 2007.

Felman, Shoshana, and Dori Laub. *Testimony: Crises of Witnessing in Literature, Psychoanalysis, and History*. New York: Routledge, 1992.

Filiu, Jean-Pierre. *Apocalypse in Islam*. Translated by M. B. DeBevoise. Berkeley: University of California Press, 2011.

Fisher, Gary. *Gary in Your Pocket: Stories and Notebooks of Gary Fisher*. Edited by Eve Kosofsky Sedgwick. Durham, NC: Duke University Press, 1996.

Fitzpatrick, Kathleen. *Planned Obsolescence: Publishing, Technology, and the Future of the Academy*. New York: NYU Press, 2011.

Fleetwood, Nicole R. *Troubling Vision: Performance, Visuality, and Blackness*. Chicago: University of Chicago Press, 2011.

Fleischer, Richard, dir. *Mandingo*. Paramount Pictures, 1975.

Foster, Thomas. "The Sexual Abuse of Black Men under American Slavery." *Journal of the History of Sexuality* 20.3 (2011): 445–64.

Foucault, Michel. *Abnormal: Lectures at the Collège de France, 1974–1975*. Edited by Valerio Marchetti and Antonella Salomoni, translated by Graham Burchell. New York: Picador, 2003.

———. *The Birth of Biopolitics: Lectures at the Collège de France, 1978–1979*. Translated by Graham Burchell. New York: Picador, 2010.

———. *Discipline and Punish: The Birth of the Prison*. Translated by Alan Sheridan. New York: Vintage, 1977.

———. *Ethics: Subjectivity and Truth*. Edited by Paul Rabinow, translated by Robert Hurley. New York: New Press, 1997.

———. *The History of Sexuality*, vol. 1: *An Introduction*. Translated by Robert Hurley. New York: Vintage, 1978.

———. *Il faut défendre la société: Cours au Collège de France (1975–1976)*. Edited by Alessandro Fontana and Mauro Bertani. Paris: Seuil, 1997.

———. "Michel Foucault on Attica: An Interview." *Social Justice* 18.3 45 (1991): 26–34.

———. *The Order of Things: An Archaeology of the Human Sciences*. Translated by Alan Sheridan. New York: Vintage, 1970.

———. "Questions on Geography." In *Power/Knowledge: Selected Interviews and Other Writings, 1972–1977*, edited by Colin Gordon, 63–77. New York: Random House, 1980.

———. *Security, Territory, Population: Lectures at the Collège de France, 1977–78*. Edited by Michel Senellart, translated by Graham Burchell. New York: Palgrave Macmillan, 2007.

———. *Society Must Be Defended: Lectures at the Collège de France, 1975–76*. Translated by David Macey. New York: St. Martin's, 2003.

Foucault, Michel, Catharine von Bülow, and Daniel Defert. "The Masked Assassination" [1971]. In *Warfare in the American Homeland: Policing and Prison in a Penal Democracy*, edited by Joy James, translated by Sirene Farb, 140–58. Durham, NC: Duke University Press, 2007.

Frankl, Viktor Emil. *Trotzdem Ja zum Leben sagen: Ein Psychologe erlebt das Konzentrationslager*. Munich: Deutscher Taschenbuch Verlag, 1982.

Freud, Sigmund. *Totem and Taboo: Some Points of Agreement between the Mental Lives of Savages and Neurotics* [1913]. Translated by James Strachey. London: Routledge, 2001.

Friedrichsmeyer, Sara, Sara Lennox, and Susanne Zantop. *The Imperialist Imagination: German Colonialism and Its Legacy*. Ann Arbor: University of Michigan Press, 1998.

Gavras, Romain, dir. *Born Free*. XL Recordings, 2010.

Genova, Nicholas De. "Theoretical Overview." In *The Deportation Regime: Sovereignty,*

Space, and the Freedom of Movement, edited by Nathalie Peutz and Nicholas De Genova, 33–65. Durham, NC: Duke University Press, 2010.

Gerima, Haile, dir. Sankofa. DVD. Mypheduh Films, 1993.

Geroulanos, Stefanos. An Atheism That Is Not Humanist Emerges in French Thought. Palo Alto, CA: Stanford University Press, 2010.

Gilmore, Ruth Wilson. "Fatal Couplings of Power and Difference: Notes on Racism and Geography." Professional Geographer 54.1 (2002): 15–24.

———. Golden Gulag: Prisons, Surplus, Crisis, and Opposition in Globalizing California. Berkeley: University of California Press, 2007.

———. "Race and Globalization." In Geographies of Global Change: Remapping the World, edited by Ronald John Johnston, Peter James Taylor, and Michael Watts, 261–74. Malden, MA: Wiley-Blackwell, 2002.

Gilroy, Paul. Against Race: Imagining Political Culture beyond the Color Line. Cambridge, MA: Harvard University Press, 2000.

———. The Black Atlantic: Modernity and Double Consciousness. Cambridge, MA: Harvard University Press, 1993.

———. Postcolonial Melancholia. New York: Columbia University Press, 2005.

Glaude, Eddie S. Exodus! Religion, Race, and Nation in Early Nineteenth-Century Black America. Chicago: University of Chicago Press, 2000.

Glissant, Édouard. Poetics of Relation. Translated by Betsy Wing. Ann Arbor: University of Michigan Press, 1997.

Godzich, Wlad. The Culture of Literacy. Cambridge, MA: Harvard University Press, 1994.

Gold, Michael. A Conspiracy of Cells: One Woman's Immortal Legacy and the Medical Scandal It Caused. Albany: State University of New York Press, 1986.

Goldman, Martin, dir. The Legend of Nigger Charley. Paramount Pictures, 1972.

Goldstein, Avram. Addiction: From Biology to Drug Policy. New York: Oxford University Press, 2001.

Goodell, W. The American Slave Code in Theory and Practice: Its Distinctive Features Shown by Its Statutes, Judicial Decisions, and Illustrative Facts. New York: American and Foreign Anti-Slavery Society, 1853.

Gordon, Avery F. "Abu Ghraib: Imprisonment and the War on Terror." Race and Class 48.1 (2006): 42–59.

———. "The United States Military Prison: The Normalcy of Exceptional Brutality." In The Violence of Incarceration, edited by Phil Scraton and Jude McCulloch, 164–86. New York: Routledge, 2008.

Gordon, Lewis Ricardo, and Jane Anna Gordon. Not Only the Master's Tools: African-American Studies in Theory and Practice. Boulder, CO: Paradigm, 2006.

Gottlieb, Susannah Y. Regions of Sorrow: Anxiety and Messianism in Hannah Arendt and W. H. Auden. Palo Alto, CA: Stanford University Press, 2003.

Gould, Stephen Jay. *Ontogeny and Phylogeny*. Cambridge, MA: Harvard University Press, 1977.

Greenberg, Karen J., and Joshua L. Dratel. *The Torture Papers: The Road to Abu Ghraib*. Cambridge: Cambridge University Press, 2005.

Grimshaw, Anna, and Keith Hart. "American Civilization: An Introduction." In *American Civilization*, 1–25. Malden, MA: Blackwell, 1993.

Gross, Raphael. *Carl Schmitt und die Juden: Eine deutsche Rechtslehre*. Frankfurt am Main: Suhrkamp, 2005.

Grosse, Pascal. "From Colonialism to National Socialism to Postcolonialism: Hannah Arendt's *Origins of Totalitarianism*." *Postcolonial Studies* 9.1 (2006): 35–52.

———. *Kolonialismus, Eugenik und bürgerliche Gesellschaft in Deutschland 1850–1918*. Frankfurt am Main: Campus Verlag, 2000.

Grosz, Elizabeth A. *Becoming Undone: Darwinian Reflections on Life, Politics, and Art*. Durham, NC: Duke University Press, 2011.

———. "Merleau-Ponty and Irigaray in the Flesh." *Thesis Eleven* 36.1 (1993): 37–59.

———. *Time Travels: Feminism, Nature, Power*. Durham, NC: Duke University Press, 2005.

Hall, Stuart. "On Postmodernism and Articulation: An Interview with Stuart Hall." In *Stuart Hall: Critical Dialogues in Cultural Studies*, edited by David Morley and Kuan-Hsing Chen, 131–50. New York: Routledge, 1986.

———. "Race, Articulation, and Societies Structured in Dominance." In *Sociological Theories: Race and Colonialism*, 303–45. Paris: UNESCO, 1980.

———. "Signification, Representation, Ideology: Althusser and the Post-structuralist Debates." *Critical Studies in Media Communication* 2.2 (1985): 91–114.

———. "Who Needs 'Identity'?" In *Questions of Cultural Identity*, edited by Paul Du Gay and Stuart Hall, 1–17. London: Sage, 1996.

Halliday, Paul Delaney. *Habeas Corpus: From England to Empire*. Cambridge, MA: Harvard University Press, 2010.

Halttunen, Karen. "Humanitarianism and the Pornography of Pain in Anglo-American Culture." *American Historical Review* 100.2 (1995): 303–34.

Hamburger Institut für Sozialforschung. *Die Auschwitz-Hefte: Texte der polnischen Zeitschrift "Przeglad Lekarski" über historische, psychische und medizinische Aspekte des Lebens und Sterbens in Auschwitz*. Hamburg: Rogner und Bernhard Verlag, 1994.

Hammonds, Evelynn. "Black (W)holes and the Geometry of Black Female Sexuality." *differences: A Journal of Feminist Cultural Studies* 6.2–3 (1994): 126–45.

Han, Sora Y. "Strict Scrutiny: The Tragedy of Constitutional Law." In *Beyond Biopolitics: Essays on the Governance of Life and Death*, edited by Patricia Ticineto Clough and Craig Willse, 106–37. Durham, NC: Duke University Press, 2011.

Haney-López, Ian. *White by Law: The Legal Construction of Race*. New York: NYU Press, 1996.

Harris, Cheryl I. "Whiteness as Property." *Harvard Law Review* 106.8 (1993): 1707–70.

Hartman, Saidiya. *Scenes of Subjection: Terror, Slavery, and Self-Making in Nineteenth-Century America.* New York: Oxford University Press, 1997.

Haslett, Tim. "Hortense Spillers Interviewed by Tim Haslett for the Black Cultural Studies Web Site Collective in Ithaca, NY." February 4, 1998. Accessed June 5, 2012. http://www.blackculturalstudies.org/spillers/spillers_intvw.html.

Hayles, Katherine. *How We Became Posthuman: Virtual Bodies in Cybernetics, Literature, and Informatics.* Chicago: University of Chicago Press, 1999.

Heidegger, Martin. *Die Frage nach dem Ding.* Tübingen: M. Niemeyer, 1962.

———. *What Is a Thing?* Translated by W. B. Barton and Vera Deutsch. South Bend, IN: Gateway Editions, 1967.

Heiner, Brady Thomas. "Foucault and the Black Panthers." *City: Analysis of Urban Trends, Culture, Theory, Policy, Action* 11.3 (2007): 313–56.

Hersh, Seymour M. *Chain of Command: The Road from 9/11 to Abu Ghraib.* New York: HarperCollins, 2005.

Hill, James, dir. *Born Free.* Columbia Pictures, 1966.

Hine, Darlene Clark. "Rape and the Inner Lives of Black Women in the Middle West." *Signs* 14.4 (1989): 912–20.

Hirschfeld, Lawrence A. *Race in the Making: Cognition, Culture, and the Child's Construction of Human Kinds.* Cambridge, MA: MIT Press, 1998.

Holland, Eugene W. "Representation and Misrepresentation in Postcolonial Literature and Theory." *Research in African Literatures* 34.1 (2003): 159–73.

Holland, Sharon Patricia. *Raising the Dead: Readings of Death and (Black) Subjectivity.* Durham, NC: Duke University Press, 2000.

Holloway, Karla F. C. *Private Bodies, Public Texts: Race, Gender, and a Cultural Bioethics.* Durham, NC: Duke University Press, 2011.

Hong, Grace Kyungwon, and Roderick A. Ferguson. *Strange Affinities: The Gender and Sexual Politics of Comparative Racialization.* Durham, NC: Duke University Press, 2011.

Hurston, Zora Neale. "Characteristics of Negro Expression" [1934]. In *Folklore, Memoirs, and Other Writings,* edited by Cheryl A. Wall, 830–74. New York: Library of America, 1995.

Hussain, Nasser. *The Jurisprudence of Emergency: Colonialism and the Rule of Law.* Ann Arbor: University of Michigan Press, 2003.

Irigaray, Luce. *This Sex Which Is Not One.* Translated by Catherine Porter. Ithaca, NY: Cornell University Press, 1985.

Iton, Richard. *In Search of the Black Fantastic: Politics and Popular Culture in the Post–Civil Rights Era.* New York: Oxford University Press, 2008.

———. "Still Life." *Small Axe* 17.1 40 (2013): 22–39.

Jacobs, Harriet Ann. *Incidents in the Life of a Slave Girl.* Edited by Lydia Maria Child. Boston: Published for the Author, 1861.

Jagoda, Z., S. Klodinski, and J. Maslowski. "Die Nächte gehören uns nicht . . .": Häftlingsträume in Auschwitz und im Leben danach." In *Die Auschwitz-Hefte: Texte der polnischen Zeitschrift "Przeglad Lekarski" über historische, psychische und medizinische Aspekte des Lebens und Sterbens in Auschwitz*, 2: 189–239. Hamburg: Rogner und Bernhard Verlag, 1994.

Jamal, Amaney A., and Nadine Christine Naber, eds. *Race and Arab Americans before and after 9/11: From Invisible Citizens to Visible Subjects*. Syracuse, NY: Syracuse University Press, 2008.

James, Cyril Lionel Robert. *The Black Jacobins: Toussaint L'Ouverture and the San Domingo Revolution*. 1938. Reprint, New York: Vintage, 1989.

———. "Black Studies and the Contemporary Student" [1969]. In *The C.L.R. James Reader*, edited by Anna Grimshaw, 390–404. Cambridge, MA: Blackwell, 1992.

———. *The C.L.R. James Reader*. Edited by Anna Grimshaw. Cambridge, MA: Blackwell, 1992.

———. "Dialectical Materialism and the Fate of Humanity." In *The C.L.R. James Reader*, edited by Anna Grimshaw, 153–81. Cambridge, MA: Blackwell, 1992.

———. *Mariners, Renegades, and Castaways: The Story of Herman Melville and the World We Live In*. 1953. Reprint, Hanover, NH: University Press of New England, 2001.

James, Joy. *Resisting State Violence: Radicalism, Gender, and Race in U.S. Culture*. Minneapolis: University of Minnesota Press, 1996.

JanMohamed, Abdul R. *The Death-Bound-Subject: Richard Wright's Archaeology of Death*. Durham, NC: Duke University Press, 2005.

Johnson, Sylvester. *The Myth of Ham in Nineteenth-Century American Christianity: Race, Heathens, and the People of God*. New York: Palgrave Macmillan, 2004.

Jones, Gayl. *Corregidora*. Boston: Beacon, 1986.

Jones, James Howard. *Bad Blood: The Tuskegee Syphilis Experiment*. New York: Simon and Schuster, 1993.

Judy, Ronald A. T. "Democracy or Ideology." *boundary 2* 33.3 (2006): 35–59.

———. *(Dis)forming the American Canon: African-Arabic Slave Narratives and the Vernacular*. Minneapolis: University of Minnesota Press, 1993.

———. "Provisional Note on Formations of Planetary Violence." *boundary 2* 33.3 (2006): 141–50.

———. "Untimely Intellectuals and the University." *boundary 2* 27.1 (2000): 121–33.

Kafka, Franz. "In the Penal Colony. " In *The Complete Stories*, translated by Nahum Norbert Glatzer. 1919. Reprint, New York: Schocken, 1983.

Ka-Tzetnik 135633. *House of Dolls*. London: Senate, 1977.

Kauanui, J. Kēhaulani. *Hawaiian Blood: Colonialism and the Politics of Sovereignty and Indigeneity*. Durham, NC: Duke University Press, 2008.

Kautsky, Benedikt. *Teufel und Verdammte: Erfahrungen und Erkenntnisse aus sieben Jahren in deutschen Konzentrationslagern*. Zurich: Büchergilde Gutenberg, 1946.

Keeling, Kara. "Looking for M—." *GLQ: A Journal of Lesbian and Gay Studies* 15.4 (2009): 565–82.

———. *The Witch's Flight: The Cinematic, the Black Femme, and the Image of Common Sense.* Durham, NC: Duke University Press, 2007.

Kelley, Robin D. G. *Freedom Dreams: The Black Radical Imagination.* Boston: Beacon, 2002.

Kim, Jodi. *Ends of Empire: Asian American Critique and the Cold War.* Minneapolis: University of Minnesota Press, 2010.

Koerner, Michelle. "Line of Escape: Gilles Deleuze's Encounter with George Jackson." *Genre* 44.2 (2011): 157–80.

Kogon, Eugen. *Der SS-Staat: Das System der deutschen Konzentrationslager.* Zurich: Europa Verlag, 1946.

Kühl, Stefan. *The Nazi Connection: Eugenics, American Racism, and German National Socialism.* New York: Oxford University Press, 1994.

LaCapra, Dominick. *History and Memory after Auschwitz.* Ithaca, NY: Cornell University Press, 1998.

Laclau, Ernesto, and Chantal Mouffe. *Hegemony and Socialist Strategy: Towards a Radical Democratic Politics,* 2nd ed. London: Verso, 2001.

Landecker, Hannah. "Between Beneficence and Chattel: The Human Biological in Law and Science." *Science in Context* 12.1 (1999): 203–26.

Langbehn, Volker, and Mohammad Salama. *German Colonialism: Race, the Holocaust, and Postwar Germany.* New York: Columbia University Press, 2011.

Langbein, Hermann. *People in Auschwitz* [1972]. Translated by Harry Zohn. Chapel Hill: University of North Carolina Press, 2004.

Lanternari, Vittorio. *The Religions of the Oppressed: A Study of Modern Messianic Cults.* New York: New American Library, 1965.

Lederer, Susan E. *Subjected to Science: Human Experimentation in America before the Second World War.* Baltimore, MD: Johns Hopkins University Press, 1997.

Lemke, Thomas. *Biopolitics: An Advanced Introduction.* New York: NYU Press, 2011.

Levi, Primo. *Survival in Auschwitz: The Nazi Assault on Humanity.* Translated by Stuart Woolf. 1958. Reprint, New York: Simon and Schuster, 1996.

Levine, Phillippa. "Anthropology, Colonialism, and Eugenics." In *The Oxford Handbook of the History of Eugenics,* edited by Alison Bashford and Phillippa Levine, 43–61. New York: Oxford University Press, 2010.

Litwack, Leon F. *Been in the Storm So Long: The Aftermath of Slavery.* New York: Knopf, 1979.

Lowe, Lisa M. "The Intimacies of the Four Continents." In *Haunted by Empire: Geographies of Global Intimacy in North American History,* edited by Ann Laura Stoler, 192–211. Durham, NC: Duke University Press, 2006.

———. "Reckoning Nation and Empire: Asian American Critique." In *A Concise*

Companion to American Studies, edited by John Carlos Rowe, 229–44. Malden, MA: Wiley-Blackwell, 2010.

Löwy, Michael. Redemption and Utopia: Jewish Libertarian Thought in Central Europe: A Study in Elective Affinity. Translated by Hope Heaney. Palo Alto, CA: Stanford University Press, 1992.

Lugones, Maria. "Heterosexualism and the Colonial/Modern Gender System." Hypatia 22.1 (2007): 186–219.

Lyons, Scott Richard. X-Marks: Native Signatures of Assent. Indigenous Americas. Minneapolis: University of Minnesota Press, 2010.

Machery, Edouard, and Luc Faucher. "Why Do We Think Racially? A Critical Journey in Culture and Evolution." In Handbook of Categorization in Cognitive Science, edited by Henri Cohen and Claire Lefebvre, 1009–33. London: Elsevier, 2005.

Majaj, Lisa S. "Arab-Americans and the Meanings of Race." In Postcolonial Theory and the United States: Race, Ethnicity, and Literature, edited by Amritjit Singh and Peter Schmidt, 320–37. Jackson: University Press of Mississippi, 2000.

Mamdani, Mahmood. When Victims Become Killers: Colonialism, Nativism, and the Genocide in Rwanda. Princeton, NJ: Princeton University Press, 2002.

Mann, Klaus. Mephisto. 1936. Reprint, New York: Penguin, 1999.

Marcuse, Herbert. Eros and Civilization. Boston: Beacon, 1955.

Márquez, John. "Nations Re-bound: Race and Biopolitics at EU and US Borders." In Europe in Black and White: Immigration, Race, and Identity in the "Old Continent," edited by Manuela Ribeiro Sanches, Joao Ferreira Duarte, and Fernando Clara, 38–49. Bristol, UK: Intellect, 2011.

Marx, Karl. "Grundrisse der Kritik der politischen Ökonomie." In Ökonomische Manuskripte 1857/58. Karl Marx, Friedrich Engels Gesamtausgabe (MEGA), vol. 2/1.1. Berlin: Dietz, 1988.

Massumi, Brian. Parables for the Virtual: Movement, Affect, Sensation. Durham, NC: Duke University Press, 2002.

Mbembe, Achille. "Necropolitics." Public Culture 15 (2003): 11–40.

———. On the Postcolony. Berkeley: University of California Press, 2001.

———. "Provincializing France?" Public Culture 23.1 (2011): 85–119.

McBride, Dwight A. "The Ghosts of Memory: Representing the Past in Beloved and The Woman Warrior." In Re-placing America: Conversations and Contestations: Selected Essays, edited by Ruth Hsu, Cynthia G. Franklin, and Suzanne Kosanke, 162–71. Honolulu: University of Hawai'i Press, 2000.

McDowell, Deborah. "In the First Place: Making Frederick Douglass and the Afro-American Narrative Tradition." In Critical Essays on Frederick Douglass, edited by William L. Andrews, 192–215. Boston: GK Hall, 1991.

McKittrick, Katherine. Demonic Grounds: Black Women and the Cartographies of Struggle. Minneapolis: University of Minnesota Press, 2006.

———. "I Entered the Lists . . . Diaspora Catalogues: The List, the Unbearable Territory, and Tormented Chronologies—Three Narratives and a Weltanschauung." *XCP: Cross Cultural Poetics* 17 (2007): 7–29.

Merleau-Ponty, Maurice. *The Visible and the Invisible; Followed by Working Notes*. Edited by Claude Lefort, translated by Alphonso Lingis. Evanston, IL: Northwestern University Press, 1968.

Mignolo, Walter D. "Citizenship, Knowledge, and the Limits of Humanity." *American Literary History* 18.2 (2006): 312–31.

Miller, Christopher L. "The Postidentitarian Predicament in the Footnotes of *A Thousand Plateaus*: Nomadology, Anthropology, and Authority." *Diacritics* 23.3 (1993): 6–35.

———. "'We Shouldn't Judge Deleuze and Guattari': A Response to Eugene Holland." *Research in African Literatures* 34.3 (2003): 129–41.

Mills, Charles W. "The Political Economy of Personhood." On the Human: A Project of the National Humanities Center, April 4, 2011. http://onthehuman.org/2011/04/political-economy-of-personhood/.

———. *The Racial Contract*. Ithaca, NY: Cornell University Press, 1997.

Mintz, Sidney Wilfred. *Sweetness and Power: The Place of Sugar in Modern History*. New York: Viking, 1985.

Mitchell, David T., and Sharon L. Snyder. "The Eugenic Atlantic: Race, Disability, and the Making of an International Eugenic Science, 1800–1945." *Disability and Society* 18.7 (2003): 843–64.

Moraga, Cherríe, and Gloria Anzaldúa, eds. *This Bridge Called My Back: Writings by Radical Women of Color*, 2nd ed. New York: Kitchen Table: Women of Color Press, 1983.

Morgensen, Scott L. "The Biopolitics of Settler Colonialism: Right Here, Right Now." *Settler Colonial Studies* 1.1 (2011): 52–76.

Morrison, Toni. *Beloved*. New York: Signet, 1987.

Moses, Wilson Jeremiah. *Black Messiahs and Uncle Toms: Social and Literary Manipulations of a Religious Myth*. State College, PA: Penn State University Press, 1993.

Moten, Fred. *In the Break: The Aesthetics of the Black Radical Tradition*. Minneapolis: University of Minnesota Press, 2003.

Moyn, Samuel. *The Last Utopia: Human Rights in History*. Cambridge, MA: Harvard University Press, 2010.

Mühlhahn, Klaus. "The Concentration Camp in Global Historical Perspective." *History Compass* 8.6 (2010): 543–61.

Muñoz, José Esteban. *Cruising Utopia: The Then and There of Queer Futurity*. New York: NYU Press, 2009.

"'Muselmann' ist offiziell eine Beleidigung." islam.de, August 26, 2009. http://www.islam.de/13731.php.

Nas. "Ether." On *Stillmatic*. New York: Columbia Records, 2001.

Negri, Antonio. "The Ripe Fruit of Redemption." Translated by Arianna Bove. Generation-online.org, July 26, 2003. http://www.generation-online.org/t/negri agamben.htm.

Nelson, Alondra. Body and Soul: The Black Panther Party and the Fight against Medical Discrimination. Minneapolis: University of Minnesota Press, 2011.

Neptune, Harvey R. Caliban and the Yankees: Trinidad and the United States Occupation. Chapel Hill: University of North Carolina Press, 2007.

Nero, Charles. "Toward a Black Gay Aesthetic: Signifying in Contemporary Black Gay Literature." In Brother to Brother: New Writings by Black Gay Men, edited by Essex Hemphill. Boston: Alyson, 1991.

Ong, Aihwa. "Experiments with Freedom: Milieus of the Human." American Literary History 18 (2006): 229–44.

———. Neoliberalism as Exception: Mutations in Citizenship and Sovereignty. Durham, NC: Duke University Press, 2006.

Oparah, Julia C. "Feminism and the (Trans)gender Entrapment of Gender Nonconforming Prisoners." UCLA Women's Law Journal 18.2 (2012): 239–73.

———. "Maroon Abolitionists: Black Gender-Oppressed Activists in the Anti-prison Movement in the US and Canada." In Captive Genders: Trans Embodiment and the Prison Industrial Complex, edited by Nat Smith and Eric A. Stanley, 293–322. Oakland, CA: AK Press, 2011.

Opitz, May, Katharina Oguntoye, and Dagmar Schultz, eds. Showing Our Colors: Afro-German Women Speak Out. 1986. Reprint, Amherst: University of Massachusetts Press, 1992.

Pasolini, Pier Paolo, dir. Salò, or the 120 Days of Sodom. United Artists, 1976.

Patterson, Orlando. Slavery and Social Death: A Comparative Study. Cambridge, MA: Harvard University Press, 1982.

Pattillo, Mary E. Black Picket Fences: Privilege and Peril among the Black Middle Class. Chicago: University of Chicago Press, 1999.

Pease, Donald E. "C.L.R. James, Moby-Dick and the Emergence of Transnational American Studies." In The Futures of American Studies, edited by Donald Pease and Robyn Wiegman, 135–63. Durham, NC: Duke University Press, 2002.

———. "Doing Justice to CLR James's Mariners, Renegades, and Castaways." boundary 2 27.2 (2000): 1–19.

———. "Introduction." In C. L. R. James, Mariners, Renegades, and Castaways: The Story of Herman Melville and the World We Live In, vii–xxxiii. Hanover, NH: University Press of New England, 2001.

Posnock, Ross. Color and Culture: Black Writers and the Making of the Modern Intellectual. Cambridge, MA: Harvard University Press, 2000.

Prince, Mary. The History of Mary Prince [1831]. Edited by Sarah Salih. New York: Penguin, 2000.

Puar, Jasbir K. *Terrorist Assemblages: Homonationalism in Queer Times*. Durham, NC: Duke University Press, 2007.

Quijano, Anibal. "Coloniality and Modernity/Rationality." *Cultural Studies* 21.2–3 (2007): 168–78.

———. "Coloniality of Power, Knowledge, and Latin America." *Nepantla: Views from South* 1.3 (2000): 533–80.

Radhakrishnan, Rajagopalan. *History, the Human, and the World Between*. Durham, NC: Duke University Press, 2008.

———. *Theory in an Uneven World*. Malden, MA: Wiley-Blackwell, 2003.

Rana, Junaid. *Terrifying Muslims: Race and Labor in the South Asian Diaspora*. Durham, NC: Duke University Press, 2011.

Rancière, Jacques. *Dissensus: On Politics and Aesthetics*. Translated by Steve Corcoran. New York: Continuum, 2010.

Rao, Anupama. "Violence and Humanity: Or, Vulnerability as Political Subjectivity." *Social Research: An International Quarterly* 78.2 (2011): 607–32.

Reich, Wilhelm. *The Mass Psychology of Fascism* [1933]. Translated by Theodore Wolfe. New York: Orgone Institute Press, 1946.

Reid-Pharr, Robert. *Black Gay Man: Essays*. New York: NYU Press, 2001.

———. *Conjugal Union : The Body, the House, and the Black American*. New York: Oxford University Press, 1999.

Richie, Beth. *Arrested Justice: Black Women, Violence, and America's Prison Nation*. New York: NYU Press, 2012.

Rifkin, Mark. "Indigenizing Agamben: Rethinking Sovereignty in Light of the 'Peculiar' Status of Native Peoples." *Cultural Critique* 73 (2009): 88–124.

Roberts, Dorothy. *Fatal Invention: How Science, Politics, and Big Business Re-create Race in the Twenty-First Century*. New York: New Press, 2011.

———. *Killing the Black Body: Race, Reproduction, and the Meaning of Liberty*. New York: Vintage, 1999.

Robinson, Cedric J. *Black Marxism: The Making of the Black Radical Tradition*. London: Zed, 1983.

Rodríguez, Dylan. *Forced Passages: Imprisoned Radical Intellectuals and the U.S. Prison Regime*. Minneapolis: University of Minnesota Press, 2006.

———. *Suspended Apocalypse: White Supremacy, Genocide, and the Filipino Condition*. Minneapolis: University of Minnesota Press, 2009.

Rose, Nikolas. *The Politics of Life Itself: Biomedicine, Power, and Subjectivity in the Twenty-First Century*. Princeton, NJ: Princeton University Press, 2008.

Ross, Kristin. *May '68 and Its Afterlives*. Chicago: University of Chicago Press, 2002.

Rozema, Vicki. *Voices from the Trail of Tears*. Winston-Salem, NC: John F. Blair, 2003.

Ryn, Zdzislaw, and Stanslav Klodzinski. "An der Grenze zwischen Leben und Tod: Eine Studie über die Erscheinung des 'Muselmann' im Konzentrationslager." In

Die Auschwitz-Hefte: Texte der polnischen Zeitschrift "Przeglad Lekarski" über historische, psychische und medizinische Aspekte des Lebens und Sterbens in Auschwitz, 1: 89–154. Hamburg: Rogner und Bernhard Verlag, 1994.

———. "Tod und Sterben im Konzentrationslager." In *Die Auschwitz-Hefte: Texte der polnischen Zeitschrift "Przeglad Lekarski" über historische, psychische und medizinische Aspekte des Lebens und Sterbens in Auschwitz*, 1: 281–328. Hamburg: Rogner und Bernhard Verlag, 1994.

———. "Zur Psychopathologie von Hunger und Hungererleben im Konzentrationslager." In *Die Auschwitz-Hefte: Texte der polnischen Zeitschrift "Przeglad Lekarski" über historische, psychische und medizinische Aspekte des Lebens und Sterbens in Auschwitz*, 2: 113–34. Hamburg: Rogner und Bernhard Verlag, 1994.

Said, Edward W. "The Text, the World, the Critic." *Bulletin of the Midwest Modern Language Association* 8.2 (1975): 1–23.

———. "Traveling Theory." In *The World, the Text, and the Critic*, 226–47. Cambridge, MA: Harvard University Press, 1983.

Sartre, Jean-Paul. *Colonialism and Neocolonialism*. New York: Routledge, 2001.

Scarry, Elaine. *The Body in Pain: The Making and Unmaking of the World*. New York: Oxford University Press, 1987.

Schmitt, Carl. *Political Theology: Four Chapters on the Concept of Sovereignty* [1922]. Translated by George Schwab. Chicago: University of Chicago Press, 1985.

Scott, Darieck. *Extravagant Abjection: Blackness, Power, and Sexuality in the African American Literary Imagination*. New York: NYU Press, 2010.

Scott, David. "Preface: Soul Captives Are Free." *Small Axe* 11.2 23 (2007): v–x.

Scott, David, and Sylvia Wynter. "The Re-enchantment of Humanism: An Interview with Sylvia Wynter." *Small Axe* 8 (September 2000): 119–207.

Sedgwick, Eve Kosofsky. *Between Men: English Literature and Male Homosocial Desire*. New York: Columbia University Press, 1985.

Seshadri, Kalpana. *Humanimal: Race, Law, Language*. Minneapolis: University of Minnesota Press, 2011.

Sexton, Jared. *Amalgamation Schemes: Antiblackness and the Critique of Multiracialism*. Minneapolis: University of Minnesota Press, 2008.

Sharpe, Christina. *Monstrous Intimacies: Making Post-slavery Subjects*. Durham, NC: Duke University Press, 2010.

Simpson, Audra. "On Ethnographic Refusal: Indigeneity, 'Voice' and Colonial Citizenship." *Junctures: The Journal for Thematic Dialogue* 9 (2007): 67–80.

Singh, Nikhil Pal. *Black Is a Country: Race and the Unfinished Struggle for Democracy*. Cambridge, MA: Harvard University Press, 2004.

Skloot, Rebecca. *The Immortal Life of Henrietta Lacks*. New York: Random House, 2010.

Smith, Andrea. "Boarding School Abuses, Human Rights, and Reparations." *Social Justice* 31.4 98 (2004): 89–102.

———. *Conquest: Sexual Violence and American Indian Genocide*. Boston: South End, 2005.

———. "Heteropatriarchy and the Three Pillars of White Supremacy." In *Color of Violence: The Incite! Anthology*, edited by Incite! Women of Color against Violence, 66–73. Boston: South End, 2006.

Smith, Barbara, ed. *Home Girls: A Black Feminist Anthology*. New York: Kitchen Table: Women of Color Press, 1983.

Smith, David Livingstone. *Less Than Human: Why We Demean, Enslave, and Exterminate Others*. New York: St. Martin's, 2011.

Smith, Iain R., and Andreas Stucki. "The Colonial Development of Concentration Camps (1868–1902)." *Journal of Imperial and Commonwealth History* 39.3 (2011): 417–37.

Smith, Linda Tuhiwai. *Decolonizing Methodologies: Research and Indigenous Peoples*. London: Zed, 1999.

Smith, Valerie. "'Loopholes of Retreat': Architecture and Ideology in Harriet Jacobs's *Incidents in the Life of a Slave Girl*." In *Reading Black, Reading Feminist*, edited by Henry Louis Gates, 212–26. New York: Meridian, 1990.

Sofsky, Wolfgang. *Die Ordnung des Terrors: Das Konzentrationslager*. Frankfurt am Main: S. Fischer, 1993.

———. *The Order of Terror: The Concentration Camp*. Princeton, NJ: Princeton University Press, 1997.

Sontag, Susan. "Fascinating Fascism." In *Under the Sign of Saturn*, 73–105. New York: Doubleday, 1980.

Spade, Dean. *Normal Life: Administrative Violence, Critical Trans Politics, and the Limits of Law*. Boston: South End, 2011.

Spiegel, Marjorie. *The Dreaded Comparison: Human and Animal Slavery*. Hong Kong: Mirror Books, 1996.

Spielberg, Steven, dir. *Amistad*. DreamWorks, 1997.

Spillers, Hortense J. *Black, White, and in Color: Essays on American Literature and Culture*. Chicago: University of Chicago Press, 2003.

———. "The Crisis of the Black Intellectual." In *A Companion to African-American Philosophy*, edited by Tommy Lee Lott and John P. Pittman, 87–106. Malden, MA: Blackwell, 2003.

———. "The Crisis of the Negro Intellectual: A Post-date" [1994]. In *Black, White, and in Color: Essays on American Literature and Culture*, 428–70. Chicago: University of Chicago Press, 2003.

———. "Interstices: A Small Drama of Words" [1984]. In *Black, White, and in Color: Essays on American Literature and Culture*, 152–75. Chicago: University of Chicago Press, 2003.

———. "Introduction—Peter's Pans: Eating in the Diaspora." In *Black, White, and in Color: Essays on American Literature and Culture*, 1–64. Chicago: University of Chicago Press, 2003.

———. "'Mama's Baby, Papa's Maybe': An American Grammar Book" [1987]. In *Black, White, and in Color: Essays on American Literature and Culture*, 203–29. Chicago: University of Chicago Press, 2003.

Spillers, Hortense J., et al. "'Whatcha Gonna Do?': Revisiting 'Mama's Baby, Papa's Maybe: An American Grammar Book'; A Conversation with Hortense Spillers, Saidiya Hartman, Farah Jasmine Griffin, Shelly Eversley, and Jennifer L. Morgan." *Women's Studies Quarterly* 35.1/2 (2007): 299–309.

Spivak, Gayatri Chakravorty. "Can the Subaltern Speak?" In *Marxism and the Interpretation of Culture*, edited by Cary Nelson and Lawrence Grossberg, 271–313. Champaign: University of Illinois Press, 1988.

———. *A Critique of Postcolonial Reason: Toward a History of the Vanishing Present*. Cambridge, MA: Harvard University Press, 1999.

———. *Death of a Discipline*. New York: Columbia University Press, 2003.

Stam, Robert, and Ella Shohat. *Race in Translation: Culture Wars around the Postcolonial Atlantic*. New York: NYU Press, 2012.

Stanley, Eric. "Near Life, Queer Death Overkill and Ontological Capture." *Social Text* 29.2 107 (2011): 1–19.

Stoler, Ann Laura. *Race and the Education of Desire: Foucault's History of Sexuality and the Colonial Order of Things*. Durham, NC: Duke University Press, 1995.

Storr, Will. "The Rape of Men." *Guardian*, July 17, 2011. http://www.guardian.co.uk/society/2011/jul/17/the-rape-of-men.

Strathausen, Carsten, and William E. Connolly, eds. *A Leftist Ontology: Beyond Relativism and Identity Politics*. Minneapolis: University of Minnesota Press, 2009.

Sundquist, Eric J. *To Wake the Nations: Race in the Making of American Literature*. Cambridge, MA: Belknap, 1993.

Szabó, István, dir. *Mephisto*. Analysis Film Releasing, 1982.

Tadiar, Neferti M. "In the Face of Whiteness as Value: Fall-Outs of Metropolitan Humanness." *Qui Parle* 13.2 (2003): 143–82.

———. "Metropolitan Life and Uncivil Death." PMLA 122.1 (2007): 316–20.

———. *Things Fall Away: Philippine Historical Experience and the Makings of Globalization*. Durham, NC: Duke University Press, 2009.

TallBear, Kimberly. "DNA, Blood, and Racializing the Tribe." *Wicazo Sa Review* 18.1 (2003): 81–107.

Tarski, Alfred. *Introduction to Logic and to the Methodology of the Deductive Sciences*, 4th ed. Edited by Jan Tarski. New York: Oxford University Press, 1936.

Tate, Claudia. *Domestic Allegories of Political Desire: The Black Heroine's Text at the Turn of the Century*. New York: Oxford University Press, 1992.

Taubes, Jacob. *Ad Carl Schmitt: Reflexive Harmony*. Translated by Keith Tribe. New York: Columbia University Press, 2011.

Theweleit, Klaus. *Male Fantasies: Women, Floods, Bodies, History*. Translated by Stephen

Conway, Erica Carter, and Chris Turner. Minneapolis: University of Minnesota Press, 1987.

Thomas, Greg. "PROUD FLESH Inter/Views: Sylvia Wynter." ProudFlesh: New Afrikan Journal of Culture, Politics, and Consciousness 4 (2006).

———. The Sexual Demon of Colonial Power: Pan-African Embodiment and Erotic Schemes of Empire. Bloomington: Indiana University Press, 2007.

Tiedemann, Rolf. Niemandsland: Studien mit und über Theodor W. Adorno. Munich: Edition Text + Kritik, 2007.

Tilley, Helen. Africa as a Living Laboratory: Empire, Development, and the Problem of Scientific Knowledge, 1870–1950. Chicago: University of Chicago Press, 2011.

Tinsley, Omise'eke Natasha. "Black Atlantic, Queer Atlantic: Queer Imaginings of the Middle Passage." GLQ: A Journal of Lesbian and Gay Studies 14.2–3 (2008): 191–215.

Toobin, Jeffrey. "Killing Habeas Corpus: Arlen Specter's About-Face." New Yorker, December 4, 2006, 46–52.

Vargas, João H. Costa. Never Meant to Survive: Genocide and Utopias in Black Diaspora Communities. Lanham, MD: Rowman and Littlefield, 2008.

Viego, Antonio. Dead Subjects: Toward a Politics of Loss in Latino Studies. Durham, NC: Duke University Press, 2007.

Visconti, Luchino, dir. La caduta degli dei [The Damned]. Warner Brothers, 1969.

Wailoo, Keith, Alondra Nelson, and Catherine Lee, eds. Genetics and the Unsettled Past: The Collision of DNA, Race, and History. New Brunswick, NJ: Rutgers University Press, 2012.

Wald, Priscilla. Constituting Americans: Cultural Anxiety and Narrative Form. Durham, NC: Duke University Press, 1995.

Wallace, Maurice O. Constructing the Black Masculine: Identity and Ideality in African American Men's Literature and Culture, 1775–1995. Durham, NC: Duke University Press, 2002.

Washington, Harriet A. Medical Apartheid: The Dark History of Medical Experimentation on Black Americans from Colonial Times to the Present. New York: Random House, 2008.

Weber, Samuel. "Taking Exception to Decision: Walter Benjamin and Carl Schmitt." Diacritics 22.3–4 (1992): 5–18.

Weheliye, Alexander G. "Feenin: Posthuman Voices in Contemporary Black Popular Music." Social Text 20.2 (2002): 21–47.

———. "My Volk to Come: Peoplehood in Recent Diaspora Discourse and Afro-German Popular Music." In Black Europe and the African Diaspora, edited by Trica Danielle Keaton, Stephen Small, and Darlene Clark Hine. Champaign: University of Illinois Press, 2009.

———. Phonographies: Grooves in Sonic Afro-Modernity. Durham, NC: Duke University Press, 2005.

Wertmüller, Lina, dir. Seven Beauties. Cinema 5 Distributing, 1976.

White, Hayden. Tropics of Discourse: Essays in Cultural Criticism. Baltimore, MD: Johns Hopkins University Press, 1978.

Wiesel, Elie. *The Night Trilogy: Night, Dawn, Day*. New York: Farrar, Straus and Giroux, 2008.

Williams, Randall. *The Divided World: Human Rights and Its Violence*. Minneapolis: University of Minnesota Press, 2010.

Williams, Robert A. *Like a Loaded Weapon: The Rehnquist Court, Indian Rights, and the Legal History of Racism in America*. Minneapolis: University of Minnesota Press, 2005.

Wilson, Waziyatawin A. "Decolonizing the 1862 Death Marches." *American Indian Quarterly* 28.1–2 (2004): 185–215.

Wolfe, Cary. *Animal Rites: American Culture, the Discourse of Species, and Posthumanist Theory*. Chicago: University of Chicago Press, 2003.

Wolfe, Patrick. "Corpus Nullius: The Exception of Indians and Other Aliens in US Constitutional Discourse." *Postcolonial Studies* 10.2 (2007): 127–51.

Wood, Marcus. *Blind Memory: Visual Representations of Slavery in England and America*. New York: Routledge, 2000.

Wynter, Sylvia. "Beyond Liberal and Marxist Leninist Feminisms: Towards an Autonomous Frame of Reference." San Francisco: Institute for Research on Women and Gender, 1982.

———. "Beyond Miranda's Meanings: Un/silencing the 'Demonic Ground' of Caliban's 'Woman.'" In *Out of the Kumbla: Caribbean Women and Literature*, edited by Carole Boyce Davies and Elaine Savory, 355–70. Trenton, NJ: Africa World Press, 1990.

———. "Beyond the Word of Man: Glissant and the New Discourse of the Antilles." *World Literature Today* 63.4 (1989): 637–48.

———. "'Genital Mutilation' or 'Symbolic Birth'? Female Circumcision, Lost Origins, and the Aculturalism of Feminist/Western Thought." *Case Western Reserve Law Review* 47 (1997): 501–52.

———. "Human Being as Noun? Or *Being Human as Praxis*? Towards the Autopoetic Turn/Overturn: A Manifesto." August 25, 2007. otl2.wikispaces.com/file/view/The+Autopoetic+Turn.pdf.

———. "On Disenchanting Discourse: 'Minority' Literary Criticism and Beyond." *Cultural Critique* 7 (1987): 207–44.

———. "On How We Mistook the Map for the Territory and Re-imprisoned Ourselves in Our Unbearable Wrongness of Being, of Désêtre: Black Studies toward the Human Project." In *Not Only the Master's Tools: African-American Studies in Theory and Practice*, edited by Lewis Ricardo Gordon and Jane Anna Gordon, 107–69. Boulder, CO: Paradigm, 2006.

———. "Towards the Sociogenic Principle: Fanon, Identity, the Puzzle of Conscious Experience, and What It Is Like to Be 'Black.'" In *National Identities and Sociopolitical Changes in Latin America*, edited by Mercedes F. Durán-Cogan and Antonio Gómez-Moriana, 30–66. New York: Routledge, 2001.

———. "Unsettling the Coloniality of Being/Power/Truth/Freedom: Towards the Human, After Man, Its Overrepresentation—an Argument." CR: The New Centennial Review 3.3 (2003): 257–337.

Young, Robert J. C. Colonial Desire: Hybridity in Theory, Culture, and Race. New York: Routledge, 1995.

———. Postcolonialism: An Historical Introduction. Malden, MA: Wiley-Blackwell, 2001.

———. White Mythologies: Writing History and the West. New York: Routledge, 2004.

Ziarek, Ewa Ponowska. Feminist Aesthetics and the Politics of Modernism. New York: Columbia University Press, 2012.

Zimmerer, Jürgen. Von Windhuk nach Auschwitz: Beiträge zum Verhältnis von Kolonialismus und Holocaust. Munster: LIT Verlag, 2007.

INDEX

Abbas, Asma, 14
abjection, 103, 105, 124, 129
Abu Ghraib prison, 86, 97
affect theory, affect, 29, 46, 67, 120, 124;
   affectable others, 140n10
African American studies, 18, 30, 94
African diasporas, 30–31, 102
Agamben, Giorgio, 1, 5–7, 9, 29, 33–36,
   38, 48, 53–56, 59, 64–65, 71–73,
   82–88, 103, 105, 108–10, 116, 118,
   119–23, 125, 127–28, 130–34
agency, 2, 11, 47, 91, 105, 108, 110,
   121–22
Althusser, Louis, 8–9, 18, 21, 23, 156n9
American Indians, 77–79, 168n44
anatomy, 40–41
androcentrism, 22
animal studies, 9–10
antihumanism, 9, 11
anti-Semitism, 105
apocatastasis, 134, 138

articulation, 4, 8, 13, 18, 23, 46, 48–51,
   57, 73, 90, 130
assemblage, racializing, 1–2, 4–6, 8, 12,
   18, 20–21, 24, 26, 28, 40, 42, 49–52,
   55, 59–62, 65, 67–69, 72–73, 77,
   79, 82, 87–88, 108, 110, 113, 127,
   133, 136
autochthonous population, Europe,
   62, 71

Badu, Erykah, 65
Balibar, Etienne, 18, 31
Benjamin, Walter, 33, 83–85, 87, 110,
   128, 133–34
biopolitics, 1, 4–9, 12, 29, 33–34, 38,
   43, 52, 53–62, 64–65, 72, 109, 113,
   124, 127, 131–32
bios, 33–34, 37, 127. See also zoe
biotechnology, 8
black diaspora studies, 29–30, 32
black feminism, 5, 22–23, 41, 94, 96

blackness, 3–4, 10–11, 18–19, 30–32, 43, 87, 96–97, 99, 111

Black Panther Party (BPP), 15, 62–63, 66

black studies, 1, 3–8, 13–14, 17–21, 25, 28–30, 32, 39, 51, 94, 135–36. See also black feminism

Bones, Ebony, 65

boomerang effect of colonialism, 61

Borkowski, Wlodzimierz, 127–30

Bourdieu, Pierre, 9

Brooks, Daphne, 90

Brown, Wendy, 76–77

Butler, Judith, 22–23, 48

capitalism, 1, 31, 42, 44

Carby, Hazel, 41

Caribbean, 29–30, 129

Césaire, Aimé, 11

Chandler, Nahum, 141n17, 144n8

Chen, Kuan-Hsing, 140n12, 156n7

citizen, 74, 127; naturalized, 114; rights of full, 76–77, 87–88; vs. slave, 102

citizenship, 38, 78

Cixous, Hélène, 9

cliterodectomy, 74

Cohen, Cathy, 41–42

Collins, Patricia Hill, 41

Combahee River Collective, 15, 23

concentration camps, 2, 12, 34–36, 53, 116, 123. See also Nazi death camps

cosmopolitanism, "cosmopolitans," 145n14

critical ethnic studies, 3–8, 13

da Silva, Denise Ferreira, 140n10, 154n30

Davis, Angela, 41, 62, 86

Dayan, Joan Colin, 50, 86–87

decolonization, 4, 7, 9, 131

dehumanization, 5–6, 11, 14, 44, 53, 72, 108, 131

De Lauretis, Teresa, 143n6

Deleuze, Gilles, and Félix Guattari, 46–51, 61; mixed-blood, 49; mixed-race, 50

depravation, 39, 88, 131

deprivation, 39, 131

Derrida, Jacques, 8–9, 155n37

desexualization, 41

deviance, 13, 34, 43, 52, 105, 108–10, 112, 130, 137

diaspora, 29–32, 42, 82, 90, 102, 105, 136

digestion, 34, 115, 122–24, 129

disability, 117

Django Unchained, 172n33

Douglass, Frederick, 91–97, 105–6, 118

Dred Scott v. Sanford, 78–79, 164n9

Du Bois, W. E. B., 20, 76, 132, 163n2

DuCille, Ann, 5

dysselection, 28, 60, 69, 72, 87–88, 90, 103, 108, 110, 138

Ellis Island, 113–15, 118, 123–24, 126

Elmina Castle, 99–100, 103–4, 108

emancipation, 10, 12, 15, 22, 117, 127, 130, 131, 133, 135, 137

eschatology, 85

"ethnic racism," Foucault lectures at Collège de France, 56, 58–64

ethnoclass, 28, 81, 137

Fanon, Frantz, 22, 25–28, 32, 83, 97, 110, 135

Fejkiel, Wladyslaw, 120–21

feminism, 5, 22–23, 38, 40, 48, 94

flesh, 2, 11, 14, 24, 27, 30, 32, 38–45, 50–52, 55, 71–73, 79, 81–82,

87–88, 90–91, 94–97, 99, 102–3,
  105–6, 108, 110–13, 116–19, 121–32,
  134–38; body/flesh (Spillers), 90
Foucault, Michel, 1, 6–9, 22, 29, 33–34,
  38, 48, 56–64, 71–72, 86, 132
Franklin, Aretha, 101–2
freedom, 2, 10, 12–16, 23, 35, 90–91, 95,
  111, 114, 117–18, 124–25, 129–31,
  133–34, 137–38

genocide, 6, 13–15, 25, 35–37, 55, 57,
  59, 82, 85, 131
Gerima, Haile, 98–101, 103–4
Gilmore, Ruth Wilson, 55, 72, 162n32
Glashaus, 137–38
Glissant, Edouard, 12, 38, 50, 93
Gould, Stephen Jay, 147n33
Grosz, Elizabeth A., 44, 47
Grzyb, Roman, 126
Guantanamo Bay, 12, 77, 124

habeas corpus, 2, 4, 11, 52, 73, 77–79,
  115, 124, 131–32
habeas viscus, 2, 4, 11–12, 52, 111–12, 113,
  119, 122, 124–25, 130, 132, 136–38
Haeckel, Ernst, 147n33
Haitian revolution, 129
Hall, Stuart, 48–49
Hammonds, Evelynn, 41
Hartman, Saidiya, 38, 89, 91–94
Hathaway, Donny, 137
Heiner, Brady, 62
Hine, Darlene Clark, 41
Holocaust, 34, 37–38, 56, 64, 85, 87,
  97, 105, 112
homo sacer, 33–35, 37–38, 53, 64, 72,
  83, 85–86, 102, 108, 110, 131, 133
Homo sapiens, species, 8, 19, 25, 28, 40,
  43, 69, 72, 81, 128, 135

human sciences, 20–21
humanism, western liberal, 9, 11, 25,
  132, 136
hunger, 52, 54, 112–14, 116–17, 120, 122,
  127–29, 136
Hurricane Katrina, 93, 97, 171–72n27
Hurston, Zora Neale, 51, 126
hybridity, 49–51, 61

immigration, 1, 13, 37, 114, 116
Immigration and Nationality Act, 114
Immigration and Naturalization Service
  (INS), 114–16
internment: of C. L. R. James, 115; of
  Japanese Americans, 77
internment camp, 12
internment center, 35
Iton, Richard, 13, 177n19

Jackson, George, 51, 62
Jackson, Jesse, 93
Jackson, Mahalia, 101
Jacobs, Harriet, 94, 112, 116–18, 124, 130
James, C. L. R., 17, 112–18, 123–24, 126,
  129–30, 176–77n13; internment,
  115; Moby Dick, 114–15
James, Joy, 62
Jones, Gayl, 97
Judy, Ronald A. T., 20, 71, 87

Kafka, Franz, 98
Keeling, Kara, 47, 105, 110
Kelley, Robin D. G., 177n19

Lacks, Henrietta, HeLa cells, 79, 81,
  165n16
Levi, Primo, 118–19
liberation, 2–4, 10, 23, 39, 65, 117,
  131–32, 136. See also freedom

Lowe, Lisa, 13
Lugones, Maria, 140n12
Lyotard, Jean-François, 9

Mandingo, 97–99, 105–11
manumission, 117, 130
Marx, Karl, 9, 18, 48, 51, 132
Marxism, 9, 48, 85
Massumi, Brian, 21, 47
Mbembe, Achille, 1, 63
McBride, Dwight, 139–40n6
McCarran-Walter Act, 114
McDowell, Deborah, 94
memory, 75, 118
Merleau-Ponty, Maurice, 44, 52
messianism, 84, 131–33
M.I.A. (Maya Arulpragasam), 65–70
militarism, 72
Mills, Charles, 116n21
mixed-blood, 49
mixed-race, 50
Moby Dick, C. L. R. James's discussion in
    Mariners, 114–15
monstrosity, 125, 137
Moore, John, 80–81
Moore v. Regents of University of California,
    80
Moraga, Cherrie, 146n20
Morrison, Toni, 10, 125
Moten, Fred, 91–94
Moynihan Report, 42
Muñoz, José Esteban, 177n19
Muselmann, 53–56, 64–65, 72–73, 103,
    105, 109, 112–13, 116–24, 126–29

Native Americans, 77–79, 168n44
Nazi death camps, 34–37, 54–55, 72,
    118, 120–22, 123
Nazism, 64, 83, 118
necropolitics, 1, 131

Negri, Antonio, 63, 83
Nirvana, 179n26
nomos, 34, 38, 56, 72
Nuruddin, Farah, 74

ontogeny, 25–27
Oparah, Julia, 41, 82

pain, 12, 14, 74–77, 79, 85, 92, 97, 102,
    105–6, 110, 115, 117, 122, 125
Patterson, Orlando, 1, 37–38
phenomenology, 27, 44, 51, 54
phylogeny, 25–27
physiognomy, 40–41
physiology, 12, 24, 27, 29, 32, 37–38,
    41–42, 44, 50–51, 60, 112, 129
plantations, slave, 2, 12, 37–38, 72, 93,
    98–99, 111, 124, 129, 176–77n13
poetics, 83, 125, 136
pornography, 109–10
pornotrope, pornotroping, 89–91, 93,
    95–99, 102–3, 105–6, 108–10, 112,
    131
posthumanism, 9–11
poststructuralism, 9, 48
potentiality, 12–13, 84–85, 121, 124,
    129–31, 137
Prince, Mary, 129
prison-industrial complex, 15, 82, 86,
    88
proletarian, 84
psychoanalysis, 25
Puar, Jasbir, 47, 155n1, 162n31

queer-of-color critique, 142n27
queer theory, 7, 47
Quijano, Anibal, 140n12

race, racial taxonomies, 67
racialization, 1–6, 8, 14, 20, 24, 26–29,

32, 38, 41, 43, 49, 51–52, 55–56, 58–60, 62, 68–69, 72–73, 78, 80

racism, 1, 4–7, 37, 54–65, 72, 87, 124

rape, 74, 76

recapitulation theory, 25, 61

reservations, Indian, 12

resistance, 2, 40, 44, 48, 91, 95, 122

Roberts, Dorothy, 51

Rodríguez, Dylan, 139n2, 150n6, 168n9

Ryn, Zdzislaw, and Stanslav Klodzinski, 54, 116, 119–20

sadomasochism, 96, 108–10

Said, Edward, 7, 21

salt, salt works, 177n14

Sankofa, 97–101, 103–6, 108, 110

Scarry, Elaine, 125

Schmitt, Carl, 33, 84–85, 87–88

Scott, David, 64, 78–79

Sedgwick, Eve Kosofsky, 171n24

segregation, Jim Crow, 20, 38, 42, 82

Sharpe, Christina, 91

Shoah, 37, 97

slave narrative, 93–94, 118, 129

slavery, 6, 10, 13–14, 19, 24, 30, 36–38, 42–43, 50, 59, 82, 85–86, 89, 91, 95–99, 102–3, 105, 108, 110–12, 117, 129, 131

slave trade, transatlantic, 13, 39

social death, 1, 37–38, 63, 72, 85, 112, 131

sociogeny, 25–27, 51

Somalia, 74

Spillers, Hortense, 2, 5, 9, 15, 17–19, 21, 23–25, 29, 38–39, 41–43, 45, 50–51, 80, 87, 90, 92–94, 96, 99, 111, 125–26, 131, 136, 138

Spivak, Gayatri, 22, 47–49

starvation, 35, 116

Styrene, Polly, 65

subjection, 2, 4, 23, 30, 87, 89–92, 94–95, 99, 102–3, 108, 110–11, 113, 129–30, 132, 135

suffering, 11–14, 52, 75–77, 82, 90–91, 93, 126–27, 130, 136

sugar, 128–29, 176–77n13

Sun Ra, Space Is the Place, 132

sweetness, 113–14, 127–29

Tate, Claudia, 41

technology, 3, 8–9, 12, 21, 42, 108

territorialization, 12, 23, 41, 46–47, 49–51; deterritorialization, 12, 46–47, 49–50, 69

terrorism, terrorist activity, 114

terrorist organization, 65

terrorist regime, 42

torture, 6, 43, 86, 97–98, 105–6, 110–12, 123, 125–27, 132

transgender, 28, 81–82

Trinidad, 115–16

ungendering, 40–41, 45, 94, 96, 99, 105–6, 108, 117

University of California, 80

vestibularity, 43–44

West, Kanye, 63, 161n22

Wynter, Sylvia, 5, 21–30, 40–42, 60, 83, 131, 135–37; new humanism, 22

zoe, 33–34, 43, 53, 80, 127. See also bios

This book is so ~~pretent~~ pretentious!!
What does "hieroglyphics of the flesh" mean?
Is this anything more than what
Spillers already says? extended,
perhaps, to Agamben, Foucault, etc
in impossibly overblown language?

What of the utopian endorsement of
desire at the end? (though not
in those terms.)

Is race + racial "experience" overstated
+ particularized unnecessarily in
compensation for its exclusion from
the grand theories of European thinkers?

An element of this leads to Tamba's
Kristen Ross' notion of the critique of
the universal (here Man) comes out
from particularized identities, but
from the place of the excluded who
don't want "in", but whose inclusion
(not merely juridical) will transform
the universal.